Networking

for

Job Search

and

Career Success

SECOND EDITION

L. Michelle Tullier, Ph.D.

JiST *Works*
America's Career Publisher

Networking for Job Search and Career Success, Second Edition
© 2004 by L. Michelle Tullier, Ph.D.

First edition was titled *Networking for Everyone*

Published by JIST Works, an imprint of JIST Publishing, Inc.
8902 Otis Avenue
Indianapolis, IN 46216-1033

Phone: 1-800-648-JIST   Fax: 1-800-JIST-FAX
E-mail: info@jist.com   Web site: www.jist.com

> **About career materials published by JIST:** Our materials encourage people to be self-directed and to take control of their destinies. We work hard to provide excellent content, solid advice, and techniques that get results. If you have questions about this book or other JIST products, call 1-800-648-JIST or visit www.jist.com.
>
> **Quantity discounts are available for JIST products.** Please call 1-800-648-JIST or visit www.jist.com for a free catalog and more information.
>
> **Visit www.jist.com** for information on JIST, free job search information, book excerpts, and ordering information on our many products. For free information on 14,000 job titles, visit www.careeroink.com.

Acquisitions Editor: Lori Cates Hand
Development Editor: Stephanie Koutek
Cover and Interior Designer: Aleata Howard
Interior Layout: Carolyn J. Newland
Proofreaders: Linda Quigley, David Faust
Indexer: Tina Trettin

Printed in Canada

09 08 07 06 05 04   9 8 7 6 5 4 3 2 1

Library of Congress Cataloging-in-Publication Data
Tullier, L. Michelle.
    Networking for job search and career success / L. Michelle Tullier.— 2nd ed.
        p. cm.
    Updated ed. of: Networking for everyone.
    Includes index.
    ISBN 1-59357-067-8
  1. Social networks. 2. Career development. 3. Success in business. I. Tullier, L.
  Michelle.. Networking for everyone. II. Title.
    HM741.T85 2004
    302—dc22

                                        2004005688

We have been careful to provide accurate information in this book, but it is possible that errors and omissions have been introduced. Please consider this in making any career plans or other important decisions. Trust your own judgment above all else and in all things.

Trademarks: All brand names and product names used in this book are trade names, service marks, trademarks, or registered trademarks of their respective owners.

ISBN 1-59357-067-8

Preface

In the career transition firm where I work, we hold a monthly networking meeting called a landing party. This is an opportunity for our clients who have landed jobs or started businesses to come back to our office and tell the story of their transition as an inspirational and educational tool for clients who are still in the midst of their own transitions. Invariably, we find that the speakers owe their successes to networking far more than to any other job search or business development method. In fact, when one of them announces that they landed a job through an online job board posting or a newspaper ad, we're always surprised because that's such a rarity.

Not only is networking by far the best way to find a new job whether you're currently employed, unemployed, or underemployed, it's also invaluable for managing your career over the long run. And if you're self-employed or hoping to be, networking is essential to the success of any business.

When I wrote the first edition of this book, which was published in 1998 as *Networking for Everyone: Connecting with People for Career and Job Success*, I tackled the project from the perspective of someone who had learned networking the hard way. As someone who is more introverted than outgoing, I had tried every which way to avoid networking in my own career. I was great at motivating my clients to network, but did I practice what I preach? Not at first. I found it uncomfortable, awkward, and difficult. Then, several years into my career and after a couple of years of running a consulting business, I wised up, bit the bullet, and started networking. Amazing things started to happen. Job opportunities knocked on my door, the media started calling to interview me, and clients came to my business instead of me having to chase after them.

By the time I wrote this book's first edition, I was convinced that networking is the way to go if you want good things to happen to you professionally. Talent, skills, training, and knowledge are highly important, but without a strong network and a well-honed networking technique, those credentials won't take you far. I also realized that networking is a process that can be learned.

Now that several years have passed, I've witnessed even more networking success stories in my own life and those of my clients, and I've been gratified by the positive feedback I've received from people who read the first edition of the book and found it helpful for reaching their own goals.

I now bring to this edition of *Networking for Job Search and Career Success* an even stronger belief in the power of networking and renewed commitment to showing others that it is a skill that can be learned. I hope you will find this book to be a trusted guide that helps you make networking work for you. I wish you success in your networking and a speedy route to your own landing party.

Michelle Tullier
Atlanta, Georgia

About the Author

As a career counselor for over twenty years, Michelle Tullier has witnessed countless networking success stories—people from all walks of life reaching their professional goals by connecting with others. As a card-carrying introvert, she has had to work hard at acquiring networking as a skill rather than relying on a natural talent for it—and she has experienced many successes in her own professional life as a result of networking. From this hands-on perspective, Michelle is particularly well equipped to advise introverts and extroverts alike on surefire networking techniques.

Michelle is a Senior Career Management Consultant in the Atlanta office of the global career transition firm Right Management Consultants, where she coaches thousands of job seekers and entrepreneurs each year. Prior to joining Right, Michelle ran a successful independent career consulting practice in New York City, attracting clients from across the U.S. and abroad, and facilitated seminars in Fortune 500 companies on networking, time management, and other career development issues. Michelle also served as a career coach for Monster.com, taught career development at New York University, and served as a career counselor at Barnard College of Columbia University. Her work in career management is complemented by management roles in e-commerce during the dot-com boom of the late 1990s and dot-com bust of the early 2000s, a harrowing, thrill-a-minute experience but one she wouldn't trade for anything.

Michelle's expertise has been featured in numerous publications, including *Fortune*, *Chicago Tribune*, and *The New York Times,* and she is the author of several books, including *The Unofficial Guide to Landing a Job* and *Complete Idiot's Guide to Overcoming Procrastination*. Michelle holds a Ph.D. in counseling psychology from UCLA and a bachelor's degree from Wellesley College.

Dedication

To Susan W. Miller, M.A., of Los Angeles for being a superb networking role model, friend, and window to a world of opportunities when I was getting my start.

Acknowledgments

Though several years have passed since the first edition of this book, I remain very grateful to LaVerne Ludden and Mike Farr of JIST for having been receptive to the initial networking efforts that launched this project. I also remain indebted to those who contributed to that edition, including Sara Bauman, Ellis Chase, Georgia Donati, Nancy Friedberg, Tim Haft, Jeanne Krier, Sheryl Spanier, and Marci Taub—the New York contingent!

Back to the present, I am so thankful to *everyone* in the Atlanta office of Right Management Consultants for their support of my writing career and for being such outstanding—and fun—colleagues. In particular, Walter Tieck contributed significantly to this edition of the book with his expert research skills, career coaching knowledge, and willingness to lend a hand. This writer cannot find adequate words to express the respect and awe I have for you as a colleague and friend. To my wonderful boss, Richmond Fourmy, I am grateful for your support and flexibility and your caring about what makes me happy professionally and personally.

A hearty thank you to my editors at JIST, Stephanie Koutek and Lori Cates Hand, for their skillful touch and for making the process go so smoothly.

On the home front, much appreciation goes to Ann Marie and John Barbone; Jennifer Goodson; Kathy Quiggins; and my parents, Patricia and Ronald Gann and Scott Tullier, for helping out with the little diva and for lots of "meals on wheels" when writing distracted me from daily life.

And the biggest thanks of all go to Michael and Alexandra for putting up with me and making it possible for me to be wife, mother, and author.

Contents

Introduction

Networking works. It's as simple as that. Whether you're looking for a new job, trying to get ahead in your career, or building a business, connecting and building relationships with other people is the best way to reach your goals. But don't just take my word for it.

Take the word of countless surveys that have shown networking to be by far the most effective job search method.

Take the word of people whose careers you admire or envy. I guarantee you they didn't get to where they are only because of their talent. I bet they also connected with key people who helped guide them along the way.

Take the word of people you do business with in your neighborhood. Did you decide to take your business to those merchants or professionals because you saw an ad in the paper or because someone you know referred you to them? Most small businesses get their customers through word of mouth, also known as—you guessed it—networking.

Networking Works

Depending on which survey you go by, at least 65 to 85 percent of jobs are found through networking. So if all you're doing to land a job is applying to online postings, sending out mass mailings of resumes, and looking through the paper, you need to start networking NOW!

You may have picked up this book because you already have some idea that networking is an important element in professional success. What you may not have an idea of is how to do it right. That's where *Networking for Job Search and Career Success* comes in. Through my many years of career counseling, including lots of networking coaching, plus my own personal struggle to learn how to network effectively, I've learned what it takes to network the right way, and I share that knowledge with you in this book.

Why You Need This Book

Networking the wrong way is worse than not networking at all. Without the proper preparation, strategy, communication techniques, and follow-through, networking can burn more bridges than it builds.

What This Book Will Do for You

The objective of *Networking for Job Search and Career Success* is to teach strategies for networking that will help you reach your career or business goals and to give you access to print, electronic, and people resources to support and enable your networking efforts. Whether you've been cultivating contacts for years or find yourself starting from scratch, and whether you're a born schmoozer or an avowed loner, this book is for you. I cover the basics for those of you who are new to networking and get into more sophisticated techniques for experienced networkers.

Toss the Cookie Cutters

You won't find one-size-fits-all advice here. One of the main goals of this book is to show how networking can work with your personal style, not against it. This book doesn't try to turn you into someone you're not. Whether you're as shy as all get-out or the life of the party, you can adapt the advice on these pages to fit your personality.

Specifically, this book will help you

- Take stock of who is in your network and see if you know the right people

- Plan a strategy for meeting the right people and building relationships

- Expand your network of contacts exponentially

- Communicate effectively in person, by phone, in writing, and online

- Deal with special situations like those faced by students or introverts

- Handle the sticky issues and pain-in-the-neck people you're likely to encounter in networking

- Keep your network going and growing

- Learn the best ways to network in a job search

- Get ahead or be more productive in your current position by finding mentors and others to help you manage your career

- Start cultivating referral sources and trusted advisors to help you establish or expand your own business

How to Get the Most Out of This Book

Networking for Job Search and Career Success is designed as a comprehensive guide. I've tried to address every issue related to the networking process, and in the appendixes I refer you to additional resources for further guidance and support.

In addition, instead of just giving random advice and tips on networking, I've organized it all into a logical sequence of chapters. I therefore recommend that you read the book from cover to cover in order to get a feel for the steps you need to take.

But if you're in a hurry, you can get a quick crash course in networking from only the first two chapters or you can zero in on any other chapter that addresses a particular concern you have at the moment.

Networking Is a Skill You Can Learn

Networking is not the sole domain of master schmoozers, quota-busting salespeople, and charter members of good-ol'-boy or -girl networks. There's no question that some people seem to have more of a natural gift for it than others. They're the ones who introduce themselves at parties, head up committees, rarely get sweaty palms when meeting someone new, and seem to have the "gift of gab." If that doesn't describe you, have no fear. By learning tried-and-true techniques and putting them into practice, you can become a skilled networker—I guarantee it.

Interspersed throughout the book you'll find worksheets, checklists, and other activities to help you get your ducks in a row and take action. I recommend completing most of these, but you be the judge of which ones are the best use of your time. You'll also find introductory pages for each of the five parts as well as summaries at the end of each chapter to help you not lose sight of the big picture.

Whichever way you choose to read and use *Networking for Job Search and Career Success*, I hope it will come to be a trusted handbook that sees you through many fulfilling and rewarding encounters with people, whether in person, online, over the phone, or through the good old U.S. Mail.

Part 1: The Basics and More: Networking Essentials

. . . .

This first section of the book consists of two chapters that form a critical launching pad for your journey to becoming a successful networker. Chapter 1 gets you off to the right start by defining what networking is and isn't (particularly useful for those of you who thought that networking only meant something to do with computers!), as well as where and how to network.

In Chapter 1 you'll find some surprises, such as that the old saying "It's not what you know, it's who you know" isn't really true. You'll learn why *what* you know—and who knows that you know it—is just as much a part of networking as the number of names in your address book. Chapter 1 also covers the reasons why you need to network, discussing how networking can help you make career decisions, land the right job, manage your career, or develop a business.

Chapter 2 walks you through the various places and ways you can network while offering tips on how to do it. I hope you'll pay particular attention to the ten key elements in the section "The Networking Mindset" in this chapter. Taking those ten tips to heart will dramatically improve your networking results, not to mention make the process more enjoyable along the way.

So, ready, set, go!

What Networking Is and Why It's Important

I use not only all the brains I have, but all I can borrow.

—WOODROW WILSON

Okay, pop quiz time. Read each statement below and decide if it's an example of networking, marking Yes or No:

1. John moves to a new neighborhood and asks his neighbors for the name of a good dentist in the area.   Yes   No

2. Lori gets together with an old friend for lunch to catch up on each other's lives.   Yes   No

3. Bob visits a professional association's Web site and posts a reply to someone's question on a message board.   Yes   No

4. Murray chats with the person seated next to him on an airplane.   Yes   No

5. Felicia and Jose ask other parents for recommendations of a good preschool for their child.   Yes   No

6. Marie is happily employed, but when a recruiter calls to tell her about a job opportunity, she gives him a few minutes of her time and saves his name and number for future reference.   Yes   No

7. Trevor volunteers to be on the planning committee for his industry's national convention.   Yes   No

What are the answers? That's easy—they're all examples of networking. As you can see from those examples, networking is simply a natural process of connecting with other people in a wide variety of ways. Chances are you already cultivate contacts and seek out information daily. Have you ever mentioned to a couple of friends that you were looking for a new place to live, deciding on which type of car to buy, or planning a vacation? In no time at all, you probably had more suggestions than you knew what to do with, and other people you'd never even met started coming out of the woodwork to put in their two cents.

Experienced networkers know that the same thing happens when they start spreading the word that they're looking for a new job, trying to build a business, or deciding on a new career direction. People who actively network find that they actually know more people, or at least have access to more people and more sources of information, than they realized and that those people and information sources provide all sorts of valuable suggestions and leads.

The key is to take these everyday experiences of connecting with people and information and see them as part of a cohesive networking strategy. This book is designed to help you do just that. First, though, let's develop a good working definition of networking and look more closely at the specific ways networking can help you in your professional life.

A New Definition of Networking

To develop a working definition of networking, it's helpful to start by looking at what networking is *not*. Networking is not about bothering, pestering, or using people. It's not about being pushy, and it's not a contest to see who can collect the most business cards or shake the most hands. It's not a one-sided, selfish, flash-in-the-pan activity. It's not asking people for jobs or hitting them up as customers for your business.

True networking—effective networking—is based on relationships that are cultivated and nurtured so that a mutual exchange of information, advice, referrals, and support takes place. If this is the definition of networking that you live and work by, you should never feel as if you're begging, being demanding, or bothering the other person. When you take the time to develop mutually beneficial relationships, networking takes on a new and better meaning. You can comfortably turn to people in your network when you need help with a career move, business decision, or transition, while the people in your network know that they can turn to you when they need assistance.

Redefining the Networking Cliché

When defining networking, many people think of the popular cliché, "It's not what you know, it's who you know." They think that knowing a lot of people, preferably the right people, is all it takes to get ahead. Well, there's more to it than that. To build on our definition of what networking is *not* as offered in the preceding section, I propose a few new twists on that familiar saying.

It's Who You Know . . .

Without a doubt, the "who you know" part of the cliché is still the cornerstone of networking. Knowing people in high places, low places, and everywhere in

> ### The New Networking
>
> Networking is not about superficial connections and brief encounters. It's about cultivating relationships with others in a meaningful way so that you have people to turn to when you need information and support and people you can help when they need someone to turn to.

between is a key to career and business success. Networking is something of a numbers game. The more people you know, the easier it is to get ahead in your career or business. Quantity cannot come at the expense of quality, however, which leads us to the next point.

It's Who Knows What You Need to Know . . .

That's a bit of a tongue twister, but it's meant to be that way to make you think more carefully about networking. As mentioned earlier, networking is not a contest to see who can collect the most business cards. In other words, effective networking is not simply a matter of getting as many people as possible into your Rolodex or contact database. Quality is just as important as quantity, if not more so. That's where "It's who knows what you need to know" comes in. When you set out to meet people, it is important to zero in on people who have the information, knowledge, or expertise that you need. Instead of meeting huge numbers of people randomly, find a balance between quantity and quality and develop relationships with those who know what you need to know— those who have the knowledge, experience, and contacts that could help you reach your goals. It's simply a matter of being strategic.

It's What You Know . . .

According to conventional wisdom, "*What* you know doesn't count; it's *who* you know that matters." Well, that way of thinking just doesn't cut it in today's world. Many relationships these days develop and thrive because people share information with each other. For example, if someone posts a question on an online message board and you are knowledgeable about that particular topic, you can make a valuable contact if you reply. Being well informed can clearly open doors for you—not just online but in life in general. What you know *does* matter.

It's Who Knows that You Know What You Know . . .

Here's another tongue twister to get you thinking more strategically about how you network. Simply put, it's a question of how visible you are or how many others know that you exist and that you have a certain area of expertise or knowledge base. Anyone who's ever tried to sell a product—whether it's lemonade at a neighborhood stand or high-ticket items in a multi-million-dollar business—knows that it's better to have customers coming to you than to have to chase after customers yourself. Well, the same principle is at work in networking. Sure, you have to make overtures to develop relationships with others, but wouldn't it be nice to have people occasionally calling you for a change?

If you're searching for a job, trying to manage your career more effectively, or looking for clients or customers for your own business, the more visible you are, the more likely it is that opportunity will come knocking on your door. Speaking in public, publishing articles (even just a letter to the editor), getting quoted in the paper, having a leadership role in a professional association, and having your own Web site are some of the many ways to gain visibility.

So, to get off to the right start in networking, you should forget you ever heard "It's not what you know, it's who you know." Instead, have "It's both what you know and who you know that count" as a guiding principle when you set out to connect with people and information.

The Psychology of Networking

One nice phenomenon people experience when they actively network is that most people genuinely want to help. Not only do I hear reports all the time from clients who are pleasantly surprised to find their networking efforts well received, but I also frequently witness this good side of human nature myself. For example, when I was a part-time professor in a university's continuing education program for several years, I often had to ask career counseling colleagues to volunteer their time as guest speakers in my evening classes. No matter how much I reminded myself that these were nice, generous people who would be happy to help if their schedules allowed, I nevertheless felt a bit apprehensive when I picked up the phone to make the request. I found, though, that 99.9 percent of the time that I asked these busy people to extend their workday by a few hours, travel to a campus in a part of town far from where they lived and worked, and share the tricks of their trade, all for no compensation, they accepted with pleasure. This experience was always a refreshing and reassuring glimpse into human nature.

In addition to reflecting generosity of spirit and basic kindness, positive results like these also reflect the idea that "what goes around comes around." Almost all the people you'll make contact with in your networking efforts are likely to have gotten where they are in their careers or businesses because someone else helped them along the way. As this happens, it creates a feeling of obligation in people and a desire to pay back a debt of sorts. This obligation can often be satisfied by helping others advance in their careers or grow their businesses.

Now, hear me out before the cynic in you says, "Wait a minute. You can't tell me that everyone on this planet is kindhearted and willing to go out on a limb for the next person!" All I am saying is that a frequent phenomenon in the networking process is that people do want to help; I'm not claiming that everyone you encounter will do so out of a sense of altruism. Some people just like the power-trip aspect of giving others advice, voicing opinions, or helping them find jobs. Others like to talk about themselves so much that they're willing to meet with anybody and everybody solely to have someone else hear them talk. And, yes, you will occasionally meet those people who just don't get it—those who don't want to help at all.

What Have You Done for Me Lately?

Social psychologists who study helping behavior have identified several phenomena that may be working in your favor when you set out to network. They have found that while some people may seem to be motivated to help others out of sheer altruism, they are actually doing so because of the potential benefits to themselves. Research has confirmed the existence of a concept that psychologists call "self-reward," which is the idea that helping others can reinforce in our own minds the notion that we are good people. It's the idea that we are motivated to lend a hand because we get an ego boost from being able to pat ourselves on the back for our good deeds. Helping can also keep us from feeling the shame and guilt that would result from not assisting others in need. As Abraham Lincoln once said when he stopped his carriage on a road to save some baby pigs from danger, "I should have had no peace of mind all day had I gone on and left that suffering old sow worrying over those pigs. I did it to get peace of mind."

Source: Reuben M. Baron and William G. Graziano, *Social Psychology* (Holt, Rinehart, Winston, Inc., Chicago, 1991), pp. 354-356.

Why Network?

Each stage of adult life brings professional challenges to overcome and goals that can be achieved only if you connect with the right people and information. Regardless of your age or stage in your career, you might be working toward any of the following four goals, which networking can help you achieve:

- **Career choice.** Throughout this book, a goal of *career choice* refers to an effort to make a satisfying and appropriate decision about your career direction. For you, that might mean choosing a first career field out of high school or college or moving to a new career field after any number of years in the work world. You might be making a choice between several career options or have one specific career field in mind and need to confirm that it's the right direction for you.

- **Job search.** If a new job is your goal, then for the purposes of this book, *job search* means that you are simply seeking employment— whether full-time or part-time, permanent or temporary. This category also includes internships and apprenticeships in addition to paid jobs. Whether you're hunting for your first job or seeking a new job after many years of experience, networking is one of the most effective job search methods.

- **Career management.** Having a goal of networking for *career management* purposes means that you want to be more productive and successful in your current job or in your career in general. What this might mean for you specifically is that you're hoping to get a promotion or a raise, to be more efficient and effective in doing your job, to plot a course for where your career path is heading, or to achieve any of a number of other career management goals unique to you and your situation.

- **Business development.** A *business development* goal applies to those who are self-employed or are contemplating self-employment as consultants, freelancers, business owners, or professionals in private practice. Your goal might be to decide if self-employment is right for you, in which case networking can provide the information and guidance you need to make such a big decision. Or, if you're already working on your own, your goal might be to network so that you can expand your business or maintain a successful one.

These four goals are themes carried throughout *Networking for Job Search and Career Success*, so when the terms *career choice, job search, career management,* and *business development* are mentioned again, in most cases they refer to the goals described here. Throughout the book, I include examples of actual people who have networked successfully toward each of the four goals.

Networking in Choosing a Career

Many people think of networking as useful primarily for job searching, not realizing how useful—and essential—networking is when you are identifying the field in which you want to work. Whether you're choosing your first career fresh out of school or changing careers in midlife, networking can help you uncover possibilities, evaluate each career option, and make a good decision.

Take the case of Jake, a high school science teacher who wanted to make a transition into the health care field. He had read a career guidebook that described health care occupations, and as a result of that reading, decided that nursing, physical therapy, and becoming a physician's assistant were growing occupations he wanted to look into further. To get his research started, he set up a meeting with a physical therapist whom a friend had put him in touch with. (The meeting he had with her is called a fact-finding mission—something you can read about in more detail in Chapter 7.) This first attempt at networking not only helped him learn more about one of his career options—physical therapy—but also made him aware of a closely related profession he hadn't known much about: occupational therapy. Keep reading to see how that happened and find out how networking comes into play in the career-choice process and how it helped Jake specifically.

Generating Career Options

Thinking of career options off the top of your head, asking friends and colleagues for career ideas, or reading about various careers in guidebooks are good starting points but are often not sufficient for uncovering the full range of options open to you. The world of work is a big place, so you want to use all possible methods to navigate around it, including networking. Talking to people who are knowledgeable about a given field or industry is a great way to do that.

For example, when Jake met with that physical therapist to discuss her profession, she happened to mention occupational therapists as a particular type of medical professional whom she sometimes comes into contact with on her job. Jake had heard of occupational therapy but didn't really know much about it, so he added it to his list of careers to research and set about getting more information. Jake's case is a typical example of how networking can generate interesting new career options. You go into a networking meeting with plans to collect information on certain career options and come out with another option or two you hadn't yet thought of.

Obtaining Career Information

Researching a particular career or occupation is an essential step in deciding whether to enter that field. As Jake found, reading guidebooks is one way to learn about the nature of the work in a given career, as well as typical salaries, qualifications needed to get into the field, and the projected employment outlook for that career field. Other sources he could have used include Web sites that profile career fields (such as the *Occupational Outlook Handbook* online at http://www.bls.gov) and literature from professional associations.

Network contacts, however, often turn out to be the best source of information. People who work in a field you're considering entering can share the trials and tribulations of their jobs, tell you what types of people tend to be satisfied and successful in that career field, and provide other useful information that you often can't get in a book or pamphlet.

Jake, for example, found out all sorts of valuable information about the field of occupational therapy when he met with an occupational therapist whom his physical therapist friend arranged for him to meet. Before the appointment, Jake learned a bit about the field from the Web site of the occupational therapy professional association. This preliminary research enabled him to come to the meeting armed with focused questions. (Examples of questions to ask in a fact-finding mission are provided in Chapter 7.) Jake left the meeting not only with thorough answers to his questions, but also with suggestions of more people to talk to, names of professional journals to read, and a list of graduate programs he could investigate.

Making a Career Decision

Your network contacts not only provide information about careers but also serve as surrogate career counselors of sorts, helping you understand how your own interests, skills, experiences, and goals might mesh with a career field you're considering.

Networking proved helpful to Jake at the decision-making stage because he found that, after two months of researching his options for a career change, he had narrowed the choice to nursing or occupational therapy but couldn't decide between the two. Their pros and cons seemed to balance one another out. So, in a career counseling session he had with me, I helped him sort out his priorities so that he would know which pros were really important to him and which cons he especially wanted to avoid. By discussing his interests, strengths, and values, he was able to come to some conclusions. He then had phone conversations with health care professionals he had met with earlier to ask them which option they thought would be a better match for him based on those priorities. From those discussions, he got a sense that nursing might be the better way to go for him because there was a nursing shortage at his local hospitals and he wanted to be sure that there would be job opportunities after he completed his training. He still wasn't 100 percent sure about his decision, though. The next section will help you see what he did to get out of this quandary.

Opening Up Opportunities to Try Out a Career

Networking can help you uncover useful ways to try out career fields, such as internships, volunteer or pro bono work, temporary projects, classes, and other opportunities. As Jake found, just reading about career options is rarely, if ever, sufficient for making an informed decision, and even talking with people for further information is often not enough to determine which direction is best for you. After all, you spend a lot of time on a job, so it helps to go in knowing what to expect.

You may also need to gain some practical experience in a new field before you can be fully employed in it. Experience can also enable you to enter a field in a higher position or get into a degree program.

So, short-term, hands-on experiences are one way to be sure that the career choice you make is right for you, and this experience also increases your chances of making a smooth transition into it.

While there are many good directories available that list internship and volunteer opportunities, and college career centers can often direct you to such experiences, networking is one of the most effective ways to uncover the best opportunities. This is especially true if you're several years or more into your current career and you do not have the luxury of taking time off from paid work to be an unpaid intern or volunteer. Networking can be a way to find out about project-based work or other short-term activities you may be able to engage in during your spare time to get your foot in the door of a new career area.

In Jake's case, networking came in handy in that one of his contacts let him know about a particular program sponsored by a local hospital that involved shadowing nurses for a week and taking an introductory class that would help him further explore the field. The experience turned out to be very valuable to Jake. He was able to decide that nursing was the direction he wanted to head, so he stayed in his high school teaching job for one more academic year while applying to educational programs in nursing. He also began volunteering at a hospital to get experience inter-acting with patients, and he did occasional science tutoring with students to make some extra money as he approached a transitional period in his career. All in all, he was pleased with his decision and was on the road to a satisfying career.

Networking in the Job Search Process

Networking as a way to generate job leads has long been one of the most popular and effective of all job search methods. You could answer classified ads every day, send out hundreds of unsolicited resumes to places you'd like to work, post your resume on the Internet, and sign up with employment agencies or executive recruiters, but you're likely to find that word of mouth is the way you hear about the job you eventually land.

The Power of Word of Mouth

Studies from a variety of sources, including outplacement firms, executive search firms, and the U.S. Department of Labor, have consistently shown that the percentage of jobs found through networking is at least 65 to 85 percent or even higher.

Although many savvy job seekers realize that networking is the name of the game, too often they think of networking in overly narrow terms. They often see networking in a job search as simply telling their immediate circle of friends, family, and colleagues to keep an eye out for jobs for them. While it can be tempting to look at friends and family as "people who can get me a job," the reality is that this narrow approach to networking inevitably leads to a lot of dead ends. Even if they would love to do so, most people do not have the power to snap their fingers and get you a job. Networking in a job search involves more than simply asking people if they know of any openings or to be on the lookout for openings for you. Networking for a job requires that you be more resourceful in the way that you utilize your contacts. It also requires that you expand your efforts beyond your inner circle of family, close friends, and colleagues.

Consider the case of Rosa, a purchasing manager for a large telecommunications company, recently laid off as part of a corporate downsizing. Rosa is a good example of someone who used networking effectively to get a job after some false starts in her search. Because opportunities were limited in Rosa's field of telecommunications, she wanted to transfer her purchasing and management skills to the more thriving, growing industry of pharmaceuticals. After spending a couple of months applying for jobs listed in the paper and posted online and contacting headhunters (executive search firms), she had reached nothing but dead ends. In the back of her mind, Rosa knew that she ought to be networking, but she didn't exactly know how to go about it. Plus, she was new in town and didn't know that many people, so she wasn't sure how to get a network going. Finally, after some coaching from the outplacement firm that her company had provided her access to after her layoff, she decided to turn to networking. Rosa called everyone in her immediate network—about 40 people—to tell them that she was looking for a job. She also attended a few networking events in her community, where she met several new people to whom she gave her resume. She called those new contacts a few days later to follow up and found that they didn't know of any openings at that time, so she asked them to let her know if they heard of anything.

After several weeks and just a couple of leads that didn't pan out, Rosa realized she had reached another dead end. What else could she have done? Everyone kept preaching, "Network, network, network," and now that she had finally done it, she wasn't seeing any better results. Rosa had the best of intentions, but her lack of strategy and flawed execution made networking less than effective for her. The following are examples of ways that networking can really transform a search—ways that ended up paying off for Rosa.

Planning Strategy

Instead of just asking your contacts to keep an eye out for jobs for you as Rosa did, why not sit down with them for advice on your search strategy? In doing so, you're developing a relationship and showing them that there is a way they can help you whether or not they are aware of actual job openings. And, most importantly, you're keeping the door open with your contacts because you've given them a more open-ended project— your ever-evolving search strategy—rather than one that has built-in limits, such as asking, "Do you know of any jobs?" (In Chapter 8, you'll read about the strategy session, which is a meeting in which you have your contacts help you plan a strategy for your job search.)

Rosa conducted several strategy sessions that helped her see what she could be doing to make her job search more effective. She got a list from her college of alumni working in pharmaceuticals and also re-contacted a few of the people she had met at that early networking event she had attended. Rosa then met with these contacts—some in person and others by phone—to get some ideas for rejuvenating her search. From these meetings, she learned that she should be attending meetings of the local chapter of a particular professional association for women in pharmaceuticals. She also got tips on how to describe her work experience in a significantly different manner to sound less "telecom-oriented." In other words, she needed to go back to the drawing board to make herself a more desirable candidate for the new industry she sought to enter.

Preparing the Tools of Your Search

When you develop your resume, cover letters, and thank-you letters and prepare for interviews, it's helpful to have input from others. This help may come not only from career counselors, job search coaches, and guidebooks, but also from people who work in the field in which you want to get a job. Who is better able to tell you what they would want to see in your resume or to conduct a mock interview with you than people who work in your target field?

Rosa, for example, identified the two people who had been most helpful and generous with their time during her round of strategy sessions and asked them for another half hour of their time. After first taking some of the action they had suggested in those sessions, she came back to them with a revised version of her resume and cover letters, as well as with a list of questions that she had found difficult to answer in the few job interviews she had had. By doing so, she received helpful critiques of her written materials, plus suggestions of ways to tackle the tough interview questions.

Uncovering Job Leads

Here's where networking most often comes into the job search process—asking others for information about jobs that are, or might be, available. This is what's really meant by the proverbial "hidden job market." Instead of just sitting at home answering ads or mailing unsolicited resumes, you talk to people and hear about jobs that haven't yet been advertised.

In the course of her strategy sessions, Rosa did find out about job openings that she was able to interview for. So, even though she was meeting with her contacts primarily for advice about her search strategy, not to ask for jobs, she did learn about actual jobs, too.

Enlisting Go-Betweens in Your Search

One notch up on the involvement scale for a contact is a person who acts on your behalf as you search for a job. Some people in your network will take the extra step of not only telling you about an opening but actively intervening on your behalf. They might hand-deliver your resume and recommend you as a candidate to the person who has the power to hire you.

> The go-between wears out a thousand sandals.
>
> —JAPANESE PROVERB

Rosa, for example, found that one particular contact she had been meeting with took Rosa under her wing and got very involved in acting on her behalf. The contact not only told Rosa about openings, but also hand-delivered Rosa's resume to a number of people in her company and spoke to them at length about Rosa's qualifications. One of these efforts led to Rosa's being interviewed and subsequently hired, so developing a relationship with that contact certainly paid off.

Helping You Evaluate Offers

When you do start to get job offers, it's useful to get advice from the more helpful and knowledgeable members of your network to help you decide whether you should accept or decline an offer. They can walk you through the process of evaluating the offer based on the terms of the deal, the nature of the job, the goals you had originally expressed to them, and their knowledge of what is considered to be a good job in their field.

This benefit of networking also came in handy for Rosa. In addition to the offer she received through one of her contacts, she also got an offer as a result of an online ad she had answered. Both were for purchasing manager positions with comparable job responsibilities, but they differed in that one had a higher salary whereas the other was at a more stable, established company. She didn't know which job to take. By consulting with several people in her network, she was able to determine which job would be the better opportunity for her, both in the short term and for reaching her long-range goals.

Emotional Support During the Ups and Downs

A less tangible, but equally important, function of networking in a job search is to attend to your emotional needs during the often frustrating and demoralizing process of trying to get a job. Any transition in life requires a support system, and the job search is no exception. A strong network can provide this support system for you.

It sure did in Rosa's case. Her search took eight months to reach a successful conclusion, a wait that seemed like an eternity to her. Though she was generally confident in her abilities and knew she would eventually land a job, her spirits certainly did flag at times. The reassurance and empathy she received not only from family and close friends but also from some of the new contacts she developed helped her get past the rough spots.

Networking and the Career Management Process

After you've obtained a job, you might think that you can stop networking and just concentrate on doing your work. Wrong! People who are the most successful tend to be those who continually cultivate and maintain rewarding relationships within and outside their workplace.

Sam, a client I worked with in my former private practice in New York, is an excellent example of effective career management through networking. As an art director for an advertising agency, Sam produced, or oversaw the production of, artwork for ads to go into magazines and newspapers. He also sometimes got involved in the creative direction of television commercials. Sam rose from a junior position at his company to management level in only a year because of his talent as an illustrator, proficiency in graphic design, and seemingly endless creativity. He knew, though, that in a competitive business like advertising, he had to nurture his talent and keep producing increasingly innovative work to keep his job secure. He also realized that talent alone would not be enough to rise to the higher levels of management that he hoped to reach.

The following are some of the ways that networking can enhance your own career management and some examples of how Sam used them to his benefit.

Being More Productive and Successful on the Job

If you have a job where productivity and success rely on generating sales or referrals of clients or customers, networking is essential. But what if your work doesn't involve selling or business development per se? Networking is still important in that it can help you find ways to solve problems, improve efficiency, and stay fresh and innovative. Good networking can also help you keep an eye on what the competition is up to.

Sam, for example, made a point of having lunch at least twice a month with creative types—illustrators, painters, graphic designers, photographers, and so on—who worked outside the advertising field. He found that viewing their work and talking with them helped to inject a new vitality into his own work. Direct involvement also helped him maintain a pool of top-notch freelancers he could call upon to work in his agency when needed. Sam also met periodically with art directors from other ad agencies, particularly from those firms that specialized in the types of clients his agency didn't service and were therefore not competitors. Doing so helped bring a fresh perspective to the way he approached his own ad campaigns.

Advancing in Your Job

Promotions, raises, and plum assignments do not always go to the people who are most deserving based on performance. They frequently go to the employees who are the most visible—that is, those whose strengths and accomplishments are well known to the people who have the power to advance others' careers. Given this reality, networking is likely to be a key element in your own advancement. Do you remember that tongue twister from earlier in this chapter—"Who knows that you know what you know"? Well, here it is in action. Just doing your job satisfactorily is not enough to get ahead; you have to be visible as well.

To make sure he didn't become invisible in his large agency, Sam took the initiative to meet frequently with his bosses to discuss what was happening in his department and to find out what objectives they wanted him to meet. On the surface, these discussions were simply standard strategy or check-in meetings between a mid-level manager and senior managers. Beneath the surface, however, these meetings were critical opportunities for Sam to ensure that upper management was aware of his successes as well as his dedication to continual improvement. In other words, he stayed visible.

Advancing in Your Career

In addition to getting ahead at your current job, you might also be concerned about getting ahead in your career in general. Are there long-range goals you're striving for? Do you hope to have reached a certain level in your field five, ten, or fifteen years from now? Do you want to be making a certain amount of money by a particular age? Do you hope to transition into a new career field or a different industry in a few years? Developing professional relationships with people who can steer you in the right direction toward your goals is essential for successful career management. Networking helps secretaries move into non-clerical positions, enables salespeople to move into management, catapults company vice-presidents to executive vice-presidents, and facilitates just about any other transition you might want to make—either with your current employer or elsewhere.

To take a proactive stance in directing his own career, Sam met a few times a year with a retired advertising executive who had led the creative departments of two of the country's top agencies. Serving as a mentor of sorts, this experienced person advised Sam about how to conduct a successful career in advertising based on his years of experience. Sam also participated actively in professional associations so that he was well known among his colleagues. As a result, he often heard of job openings before they were advertised. He chose not to pursue most of them, but at least he knew that

> ### Neanderthal Networking?
>
> Networking may have its origins in the self-preservation instinct that has led human beings since prehistoric times to band together to fend off enemy aggression.

when he *was* ready to make a move, he would have a well-developed network to turn to. After all, an important element in career management is cultivating contacts now, even if you might not need them until later.

Networking in the Business Development Process

Whether you are already operating a booming enterprise or are only at the "be my own boss" daydreaming stage, networking is essential to your success. Seeking the advice and guidance of people who are already self-employed (as consultants, freelancers, business owners, or professionals in private practice) can help you make sound decisions about how to start, expand, or maintain a successful business.

Networking certainly helped Monica, a Web site developer for the e-commerce division of a magazine publishing conglomerate. Monica was getting tired of the bureaucracy and politics where she was working and began to think that maybe she could strike out on her own as a freelance Web site designer/producer. She often designed home pages for friends in her spare time, so she had some idea of what it might be like to freelance but wasn't sure how to get started. Monica knew her skills lay in technical and creative areas, not in business, so she was at a loss as to how to develop a successful business of her own. Monica's story is a superb example of how connecting with the right people and information can turn a vague idea into a successful reality.

We'll follow Monica's story as we look at some of the ways that networking can facilitate the process of starting, growing, and maintaining your own business.

Deciding to Go into Business for Yourself

The thought of being your own boss can be exciting but can also bring up a host of concerns. Can I make enough money to survive? Do I really know how to run a business? Is there a market for my product or service?

If you're thinking of becoming self-employed as a small business owner, consultant, freelancer, or professional in private practice, networking can help you answer those questions and make the right decision. Turning to knowledgeable people and valuable sources of information (the "who you know and what you know" idea) can help you survey the demand for your product or service, identify what you really need to know about running a business, and carefully assess the financial risk involved.

Monica, for example, embarked on a thorough research process to find out everything she could about running a business. She read all the latest books on small business operation, consulting, and freelancing. (Many of these are listed in Appendix D.) She became a regular visitor to Web sites devoted to self-employment and home-based business (see Appendix C for a list of sites), and she spoke with several computer consultants to learn about the ups and downs of their work. After a few months of research, Monica felt she was equipped with enough information to make a good decision. She decided that she definitely would strike out on her own but also decided that she would do so only after carefully planning a strategy for how she would start and build her business.

Building a Business

You've probably heard all the dismal statistics about how many businesses fail in the first year (usually about 80 percent of them, according to the U.S. Department of Labor). Why the poor success rate? It's because most people dive into self-employment on a wing and a prayer without the careful planning and budgeting that's necessary to survive and thrive. Launching a business—whether it's a small freelance operation run out of your home or a full-fledged corporation with employees and a suite of offices—requires that you first map out a detailed business plan to guide your every step.

After all her research at the decision-making stage, Monica knew that quitting her job on an impulse and setting up shop as a consultant with nothing more than a business card and a phone line would be a recipe for disaster. Therefore, she created a rough draft of a business plan using some do-it-yourself business plan software and then took it to the advisors at SCORE, a branch of the U.S. Small Business Administration that provides advice free of charge. (See Appendix C for ways to locate a SCORE office near you.) They reviewed her business plan and pointed out some areas that needed work. Monica also went back to a couple of the computer consultants she had spoken with earlier to get input on her plan from the perspective of people actively working in her field. With all of this help, she was able to put together a solid business plan that was professional enough to impress a bank, which lent her some start-up capital for equipment she needed to purchase.

Expanding a Business

In *Field of Dreams*, a voice said, "If you build it, they will come." Well, anyone who's self-employed knows that just building a business isn't enough. You have to build it and spread the word about it, and then "they" will come. That, of course, is where networking comes in handy. To grow a business, you have to make people aware of what you have to offer. In a previous section, you saw that in the career management process, you can't just do your job well—you have to be visible too. The same holds true for running a business or being a consultant.

I know that when I started my private practice in career counseling, I hoped that if I simply provided high-quality service to my clients, word would spread and my practice would grow exponentially. Well, word of mouth among clients did help, but it wasn't enough. I also had to become involved in professional associations, take the initiative to get out and meet people who could refer clients to me, do public speaking, and generally be as visible as possible. The same was true for Monica after she launched her consulting business. While satisfied clients did refer business to her, she soon learned that she had to find the time to cultivate a wider circle of referral sources, so she became active in her local Chamber of Commerce and also joined two professional associations made up of people from a wide variety of businesses. Doing so made greater numbers of people aware of what she had to offer, and she soon became a household name in her community.

Maintaining a Business

Working on your own can be enormously rewarding. You have considerable, if not total, control over when and how you work. Your income potential is not limited to the salary an employer has dictated for you. You have the satisfaction of seeing your visions become realities. All in all, self-employment can be very gratifying. There is, however, a downside. Successful businesses inevitably have seemingly inexplicable dry spells. The pressure of being solely responsible for your own paycheck, or for meeting a payroll if you have employees, can become overwhelming. The long hours you have to put in can be exhausting. The constant need not only to do your job but also to bring in business can be stressful.

Maintaining a business takes perseverance, hard work, and a little faith that it's all worth it in the long run.

Monica reached this point only one year into her consulting business. She was exhausted by the long hours she had been keeping and felt that she was just barely keeping her head above water financially. She could see that the business was growing. Momentum was building steadily, but she hadn't yet reached the point where she could relax for even a moment. To get over this rough patch, Monica consulted two people who had been serving as mentors for her. One was an experienced consultant who had nothing to do with the Internet industry but was an excellent source of advice, inspiration, and moral support. The other was actually a paid mentor—a business strategy coach she met with for hourly sessions (such coaches are discussed in more detail in the "Allied Forces" section of Chapter 4). These advisors helped her find ways to focus her efforts and redefine her business goals so that she could be more streamlined in the way she worked. Doing so enabled her to see greater rewards for less output of time and energy. Her meetings with the advisors also helped her realize that every business has rough patches and that it just takes a little patience and perseverance to get past them.

As you can see from the cases of Jake, Rosa, Sam, and Monica, connecting with people and information is a crucial part of any career or business endeavor. Whether your goal is career choice, job search, career management, or business development, networking can help you reach that goal.

Quick Summary

What Networking Is Not

- Bothering, pestering, or using people

- A contest to see who can collect the most contacts

- A one-sided, one-shot deal

- Asking for a job or directly soliciting business

What Networking Is

Networking is a process of cultivating and maintaining relationships in which a mutual exchange of information, advice, and support facilitates the growth, success, and happiness of all involved.

Why Network?

- To choose a career direction

- To generate career options

- To obtain information about careers

- To make career decisions

- To find opportunities for trying out career options

- To obtain a job

- For help planning your job search strategy

- For help preparing the tools of your job search

- To uncover leads

- To find people to act as agents for you

- To find people to interview or hire you

- For guidance as you evaluate job offers

- For emotional support

- To help you manage your career

- To be more productive and successful on the job

- To make decisions about going into business for yourself

- To develop and grow a business, consulting practice, or other self-employment enterprise

Where and How to Network

Networking opportunities can be as impromptu as chatting with the person seated next to you on a plane, as formal as having an official scheduled networking appointment in someone's office, and as big as attending a large professional event where there's lots of mixing and mingling. It doesn't matter where you're networking or whether you're doing it with one person or with hundreds, the key is to network in a variety of places and to do it effectively. This chapter explores the various avenues for networking along with do's and don'ts for your networking technique.

Where to Network

Networking can essentially take place anywhere. That's a good thing, but I know it can also be a bit daunting as you start to develop your own networking plan, so I'll rein it in a bit and look at what "anywhere" can mean specifically. Basically, most networking encounters fall into the following six categories:

- One-to-one meetings

- Professional groups

- The Internet

- Education and training

- Social/recreational/community settings

- Serendipity

Let's look at each of these categories in more depth so that you can start getting some ideas for networking opportunities you could be seeking out as well as for some that might have been right under your nose all this time. Then, later in this chapter, I'll walk you through some critical do's and don'ts for how to make the most of the networking avenues.

One-to-One Meetings

One-to-one meetings with network contacts can range from an informal conversation with a friend, family member, or co-worker to an exchange of e-mail with a distant professional colleague to a formal appointment with someone you've never met. Chapters 7, 8, and 9 focus on three particular types of one-to-one meetings you might have depending on your needs and goals and offer tips on protocol and strategy for requesting, scheduling, and conducting such meetings.

One-to-one meetings are often the most productive networking encounters in that they obviously give you quality time with one person to develop rapport, grow a relationship, and have an in-depth discussion of your needs and goals, as well as of how you can help each other.

Beware of relying too heavily on one-to-one meetings in your networking, though. Too many clients I've worked with over the years have been under the false impression that connecting with people one by one is all they need to do. While one-at-a-time connections should certainly be a major part of your networking effort, keep in mind that this is the most labor-intensive way to network. You need to add some group events to the mix to make sure that you are covering more ground and expanding your network more exponentially than is possible with the one-by-one approach.

Professional Groups

Professional group opportunities for networking come in a variety of shapes and sizes. Here are some of the most common ones:

- **Conferences and conventions.** Regional or national conferences or conventions in a given profession or industry (or ones that encompass a number of industries or career fields) are often excellent opportunities to expand your network. Professional and trade associations are most typically the sponsors of these events. For ideas of associations that might be hosting events you could attend, see Appendix B. Most associations post a calendar of local and national events on their Web sites.

  If you're currently employed or are self-employed and have a travel or marketing budget, be sure to take advantage of conferences and conventions that your employer or business can foot the bill for. These are great ways to not only stay on top of developments in your field but also to make valuable connections. If you are unemployed and seeking a job and need to keep an eye on your expenses, watch for events that are local or require minimal travel.

Working Your Wallet

If hefty conference registration fees make your wallet groan, be aware that some conferences allow you to register for only a portion of a multiple-day conference, such as just for one day. Pick the day or days that have the most relevant agenda items for you to get the most value for your networking dollars.

- **Career or job fairs.** As with conferences and conventions, attending career fairs or job fairs (the names are used somewhat interchangeably) can be a valuable way to expand your network. Most people think of career fairs as only a way to find out about and apply for job openings, but they are also a valuable networking avenue. Even if the employers attending aren't ones you had thought of working for or if employers that do interest you are there but not interviewing for positions that fit your background and goals, you can still have worthwhile conversations there. You never know what positions they might have in their back pocket or what may come available shortly after the fair.

Career and job fairs are often sponsored by professional and trade associations. These kinds of fairs can be found through the associations listed in Appendix B. Other fairs are community-based, sponsored by various nonprofit organizations related to employment or by governmental agencies. These are often advertised in city and neighborhood newspapers, as well as on television and radio.

- **Professional associations.** We've seen that professional associations play a role in your networking in that they often sponsor conferences, conventions, and career fairs you might attend. In addition to that, professional associations usually have local or regional chapters with a schedule of regular meetings, often monthly. These can be a great way to get to know people in your field and for them to get to know you. Also, professional associations publish newsletters and journals, which you could write for or be quoted in, and they sometimes have chat rooms and message boards on their Web sites where you can meet and communicate with other members. If you don't already know of the associations for your field, check Appendix B.

- **Networking groups.** Across the country, there are many groups formed for the express purpose of networking. Some are informal groups like breakfast clubs or happy hour groups that you'll probably only find out about through word of mouth; others are more formalized networking groups that announce their meetings in newspapers or through an online presence. Whether formal or informal, they usually include people from similar industries or with similar functional roles who get together to share best practices, job leads, and support. While some are quite large and may be under the umbrella of an international networking organization, many are informal, independent groups formed by a few people with common interests. Some groups have members who are all in the same industry, while others cross over industries but have a common function like sales or management. Others are for entrepreneurs, while still others are for women or people of the same ethnic group.

You're probably starting to get the picture that there is no one type of networking group. The point is to keep your eyes and ears open for them and be willing to give them a shot.

A Host with the Most: Monster Networking

Who better to introduce you to an online network of millions than Monster.com? With their networking feature, the folks at Monster now take care of the full range of your job seeking and career management needs. Not only can you connect with employers through Monster, but now you can join their online networking database, a community where professionals across all industries and levels exchange information about jobs, share knowledge and expertise, and help each other reach their goals. Membership is free, but for a nominal fee you can enjoy increased perks and access. Particularly valuable features of Monster Networking include the ability to save your searches of member profiles as well as suggestions from Monster of people they think you ought to meet. And, lest you worry that it's all quantity and not quality, Monster Networking simulates trade and professional association chapters by grouping members into like-minded teams based on occupation, industry, or career level so you can zero right in on the people who would add the most value to your network and whom you might help in return. You can access Monster Networking at http://www.monster.com.

The Internet

In a sense, the Internet shouldn't even be a separate category because it can simply be the vehicle for communicating in many of the other networking categories. You can, for example, conduct one-to-one meetings online, participate in group networking events through chat rooms and newsgroups, or attend seminars in Web site auditoriums. But there are some online networking avenues that don't fit into our other five categories. There are online networking opportunities that aren't sponsored by professional associations or any particular networking organization. Google (http://groups.google.com) and Yahoo (http://groups.yahoo.com) are examples of portals that connect you with online discussion forums and newsgroups for networking.

At a Crossroads in Your Online Networking?

Without a doubt, the best guide to career-related Web sites is CareerXroads, by Gerry Crispin and Mark Mehler. Not only is it the most comprehensive, it also provides brief reviews of sites so that you know where to concentrate your efforts before you start pounding the cyber-pavement. CareerXroads is available as a print book or through online searches (for a fee) at http://www.careerxroads.com.

Education and Training

Academic and training settings are great places to network. Whether you have your B.A. from Harvard and an M.B.A. from Stanford or your education is mostly through work-related training programs, education is an important category in your networking strategy. If you earned a degree from a college or university, check with your alumni office as well as the campus career center to find out about alumni networking events in your area or online. If you are taking, or have taken in the past, classes or seminars through a continuing education program or job skills training institute, your classmates, instructors, and guest speakers can often expand your network significantly.

Social/Recreational/Community Settings

Old School Ties

With 130,000 schools and 35 million alumni participating, you're likely to find an old friend or make new ones at Classmates.com (http://www.classmates.com).

Valuable contacts are made and relationships nurtured in such ordinary settings as health clubs, cocktail parties, neighborhood meetings, and many other gatherings. Think about any organizations you belong to or would enjoy getting involved with that are civic, community, non-profit, religious, sports-related, social, hobby-oriented, or recreational. Some of the best networking takes place in settings that are not professionally or business oriented. A word of caution, however—networking in social and community settings has a networking etiquette all its own. The how-to's of tactfully mixing business and pleasure are addressed later in this chapter.

Holy Networking!

Many religious institutions now offer structured networking opportunities, particularly for job seekers. Crossroads Career Network is a good example of an organization that offers free presentations by career transition professionals and networking meetings through churches in several states. You don't have to be a member of the church to attend. See http://www.crossroads-career.net for more information.

Serendipity

Sometimes networking just happens. You never know where the next great contact, lead, or tidbit of information is going to come from, so it's important to be open to all possible opportunities, not only to those that are part of your premeditated networking plan.

Think of all the places in which you interact with people who might become valuable members of your network. These include the office waiting rooms of doctors, dentists, accountants, lawyers, and other professionals; your barber shop or beauty salon; real estate offices; buses, trains, and planes; and the gym or health club. The list is endless— wherever you are, you can network with people.

How to Network

Whether you are interacting with people at a formal networking event or simply in an impromptu situation, it's important to keep certain guidelines in mind to make the most of each encounter. Now that you've been introduced to the six basic categories in which networking takes place, the remainder of this chapter covers do's and don'ts for networking in those settings.

The Networking Mindset

First, regardless of the setting, it is critical that you adopt the right mindset for networking. Like many endeavors in life, networking is just as much attitude as it is technique or talent. To network effectively in any circumstance, keep the following ten cardinal rules in mind as you adjust to a networking attitude:

1. **It takes patience.** If only I had a nickel for every time I've heard "Well, I went to a networking meeting and nothing came of it," or "I met someone who seemed like they'd be a great contact, but they haven't done a thing for me." Networking takes time! No matter how much you're in a hurry to get a new job, get ahead in your career, or grow a business, you can't rush networking. If you plant lots of seeds and allow some time for relationships to build and leads to pan out, you'll see results. It simply takes patience.

2. **It's a learned skill.** Okay, this time I wish I had a dime for every time I've heard "But I'm just not the networking type." There is no such thing as the networking type! Sure, some people are born with an outgoing personality and gift of gab, but even for them, effective, appropriate networking is a learned skill. No matter how natural or unnatural networking may feel to you, it is a skill you can learn. Believe me, if I can do it, you can, too.

3. **You have to believe in the process.** Networking works. Period. I can give you hard statistics (up to 85 percent or more of all jobs are found through networking), and I can tell you endless stories of how networking has worked for the thousands of clients I have directly worked with as a career counselor or the thousands more I've heard about through my colleagues. No matter how long and winding your networking road may seem, no matter how remote a contact may be, you have to keep the faith that it will work for you.

4. **You must be strategic.** On the one hand, networking is a natural, simple process of connecting and building relationships with other people, just as you do in everyday life without even realizing it. On the other hand, though, networking is not to be ventured into casually. Effective networking requires a strategy, a plan, and a clear vision of your goals. Strategies for networking are provided throughout this book, beginning with some of the techniques I describe in the remainder of this chapter. Even though it's great to be relaxed about networking and see it as a fun endeavor, make sure your attitude is not too casual.

5. **It requires a diversified plan.** Far too often I see motivated, diligent networkers find that their networking just isn't paying off because they're putting all their eggs into too few frying pans. They do things such as relying only on their existing networking, contacting the same people over and over, or only attending monthly meetings of one professional group, thinking that that's enough. Your networking strategy must pull from all six of the categories I describe earlier in this chapter because you never know where that one best contact or referral source will come from. So take off the blinders and think diverse and varied.

This Coupon Entitles You to ... Nothing

Harsh as it may sound, no one owes you anything when you're networking, especially people who don't know you very well. When you work hard at learning how to network and when you finally get up the nerve or the energy or find the time to network, it's easy to lapse into an attitude of entitlement. "If I went to all the trouble to track down this guy, the least he can do is find me a job." Again, no one owes you anything. Enter every networking encounter with the belief that good things can and probably will come of it but also with the understanding that there are no guarantees.

6. **Do it with courtesy.** You can never go wrong with being kind, considerate, and polite in every single one of your networking endeavors. It's a surprisingly small world out there, so if you're having a bad day or are just fed up with networking and really don't feel like being nice, think twice before acting in any way you will regret. Don't treat even one person with anything less than all the courtesy you can possibly muster up. (Chapter 10 covers how to deal with some of the more difficult people and sticky situations that can really put this rule to the test.)

7. **Think creatively.** No matter how skimpy your Rolodex, how remote your hometown, or how shy you are, there is always a way to get to the people and information you need to reach to network effectively. Networking is not a matter of making cold calls and saying "Hi, I'd like to network with you." Networking is about being creative about

who to contact, how to approach them, and how to build the relationship. Creative tips are offered throughout this book, but I have by no means thought of them all. Let my tips be a catalyst for your own creative thinking.

A Date with Your Networking Destiny

Take a moment right now (okay, please take a moment at your earliest convenience) to pull out your appointment book, planner, PDA, online calendar, or stone tablet and set a date about six months from now to reread—or at least re-skim—this book. If you've settled into a new job or business or have gotten busy and comfortable in your old job by then, you might easily forget to keep your networking going. Or, if you're still trying to reach your goals six months from now and have run out of creative ideas for jump-starting your networking, revisiting this book may be just the catalyst you need.

8. **Giving.** Networking is a two-way street. You must keep this in the forefront of your mind as you network. Make a habit out of asking people how you can help them, and mean it when you say it. And, if some people just never seem to need anything from you or from anyone you might know, then at the very least make sure they know how much you appreciate them. (Chapter 13 covers the art and science of showing appreciation and giving thanks to your network.)

9. **Show integrity and reliability.** You can stammer through a networking phone call, forget someone's name, sound bewildered about how to get a job or start a business, or otherwise goof up, but one area where you must be infallible is in your level of integrity and reliability. You will be judged more on how honest, ethical, punctual, and reliable you are than on how the i's are dotted and t's are crossed in your resume. Show up when you say you'll show up, leave when you've taken up enough of their time, follow through on your promises, don't bad-mouth anybody or anything, and never, ever lie.

10. **Make it easy for people to help you.** Networking is like connecting the dots. You meet with Sally, who refers you to Tom, who refers you to Jorgia, and so on. You aren't a job seeker with a network, you're the

manager of a sales team. Sally, Tom, Jorgia, and all the people they know are on your sales team. In the business world, does a sales rep selling a very complicated product know every single thing about the product? Usually not. They've got technical support for that. Instead, they know just enough about the product to know how to tell a potential customer what it is, what it does, and, most importantly, what it can do for the customer. That's what you have to do in networking to make it easy for people to help you. You have to have your personal pitch down pat (I call this a *self-marketing sound bite* and I explain it in Chapter 5), and you have to be specific when you tell people what you need and what you have to offer. This enables them to more easily spread the word about you and what you're trying to accomplish.

Now that you have these ten rules for the right networking attitude, let's look at some techniques to use when networking in specific circumstances.

Do's and Don'ts for Group Networking Events

Whether you are attending a national professional conference, a major trade show, or a ten-person breakfast meeting of a small networking club, the following strategies are effective in almost any group setting:

- Shake hands with everyone you meet. Use a firm but not bone-crushing grip.

- Introduce yourself as you shake hands, clearly stating your first and last name. Don't wait to be introduced by someone else or to have to be asked for your name.

- If you're standing with one or more people when a new person approaches, take the lead in introducing everyone to each other.

- To remember the name of someone you've just met, focus carefully on the name when you're first introduced (we usually have a million other thoughts running through our minds and don't even listen to the name). You should also try to use the name in the first few minutes of conversation to reinforce it in your mind.

- When wearing a name tag, wear it on your right side. This is a more natural place for people to cast their eyes as they shake your right hand with their right hand.

- Have a few opening lines or questions in mind so that you can discuss something other than the weather or the latest sports scores when you first begin to converse with someone you don't know well. Remember that you can never go wrong with asking the person about themselves. This is much preferable to launching into a spiel about yourself.

- Take plenty of business cards and keep them within easy reach. (It's always a good idea to wear clothes with pockets.) If you are self-employed, take your promotional materials to hand out, and if you are job hunting, always have your resume handy, but remember not to hand these out too early and not to force your material on someone who doesn't seem interested.

- When people give you their business cards, store them in a different pocket from where you carry your own so you won't have to fish through a jumble of cards when handing out your own card.

- As soon after each networking encounter as possible, make notes on the back of each business card you receive so that you don't get confused about who each person was and what was discussed.

- Don't spend too much time with any one person. You don't want to come across as clingy. Plus, you should try to meet a range of people. Even if you are attending an event primarily to connect with just one person, it's not a good idea to monopolize that person's time. Also, you never know how you might benefit from interacting with some of the other people in attendance.

- If possible, identify in advance the people whom you want to meet or get reacquainted with so that you'll be sure to connect with them. This tip is especially important when attending very large events. It is easy to get a little overwhelmed when you're faced with a large crowd of people and forget which ones you came to meet.

● Set objectives concerning the type or number of people you want to meet, the information you want to collect, points about yourself that you need to convey, or resources you need to find.

● Keep one running list of things you need to do after the meeting to follow up—that is, letters or e-mails to write, calls to make, Web sites or books to look up, projects to take on, and so on. This is especially important at a meeting that lasts more than one day because you can easily lose track of follow-up notes and reminders scattered here and there in the materials that you collect over the course of the event. You can keep your list in your appointment book or planner or on the notepad that is often provided in conference materials.

Staying Organized at Conferences

When attending a conference, particularly one out of town that lasts for more than a day, take along several file folders or accordion files to keep track of the mountains of information that you are likely to collect over the course of the event. Label the files according to functions, such as "to file," "to follow up," "to read," and "to do." That way, when you get home or back to your office, you can pull out the "to follow up" file, for example, and get all your correspondence and phone calls taken care of easily since the names, e-mail addresses, phone numbers, and other relevant information are all in one place. You'll also need a few files in which you can place miscellaneous information that might not fit into the functional categories. When you return to your hotel room at the end of each day, take some time to sort through the session handouts, promotional materials, and business cards you collected that day. Throw out what you don't need to lug home and file the rest.

The do's and don'ts listed previously apply to most any group event, but there are also a few strategies to keep in mind for each specific type of gathering you might attend. Tips for various settings are provided in the following sections.

How to Network at Conferences and Conventions

When attending a conference or convention, consider the following tips:

- Take some time at the start of the conference to study the agenda and mark the sessions and events that you want to attend. This will help you maximize your time at the event because you will be sure to hit the most promising sessions. Mark sessions you're interested in but have to miss because a more important one is being held simultaneously in another color. (It is helpful to carry with you highlighter pens or markers in a couple of different colors.) Since even parallel sessions often don't end at exactly the same time, you can go by the rooms where those conflicting sessions were held to see if anyone is still there. (They usually are.) This gives you a chance to pick up any leftover handouts and perhaps to meet the session leaders and some attendees.

- Also, take time at the start of the meeting to go through the list of participants (both attendees and exhibitors) and mark the people you want to meet or re-meet. Transfer the names to a separate sheet of paper or index card to have a handy list you can consult throughout the conference. Check off the names of people you meet so you can track your progress.

- Some conference exhibit halls have a freebie table where anyone can leave promotional or educational handouts without paying the often exorbitant exhibitors' fees. These are great for entrepreneurs on a tight budget, so be sure to take a stack of your brochures or other literature to leave on such a table if there happens to be one.

- Try not to skip the scheduled social events at conferences, as they often provide a more relaxed setting in which to meet people. While an occasional evening alone in your hotel room with room service can be relaxing and rejuvenating, it doesn't offer much in the way of building relationships. Sometimes to network effectively, you have to do what doesn't come naturally. (You can always relax in the room after the gathering, and then you won't have to feel guilty about it!)

- At conference meals, try to sit with people you don't know and with a different group at each meal.

- Also, take part in any side trips to local sites that are sometimes arranged for conference attendees. These often take place outside the formal conference agenda (sometimes before the official start " of the conference or after it ends), so they may require some advance planning regarding your travel arrangements, but they are often worth the extra effort.

Bonding in Unexpected Places

Some of the best networking at a conference takes place on field trips. I once attended a conference of a few hundred educators, many of whom were excellent potential referral sources for my career counseling practice. Of the thirty or so people I got to know at the conference, which ones turned out to be my best referral sources? Not the ones I met at the sessions or conference meals, but rather several people I met briefly on a crowded van ride from a museum back to the hotel during an outing at the end of the conference. There's something about a shared experience outside the professional arena that bonds people together in a powerful way.

How to Handle Networking Group Events

These events range from small meetings in which a handful of people get together to give each other tips and advice to large "networking socials" where a hundred people or more might mingle over cheap white wine and hors d'oeuvres. Whichever type of event you attend, certain rules of etiquette and strategies prevail:

- **Don't be selfish.** Make sure you're being true to the give-and-take nature of networking by sharing advice and leads as well as receiving them.

- **Follow through.** Since fellow members of the group often go out on a limb to provide you with contacts, be sure to follow through on the leads they give you or graciously explain why you don't plan to do so.

- **Promote yourself.** If you meet regularly with a group of people, you might start to take for granted that they know you're great at what you do. Don't assume anything! Familiarity can breed forgetfulness, so keep the group apprised of your successes, accomplishments, and strengths so that they have an incentive to help you.

- **Be positive.** These groups can take on a gripe-session quality over time, so be sure the supportive environment doesn't lure you into sounding negative or pessimistic. Remember, you always want to convey an air of enthusiasm and confidence to maximize your effectiveness while networking.

- **Focus on quality over quantity.** Networking is something of a numbers game, and large gatherings are great places to expand your network exponentially. Don't, however, get caught up in the free-for-all atmosphere of a large networking event and race around the room trying to meet as many people as possible. Keep an eye toward quality, making sure you have at least a few substantive conversations, and really make an effort to get to know people.

Networking at Professional and Trade Association Meetings

Associations often hold events in which networking is not the main objective, but is simply a by-product of the gathering. These types of events include lectures, seminars, discussion groups, and other professional development activities. Since networking is not the main aim, it is particularly important to have a strategy for creating networking opportunities while participating in the event. Things to remember include the following:

- **Be subtle.** Remember that the visibility you gain simply by attending a professional meeting can be powerful. You don't need to bowl people over with your presence and thus be seen as disinterested in the main purpose of the event, especially if that purpose is educational or charitable.

- **Share war stories and successes.** These gatherings are excellent opportunities to interact with like-minded colleagues. If the aim of the event is to help members develop their professional skills, knowledge, and expertise, such as with a continuing education seminar, a lecture by a guest speaker, or a best practices discussion, then the atmosphere is often one of collaboration and commiseration. Take advantage of this chance to bond with your colleagues by talking about what you know more than who you are. (By showing them what you know, you'll be telling them indirectly who you are!)

- **Look for ways to distinguish yourself.** In professional and trade associations, you are networking with a fairly homogeneous group in terms of career interests and pursuits. Make sure that you let people know exactly what you do and find out about others' jobs or businesses so that you know how to help them in the future.

- **Take on a leadership role.** Just attending professional and trade association events is not enough. To gain true visibility, you need to volunteer for some kind of official role or even run for elected office.

How to Network at Career and Job Fairs

You often are able to find out in advance which employers are coming to a fair and what sorts of positions they will be interviewing for. If the employers and their jobs fit with your goals, then it's obvious that attending would be worth your time. But what if they don't fit the bill exactly? Go anyway! I can't even begin to count the number of times I have seen job seekers almost grudgingly attend a career fair with no expectation of anything coming from it, only to find that they made valuable connections. Rarely do you actually *get* a job just by showing up at a fair. Jobs result from fairs because you networked effectively with the *people* at the event—both the employer representatives and your fellow participants.

A few strategies to keep in mind specifically for these events:

- **Research.** If it's possible to find out in advance which organizations will be represented at the fair (it usually is), try to do some research on the ones that most interest you. Most corporations, not-for-profit organizations, and government agencies have Web sites, so you can learn the basics about a large number of organizations in a fairly short time. Doing so will enable you to have more substantive conversations with those organizations' representatives at the fair.

- **Perfect your self-marketing sound bite.** Job fairs are often crowded, hectic environments with all-too-brief and superficial interactions, so you have to make an impact on prospective employers in less than ideal circumstances. A strong, concise personal pitch is one way to do that. It enables you to convey who you are, what you have to offer, and what you're looking for to a recruiter who has very limited time to spend with you. In Chapter 5, you'll find detailed guidelines for developing this personal pitch, which I call a self-marketing sound bite.

- **The early bird gets the worm.** Try to arrive right at the start of the fair when it's likely to be a little less crowded and when the recruiters are fresh and don't yet have that glazed-over look. If you must arrive after the event is well under way, be sure to allow yourself ample time there so that you can meet everyone you want to meet. Be prepared for long lines at some of the employers' booths and don't expect to be able to pop in and pop out.

- **Distinguish yourself.** Making yourself stand out is important in any group setting, but it is particularly important at job fairs. Recruiters can meet hundreds of job seekers at fairs, so it's important to distinguish yourself from the pack. Besides just introducing yourself and providing your resume, add some bit of information that's likely to stick in the recruiter's mind. You might mention some fact about the organization that attracts you to it (here's where that research comes in handy) or give a brief example of one of your accomplishments.

- **Follow up immediately.** Follow-up is particularly important after job fairs. When recruiters get back to their offices, the faces that go with the resumes on their desks are mostly one big blur. Sending a carefully crafted letter mentioning something specific that you talked about can put a face with your resume. By the way, don't take this advice too literally and send a photo! That's a no-no for all job seeking except modeling and the performing arts.

How to Find Career Fairs

CareerFairs.com (at http://www.careerfairs.com) is a one-stop source of career fairs around the United States. You can search for fairs by month, state, or industry/profession keyword. And if you aren't able to attend a fair, you can submit your resume to the CareerFairs.com database for free.

Eateries

Networking over meals or drinks falls into that murky area in which social and professional pursuits overlap, making it difficult to know how to balance social courtesies with your own career or business objectives. All of these situations require that you be extra clear about your goals and networking objectives so that you can subtly but assertively work them into the conversation, all the while making sure not to turn a casual social occasion into a hard-driving business meeting.

When mixing networking with food and drink, keep the following in mind:

- **Choose a convenient location.** When deciding where to go, try to choose a place convenient to the other person if you're initiating the get-together. After all, it's the courteous thing to do. If the other person has initiated the invitation, or if the get-together is a mutual idea, be sure to be flexible in any discussion of where to meet. Try to find a mutually convenient place, or better yet, make the generous gesture of offering to meet near where the other person lives or works.

- **Keep the cost appropriate.** Take into account the income bracket of the other person and be sure that no one suggests a place that will be too much of a financial burden on anyone. If you need to choose an inexpensive restaurant and are embarrassed to reveal that you're on a tight budget, suggest a place that you know is reasonable, but cite its convenience, quiet atmosphere, great soup, or another feature that gives you an excuse for proposing it.

- **Understand who should pay.** In most routine networking situations, each party should expect to foot his or her own portion of the bill. But, if in doubt, the rule of thumb is that whoever does the initiating should offer to pay the bill—and should be prepared to do so. If, however, you're just getting started in the working world and ask to go out with someone older or more experienced than you, then that person might offer to pick up the bill, and it's okay to let them do so (though you should at least protest a bit).

If you were invited by the other person, you should still be prepared to pay in case they don't offer, so make sure you have adequate cash or a credit card with you. Be aware that many people who network frequently get in the habit of going dutch, which is a good policy so that neither of you feels obligated to the other.

- **Make the food a secondary focus.** When someone wants to get together over a meal, try to opt for just a coffee break instead. The focus should be on talking with each other, not on consuming lots of food and drink, which can distract from the conversation. This is often unavoidable, however, as some people have time to meet with you only during a lunch break or for breakfast. So, if you must network over a meal, it is better to eat light so that you can focus on the conversation; you can always grab something later to satisfy your hunger.

- **Order food that's easy to eat.** Since the focus of the meeting should be on conversation, not the food (unless you're both in the food or hospitality business!), order something that won't be awkward to eat. Spaghetti dangling over your chin or cheese from French onion soup stretched across the room doesn't do wonders for your professional image. Also avoid food that will cause a spectacle. Anything that the servers have to light on fire or that requires you to wear a bib is a bad idea, as are orders that inspire the restaurant staff to ring bells and sing to you.

- **Hold your liquor.** In many professional circles, drinking is not a smart move since there's no telling what you could end up saying or doing that you might regret. If you do go to a bar with someone or have a drink with a meal, keep an eye on how much you imbibe and stay well below the limit at which you are usually affected. A networking meeting with someone you've never met is not the time to discover what the fuss over martinis is all about.

● **Watch out for no-business policies at clubs.** If someone invites you to a country club or other private social club that you're not familiar with, don't assume you'll be openly doing business. Some exclusive clubs have a policy of no business in their dining rooms and will seriously frown on the fact that you've spread papers and other business paraphernalia across the table.

Social Gatherings

Social events, such as weddings, parties, charity functions, and small gatherings, need to be handled delicately. Here's how to do so:

● **Strike the right social and business balance.** It's extremely important that you don't push people into talking business when they would rather be socializing. Read situations and people very carefully, and be sure not to cross the line between low-pressure networking and being overbearing. Also, it's particularly rude to rope an event's host into a business discussion. The mother of the bride, for example, probably has other priorities than discussing your career.

● **Initiate a business contact and make plans to follow up.** Related to the first point is the idea that you should simply broach the subject of your career or business with someone at the social gathering and then turn back to discussing non-business topics. Just make sure that you get people's office phone numbers or cards so you can continue the conversation at a more appropriate time and place.

● **Don't try to do business if you've had one too many.** As mentioned earlier, drinking too much can really foul up professional interactions. While you might enjoy the fact that a drink or two rids you of your inhibitions and makes networking a little less intimidating, don't get yourself in an embarrassing situation by having too much at a party where potential professional contacts are around.

● **Keep your follow-through expectations realistic.** In the relaxed atmosphere of social gatherings, lots of promises are made that aren't always kept after the party's over. Keep your expectations realistic and realize that even though on Saturday night your date's Uncle Louie said he'd get you a job, he may not even remember who you are when you call his office on Monday.

Classes, Lectures, and Seminars

Educational settings are great places to network. When you have a chance to connect in such environments, be sure to do the following:

- **Get to know the instructor.** The people who teach classes and lead workshops are often a great source of contacts and resources. Be sure you are known to them as more than a name on a class roster. Make an effort to talk with the instructor during office hours or in a setting other than class.

- **Get to know your classmates.** As with instructors, your fellow students and workshop participants can often lead you to people, places, and information that can get you closer to your goals. Try to get together with people after class.

- **Use class materials as sources of contacts.** The textbooks, articles, and handouts used in most classes are a largely untapped source of networking opportunities. Pay attention to who wrote the things you're reading or to people mentioned in what you read. Some of them might be more approachable than you think.

- **Be on the lookout for organizations cited in your class materials.** For example, if a research study is listed as being funded by a particular foundation and you're exploring careers in foundation work, you've just found a place to approach for information or to apply for a job.

Using the Internet to Network

The Internet has revolutionized the way that networking takes place. If you're a cyberspace neophyte, you probably hate hearing statements like that. It can be overwhelming if you don't know where to begin or how to make the most of this vast network. You might think to yourself, "So what if I can communicate with billions of people and find ten million search results that match my interest areas? I just want one good contact who can help me make a career decision and lead me to a job." Well, those of you who are skilled Net surfers know that the process of tracking down people and information on the Internet *can* be frustrating, but it can also be amazingly convenient and thorough as well.

Many of the Web sites listed in Appendix C are good sources of online information on career and business topics, and there are books listed in Appendix D that cover online job searching and other uses of the Internet for networking. While Web sites are one very important networking avenue in cyberspace, be sure to make full use of electronic networking through these additional tools:

- **Use e-mail**. Of all the possible networking methods, e-mail may be the most convenient one. With the click of a button, you can contact anyone anywhere. With e-mail, there's no excuse for not checking in frequently with people in your existing network or for not contacting people you don't know but would like to add to your network. It's becoming more and more common to see e-mail addresses publicized. Authors of books and articles sometimes list their addresses in their creations, letters-to-the-editor sections in magazines and newspapers often include e-mail addresses so that you can enter into a dialogue with people who write on topics that interest you, editors and reporters of magazines and newspapers can also be reached this way, and Web sites of corporations and other organizations often connect you with people who a few years ago would have been untouchable. Tips and protocol for e-mailing are offered in Chapter 6 to help you take advantage of this powerful communication method.

Be Thankful You're Networking in the 21st Century

As the Internet becomes commonplace, most of us are already taking for granted the ease with which we connect to people around the globe. A thousand years ago, networking was slow sailing—literally. In A.D. 1100, the Arabs invented the lateen, a triangular sail that allowed ships to sail against the wind and sped things up a bit, but that travel was nothing like the speed and ease with which words and ideas fly through cyberspace these days. You wouldn't have fared much better globetrotting in the 1930s either, when the British concocted a grand plan for regular passenger service by blimp to faraway lands in their world empire. On the maiden voyage, the first blimp made it only as far as France when an accident felled not only that trip but also the whole plan. Virtual travel has both these methods beaten by a mile.

Source for historical facts: *World Access: The Handbook for Citizens of the Earth* by Kathryn and Ross Petras. Fireside/Simon & Schuster, 1996.

Caution—This Is a Very Public Forum

If you're using the Web for job hunting, be careful when you post your resume online. While doing so can be a great job search method—in that it lets your resume work for you 24 hours a day with little or no effort on your part—keep in mind the downside of this visibility. Is there a boss, competitor, or client whom you'd rather not make aware that you're looking to make a move? They can easily see your resume online, and the consequences might not be pretty.

- **Join newsgroups.** Newsgroups are kind of like virtual community centers—places you can go to talk with people who share an interest of yours and to read information on a given topic. People post questions, announcements, and other information on message boards that you can review and respond to. You can also be a silent member (also known as a lurker), just reading other people's dialogues or the posted articles and notes without actively participating. You can also branch out from a newsgroup to carry on a private correspondence by e-mail with someone you meet through the newsgroup.

  When first getting involved with a newsgroup, be sure to read the FAQs (Frequently Asked Questions) for new members so you won't break any cyberspace etiquette rules.

A Date for Saturday, a Job for Monday

There has been an explosion of social network sites on the Web where you can tap into huge networks of people around the country or the world. Most of them are basically high-tech, do-it-yourself dating services, but four sites are gold mines for potential business and job hunting contacts: http://www.linkedin.com, http://www.ryze.com, http://www.tribe.net, and http://www.zerodegrees.com.

- **Use the Web's people and business directories**. There are many Web sites that let you track down an address, phone number, and e-mail address for just about any person or business. These include Big Yellow, at http://www.bigyellow.com/; Yahoo! People Search, at http://people.yahoo.com/; Galaxy, at http://www.einet.net/galaxy/Reference.html; Switchboard, at http://www.switchboard.com/; and WhoWhere?, at http://www.whowhere.lycos.com/.

When Networking Just Happens

Remember that our final networking category was the serendipity factor—those unexpected times when networking just happens, often because you make it happen. To handle these serendipitous situations with aplomb, keep the following do's and don'ts in mind:

- DO start a conversation with a simple hello or neutral comment or question instead of trying to be overly witty (unless you truly are witty!) or opening with a comment that could be controversial.

- DO stretch past your comfort zone and make contacts even if you don't feel like doing so.

- DO exchange business cards with anyone who seems to be a worthy candidate for your network.

- DO maintain a professional tone, vocabulary, and posture so that your overtures can't be misconstrued as romantic or inappropriate in any other way.

- DON'T be a pest. Don't bother anyone who seems busy, depressed, or distracted or doesn't continue a dialogue that you initiate.

- DON'T put your foot in your mouth by saying something that might be controversial or offensive; wait until you know more about the person before you move into potentially sensitive areas.

- DON'T open a conversation with anyone who looks menacing or dangerous, and exercise caution even with seemingly friendly people. And don't ever go anywhere alone with someone you've just met.

Chapter 6 offers additional tips on how to handle specific encounters, including techniques for oral and written communication.

Express Train to Networking Success

In addition to a carefully orchestrated networking strategy, don't overlook the power of the serendipity factor. Impromptu encounters with people can become rewarding networking opportunities in ways you never could have anticipated.

I once struck up a conversation with a woman sitting next to me on a train headed into New York City from a Long Island beach town. It turned out that Martha worked on Wall Street and was thinking of making a job change as well as a transition into a different specialty area within finance. After talking about her career situation and also having a pleasant conversation on other topics, we arrived at our destination. Before departing, we exchanged business cards and promised to keep in touch. Shortly after that encounter, I received a phone call from Martha requesting a career counseling session with me to continue the discussion we had had on the train. Just acquiring Martha as a client would have been sufficient reward for that chance encounter on the train, but there were other benefits as well. One of my other clients benefited in that I was able to refer him to a headhunter (an executive recruiter) whom Martha knew well. This headhunter typically dealt only with experienced candidates, but as a favor to Martha, he made the effort to find an excellent entry-level job for my client, a recent graduate who had been trying for months to break into finance at the height of the recession in the early 1990s. And, to top it all off, that executive recruiter ended up referring several clients to me over the months and years that followed. The serendipity factor certainly paid off in this case!

So, the next time you hesitate to start up a conversation with the friendly-looking person next to you or to accept an invitation to go somewhere, think twice. You never know what good things might happen if you deviate a bit from your carefully crafted plan. These chance encounters are just as important in the networking process as your carefully planned strategies are.

Quick Summary

Networking can take place just about anywhere, from casual conversations to major conferences with scheduled networking events.

This chapter discussed two main types of networking settings:

- Structured networking events, including conferences and conventions, networking clubs, professional and trade association meetings, and career and job fairs.

- Unstructured settings in which networking is not the main focus but can be if you make an effort. These include restaurants and bars, social occasions, classes and other educational settings, and the Internet.

This chapter also covered do's and don'ts for your conduct in all these typical networking settings, as well as for making the most of the serendipity factor.

Where to Network

- One-to-one meetings

- Conferences and conventions

- Career or job fairs

- Academic/training settings

- Networking clubs/groups

- The Internet

- Social/recreational/community settings

Networking Methods

- In person

- Via e-mail and other online communications

- By writing letters and notes

- Through public speaking opportunities

- Over the telephone

Part 2: Making It Work: Keys to Effective Networking

The chapters in this section build on what you learned in Part 1. This is where you roll up your sleeves and get to work. Half the battle in networking is to do the right kind of preparation—and the right amount of it. These chapters help you do that.

Chapter 3 shows you ways to keep track of who you know and what you know with simple organizational and time management systems that actually work!

In Chapter 4 you'll take stock of who is already in your network and learn valuable ways to expand that network—particularly helpful for those of you who are concerned that "who you know" is a very short list.

Next, you'll put together essential materials in Chapter 5 that will enable you to communicate who you are and what you have to offer. No matter what your reason for networking is, marketing yourself effectively is a key component, so this chapter is a must.

Finally, Chapter 6 covers the ins and outs of communication. After all, that's what networking is all about—communicating with others in person, by phone, in writing, and online to convey your needs and to help others with theirs.

Getting Organized: Don't Skip This Chapter!

Out of intense complexities intense simplicities emerge.

—WINSTON CHURCHILL

Where did I put that phone number? What did I do with that article I wanted to send Jennifer? When did I last talk to Glen and what did I say? How will I ever find time to get to that meeting tonight? If your organizational system consists of stick-on notes dotted all over your desk and a computer desktop riddled with random files, as well as way too many items on your to-do list, you probably ask yourself a lot of these questions. It's time to put some better organizational and time management systems in place. Being organized with your papers, computer files, and time is critical to success in networking. Even if you're the organized type, networking poses special challenges with all the new people, places, and activities to keep track of. As a first step in preparing yourself to network, this chapter offers tips and techniques for keeping track of who and what you know as well as for finding the time to keep up with all those people and all that information.

You'll find three main sections in this chapter:

- Keeping Track of Who You Know

- Keeping Track of What You Know

- Keeping Track of Your Networking Activities

In Chapter 4 you'll be taking an inventory of your network by jotting down names of people in various networking categories on the worksheets provided in that chapter. The first section of this chapter focuses on developing a more permanent, detailed system for keeping track of who you know. You learn about contact management systems—databases that keep records of your contacts. I also guide you through the process of setting up "to-be-entered" files and "key people" files—two additional handy organizational tools for keeping track of who you know.

Keeping Track of Who You Know

Maintaining accurate and organized records of the people you know (or could get to know) is essential to successful networking. The first step in that process is to develop a contact management system—an easily accessible, detailed database of the people you know or hope to know.

Setting Up a Contact Management System

You have two basic choices for your contact management system: You can keep it on paper or electronically. The most efficient way to compile and access your network is to have it as a database in your computer and/or PDA (personal digital assistant, such as a Palm device). This need not be a complex, sophisticated marvel of computer programming. There are many software packages easily found at your neighborhood computer store that help you set up a simple but powerful contact management system. If you're proficient in Microsoft Excel or another spreadsheet application, you could also set up spreadsheets listing your contacts.

If you don't have access to a computer or would prefer not to keep your contacts that way, your other option is to put them on paper. I recommend an index card system instead of listing people in notebooks or folders. Using index cards simulates a computer database. You can file the data on your contacts in various sections of an index card box according to the category in which the contact falls. You can also add a fairly substantial amount of information to the cards (compared to a list in which you have limited space to record information on each person).

Whether you use old-fashioned paper or a "high-tech" system, you'll want to list various data for each of your contacts. This includes the following:

- First name

- Nickname (if applicable)

- Last name

- Title (Mr., Ms., Dr., etc.)

- Job title

- Employer

- Address (office and/or home)

- Telephone numbers (office, home, cell)

- Fax number

- E-mail address

- Career field (industry and/or functional role/title)

- STARS category(ies) (The STARS system is explained in Chapter 4. For now, just know that this needs to be a field in your contact management system.)

- Referred by

- When and where you met

- Personal information (for example, birthday, names of spouse or children, personal interests, hobbies, and so on)

- Notes (for miscellaneous information that doesn't fall into the other data types)

Whichever type of contact management system you use—electronic or paper—make sure it works well for you. You aren't likely to make use of a system that is cumbersome or difficult, so set up a system that matches your personality and work style. Some criteria to consider when purchasing or setting up a contact management system are the following:

- Is it accessible?

- Is it easy to use?

- Is it manageable?

- Is it expandable?

- Does it fit my comfort and proficiency level with technology?

- Is it portable?

What Can I Do with All Those Business Cards and Random Slips of Paper I Collect?

Linda Rothschild, Chief Executive Organizer of ~~CROSS IT OFF YOUR LIST~~, a New York–based professional organizing and lifestyle management company (http://www.crossitoffyourlist.com), has a helpful system to distinguish between people she classifies as resources versus actual members of your network. She says, for example, "You might have names of ten people who can repair your computer, but when it comes time to need a computer repaired, you'll choose one person, and that's the name that goes into your central database. All the rest stay in what I call your re-source file, a box of index cards sorted according to the type of resource. You can staple business cards to the index cards or just write directly on the card and then file it under the category for that type of resource."

According to Linda, "Your database should be clean, containing only the names of people you actually have some contact with or plan to contact in the near future. Everyone else goes in the resource file. Otherwise, you'll have thousands of entries cluttering up your system."

Keeping a To-Be-Entered File

As you collect business cards or names of new contacts on little slips of paper, you don't always have time to enter them in your contact management system right away. As a result, valuable information can easily get lost—cards forgotten in the pockets of jackets sent to the cleaners, pieces of paper that slip through that crack between your desk and the wall, and so on. The way to solve this problem is to have one place where you keep this kind of information temporarily until you can enter it into your contact management system. Take an accordion file folder (the kind that's like a regular file folder but is closed on the sides and expands to half an inch or an inch in depth) and keep it in an easily accessible spot on or near your desk. Every time you write down a name or receive a business card, brochure, or other piece of paper, drop it in your to-be-entered file. If you travel a great deal or tend not to be in one place most days, keep a file folder or envelope in your briefcase or bag to use as your to-be-entered file.

This also works well when you receive a change-of-address notice. It's best to update your contact list immediately when you learn of an address change, new phone number, etc., but that's not always possible. The to-be-entered file serves as a safe resting place until you have time to enter the new information.

The Value of To-Be-Entered Files—Learning the Hard Way

During her job search, Frances learned the hard way that she needed to keep better track of all the names she was collecting during her networking activities. Midway through her search, she attended a professional association meeting where she met several people who said they would be happy to help her out in any way they could. She collected business cards from all of those potential strategists and targets, and on the back of each card she wrote some notes to herself, indicating how she should follow up

(continued)

(continued)

with each person. When Frances got home, she took the cards out of her pocket and dropped them on a table on top of a stack of newspapers. She thought to herself that she should probably enter the names and addresses right away in her contact database so she could send follow-up e-mails and make calls over the next couple of days.

Well, several days passed before she got around to writing the letters, and in the meantime, more newspapers had been piled on top of the cards. You can probably imagine what happened at this point! Yes, she threw out the stack of newspapers for recycling, forgetting that the cards were buried within them. By the time she realized what had happened, the papers—and the valuable business cards—were long gone. If only she had had a to-be-entered file, she could have come home from the meeting and taken two seconds to drop the cards in that file where they would have been safe and ready to retrieve when she got around to doing the follow-up.

Setting Up Key People Files

As you interact with various people during your networking, you'll probably find that there are some people or organizations you have frequent contact with and others you rarely deal with. It's helpful to identify the key people whom you talk to, meet with, or correspond with, and set up "key people" files for these contacts. A key people file is simply a file folder labeled with the person's name. As you communicate with key people, you can file copies of letters, e-mails, faxes, and notes from phone calls to keep a running record of your communication with that person. You might also keep an electronic folder for each person where you store electronic communication.

Keeping Track of What You Know

Networking for any purpose, whether for career choice, job search, career advancement, or business promotion, inevitably involves a lot of research. Magazine articles, information from Web sites, and notes you take when speaking to people all have to have a place to go.

There are also the materials that you haven't gotten to yet—journals to peruse, newspaper clippings to read, Web sites to browse, and so on. It can seem as if you'll never catch up. Keeping up with information relevant to your field is important so that you are informed and knowledgeable as you interact with others. Remember, it's not just who you know, it's what you know that counts as well.

Keeping close track of what you know is also important for remaining true to the notion of networking as a two-way street. If you are able to serve as a sort of information clearinghouse, you are keeping tabs on information not only for yourself but for others as well. Imagine that someone calls and says, "Do you know of a good book on...?" or "Have you ever come across a service that does...?" If you've kept track of such resources, you'll have an answer without a lot of fuss, and your networking becomes a give-and-take process, not just a one-sided, selfish activity. To be able to do that, you should consider setting up topic files and resource files as described in the following section.

Setting Up Topic Files and Resource Files

Next to rocket science and brain surgery, setting up a decent filing system has to be one of life's greatest challenges. They're always too complicated or not complex enough, hard to maintain or never even used at all. The complete art and science of filing is beyond the scope of this book, so I recommend turning to some of the excellent books on organizing listed in Appendix D or contacting the National Association of Professional Organizers listed in Appendix C. I also cover filing extensively in my book *The Complete Idiot's Guide to Overcoming Procrastination*.

For now, I'll offer one simple piece of advice that can help you get started managing all the information you collect: Think of files as topic files or resource files. Topic files are the places you keep articles, handouts from seminars, and any other materials that inform you about a topic that's of interest to you. Examine the articles or other papers you have lying around in piles and see how you can sort them into topic files.

Resource files are slightly different in that they are arranged more around a function than a topic. They are where you might keep brochures, flyers, or other information on people or places that provide services or products of use to you. Some of the people whose materials are in your resource files might also be listed in your contact database.

Organization Pays

Mike Hart, a project manager with an urban planning and preservation organization, is a great example of organized networking in action. Mike is always on the lookout for articles in newspapers, magazines, and professional journals that are of interest to him, whether relevant to his current job or just related to his other interests. He immediately clips the article, tracks down the telephone number and/or e-mail address of the person or organization featured or quoted in the article, and attaches the contact information to the article. He then files it in the appropriate topic or key person file, either paper or electronic.

Doing this provides him with continuous reference files to turn to whenever he needs them. The organization has paid off. Once he had to write a cover letter for a job and found that he had kept several articles on the person he was writing to. His mention of the information in the articles showed the prospective employer that he had been following that person's work and was serious about working for him. His advanced planning came in handy: He got the job. "Networking is something you carry with you all throughout your life, not just something you do when you need a job," Mike says.

Keeping Track of Your Networking Activities

As you've learned by now, effective networking is based more on quality than on quantity. There is some value, however, to keeping track of how much networking you've done. When you're networking in connection with one particular project—a job search, for example—it's important to keep a running record of all your networking efforts. The project

section is one way to keep that record,
have attended, people you've spoken

l of your networking activities asso-
her than by project. The record-of-
ion is one of the best ways to keep a
th one person. But first, let's look
r of keeping organized notes on

ting Records

eting record that you can use
working meeting as well as
nmend setting up a form like
application and printing it
clined, simply make one up

Date: _____
Title: _____
Address: _____
E-mail: _____
What we discus

Key information g

(continued)

(continued)

Key information gained about the person I met (experience, how he/she got into the field or company, personal info) _____

_____

_____

_____

What this means for my decisions or strategy: _____

_____

_____

_____

People he/she referred me to for networking: _____

_____

People he/she referred me to for possible job (or business) opportunities: _____

_____

_____

Overall evaluation of the meeting: _____

_____

_____

Next steps (I am to do): _____

_____

Next steps (the other person is to do): _____

_____

_____

Using Record-of-Contact Logs

Record-of-contact logs are for use primarily with the key people files described earlier in this chapter. In addition to keeping a paper trail of communication in each key person file—for example, copies of letters, faxes, e-mails, and so on—it is also helpful to have one sheet of paper in the file that shows a record of communication with that person. That sheet of paper is a record-of-contact log—a form you can easily create using the sample below as your guide. The sample log provided here shows a record of one job seeker's networking activity with one person, Veronica Martin.

Contact Name:	Veronica Martin, VP, Information Systems
Address:	Dept. of Information and Technology
	Hope Hospital 3535 City Blvd., Richmond, VA 11111
Phone:	(555) 222-2222
Fax:	(555) 222-2223
E-mail:	vmartin@fauxmail.com

Date	Type of Communication (phone, e-mail, mtg., etc.)	Summary of Communication	Follow-Through Needed?
3/14	Phone	Introduced myself. Told her of my interest in transition to health care.	E-mail 3/18 to confirm mtg.
		Set up meeting for 3/19 at 4:00.	
3/18	Sent e-mail	Confirmed that I will meet her tomorrow at 4:00.	
3/19	Meeting	Very helpful mtg. See notes in file.	Send thank-you ASAP
3/21	Letter	Mailed thank-you letter.	Copy on file.

Using Project Progress Logs

If you need to keep track of networking related to one project—such as a job search or promoting a new development in your business—you need a log that lists all of your networking efforts related to that particular project. This enables you to have one running list of people you've contacted, events you have attended, mailings you have sent out, and so on. The project progress log is not as detailed as the record-of-contact log in that the former does not include summaries of communication or follow-up notes. That information should be kept only on the record-of-contact logs in the key people files.

The project progress log is intended only as a basic record sheet that you can glance at quickly to get a sense of your overall networking progress. For example, each time our job seeker contacted Veronica at Hope Hospital as indicated on the record-of-contact sheet in the preceding section, he would make a brief note of each contact with her on his project progress log as well. He would also list anyone else he spoke to in his search. Then, at the end of a week or a month when he wanted to take stock of how much networking he had been doing, he could look at his project progress log and see how many people he had contacted to date and what the status was with each.

You can develop a form similar to the following sample to suit your own purpose. The sample here shows entries that a job seeker made during a few days of his job search.

Date	Name	Nature of Communication	Next Steps
9/10	Joe Adams	Phone conversation	Call 3 people he referred me to.
9/10	Ann Richardson	Phone conversation	Call in Nov.
9/10	Sue Mullin	Phone conversation	E-mail resume
9/10	Bob Taft	Left him message	Try again 9/12
9/12	Bob Taft	Left second message	Try again 9/20

Quick Summary

Putting organizational and time management systems in place is an important step toward becoming an effective and efficient networker. This chapter described systems for keeping track of people, information, and networking activities and offered tips on finding the time to network.

To help you keep track of who you know, three systems were discussed:

- **Contact management systems.** A contact management system is a database of people in your network kept on index cards or in your computer.

- **To-be-entered files.** These are accordion folders in which you can quickly drop business cards or slips of papers with names for safekeeping until you have time to enter them in your contact management system.

- **Key people files.** These are file folders in which you keep records of communication with people you interact with frequently or periodically. They contain copies of letters, faxes, and e-mails and notes from phone conversations.

To help you keep track of what you know, two types of files were suggested:

- **Topic files.** These contain information (for example, newspaper and magazine articles and printouts from Web sites) on topics of interest to you or related to your career or business.

- **Resource files.** These contain information (for example, business cards, brochures, and flyers) on people and organizations that provide products or services you need to know about.

To help you keep track of your networking activities, two types of forms were suggested:

- **Record-of-contact logs.** These are forms on which you keep a record of all communication with a particular person. The logs include the name of the contact, the nature of the contact (phone, in-person, etc.), the results of the communication, and any follow-up needed.

- **Project progress logs.** These are forms on which you keep a running list of people you talk to or meet with and events you attend. These logs help you keep track of the volume of networking you have done.

Identifying and Expanding Your Network

I read somewhere that everybody on this planet is separated by only six other people. Six degrees of separation. Between us and everybody else on this planet. The President of the United States. A gondolier in Venice. Fill in the names.

—OUISA IN *SIX DEGREES OF SEPARATION* BY JOHN GUARE

Does your network consist of not much more than the ten names programmed for speed dial on your telephone? Or are you the type who has a Rolodex or electronic database stuffed to the gills with hundreds of names and business cards? It doesn't matter which camp you fall into—or if you're somewhere in between. Everyone must begin at the beginning, and that beginning is to take an inventory of your network.

In this chapter, you'll search your memory banks and go through records and files in your office or home to take stock of the people you already know. You will also learn ways to cultivate new contacts and expand your network well beyond the size you ever imagined possible.

And because an effective network is as much about quality as quantity, you'll also learn about the STARS system, a way of examining exactly who makes up your network and ensuring that your network is robust and well rounded. The STARS system involves classifying people as strategists, targets, allied forces, role models, or supporters based on the role each person plays in helping you reach your goals. You'll learn more about what I mean by those terms a little later in the chapter. First, though, you need to take stock of who you already know.

Taking Stock of Your Network and Potential Network

When you take stock of the people you know or have known of in the past, it's helpful to tackle the task by thinking in terms of categories of contacts. The following pages walk you through several broad categories: personal, work, education, professional groups, career services, personal and professional services, and multimedia. Each of the categories is explained in detail, including descriptions of subcategories. You'll also find worksheets following each category description so that you can start writing down the names of people you know (or could get to know) in each category. Doing so enables you to have the makings of an inventory of sorts—a comprehensive listing of your network.

In Chapter 3 you learned about setting up a contact management system electronically or on paper, so you might choose to use your contact management system rather than the worksheets in this chapter to record your network inventory.

Supplies You'll Need to Identify Your Network

To compile an inventory of your contacts, you'll need a few things. First, think of all the places—besides your brain—where you'll find names and contact information for people you already know or at least know of. You should gather all of the contact information that you can lay your hands on. You'll probably find it in

- Contact lists in your computer and/or electronic planner
- Paper address books (current and old ones)

- Rolodex or business card files

- Holiday card and birthday lists

- Company directories (current and past jobs)

- A directory for your school or college (current students or alumni)

- Files of clients, customers, vendors, or other professional contacts

- Membership rosters of professional or community groups you belong to or have belonged to in the past

As you fill in the worksheets that follow each of the contact categories, be open to including anyone or any group that comes to mind. Now is not the time to say things like "I don't know if they could really be of any help," or "I haven't spoken to him in years, so I can't include his name." Don't censor your list. It's very likely that people you haven't kept in touch with or are just barely acquainted with can be a valuable part of your network. And people who you think don't have much information or many resources may have more than you expect. So include them all—at least for now.

Personal Contacts

This category includes family, friends, acquaintances, and neighbors, as well as people you come across through involvement in clubs, community activities, sports, religious organizations, and other affiliations.

Some people hesitate to call on family and friends for help in reaching their own career or business goals. While it is important not to rely too heavily on people close to you, there is nothing wrong with enlisting their help on a basic level. Say you're looking for a job in accounting and your brother-in-law is a big shot at a major accounting firm. It's understandable that you might feel uncomfortable if he were simply to get you a job, but you could at least let him give you some advice or put you in touch with some of his colleagues. That way, you can feel good about the fact that your relative only steered you in the right direction, while you alone ultimately landed the job. In competitive situations, it's essential that you utilize all possible sources of leads, advice, and contacts, so you may need to stretch past your comfort zone when dealing with family and friends who could help.

You might also need to stretch a bit if you are uncomfortable contacting people you don't know all that well, such as friends of friends or acquaintances you know of through an organization like your church or a community sports league to which you belong. If you approach them with tact and courtesy and don't expect the world, most people will be happy to help out, even if they don't know you very well.

Take a look at the categories of personal contacts on the worksheet that follows and make note of people you know in each category. (In the case of clubs or other groups, it may not be practical to list all members in this small space, so just list the name of the organization. Also, for categories like Friends and Acquaintances in which you may have a lot of names to list, you might want to list several key people to get the listing started and then write something like "See address book" to refer you to the rest.)

In addition to writing down names of people you know in each category, think about how you could expand your network by getting involved with some of the organizations, activities, or people mentioned in these categories.

Personal Contacts Worksheet

Family:

_____

_____

_____

_____

_____

Friends and acquaintances:

_____

_____

_____

_____

_____

Clubs and organizations (include social clubs, country clubs, book clubs, parents' groups, sports teams, gyms/health clubs, fraternities/sororities, and other such groups):

_____

_____

_____

_____

_____

Community groups (fundraising or other services for charities; advisory or governing bodies of organizations, such as Boards of Trustees; neighborhood associations and other civic groups; foundations and other philanthropic groups; cultural organizations; or parent-teacher groups):

_____

_____

_____

_____

_____

_____

(continued)

(continued)

Religious organizations (churches, mosques, temples, religious study groups, social groups, or youth groups):

_____

_____

_____

_____

_____

_____

Work Contacts

Your current and past work experiences are excellent sources of network contacts. Bosses, co-workers, clients, and customers should all be considered as potential network members. This category is not limited to paid jobs, either. It also includes volunteer work, internships, and other professional assignments.

Pull out your current resume as well as old ones, along with any company directories you've saved from past jobs, and think about who you know from all your jobs, internships, and other work-related projects. Write as many people as you can think of on the worksheet that follows.

Work Contacts Worksheet

Co-workers (current and former):

_____

_____

_____

_____

_____

Supervisors/managers (current and former):

_____

_____

_____

_____

_____

Subordinates (current and former):

_____

_____

_____

_____

_____

Associates (clients, customers, vendors, suppliers, freelancers, consultants, temps, people at other organizations in your industry, investors, and shareholders):

_____

_____

_____

_____

_____

_____

Volunteer work colleagues and supervisors:

_____

_____

_____

_____

_____

Education Contacts

Whether you are a current student or an alumnus, educational institutions offer ready-made networks. Your classmates from high school, college, or graduate school are often very willing to help you reach your career or business goals.

Don't forget about other educational settings as well. If you've taken any continuing education or other part-time, non-degree classes or have been through vocational training or professional development programs on your own or through an employer, you've undoubtedly met people (classmates, instructors, and guest speakers) who could be valuable members of your network.

Think about the people you know (or used to know) through educational settings and list them on the Education Contacts Worksheet. (You may not be able to list all the individual names, but you can include a reference to an alumni directory or class roster.)

Education Contacts Worksheet

Alumni (high school, college, or graduate school):

_____

_____

_____

_____

_____

Teachers and professors (high school, college, or graduate school):

_____

_____

_____

_____

_____

Advisors, deans, and coaches (high school, college, or graduate school):

_____

_____

_____

_____

_____

Continuing education courses/seminars/workshops (classmates, instructors, or guest speakers):

_____

_____

_____

_____

_____

Job training/professional development programs (classmates, instructors, or guest speakers):

_____

_____

_____

_____

_____

Professional Groups Contacts

If you don't already belong to professional or trade associations, consider joining any of the organizations for your career field or industry. Attending meetings, conferences, seminars, and social events sponsored by such groups is an excellent way to expand your network. (See Appendix B for a sampling of associations if you need to find ones to join.)

You might also want to join organizations whose sole focus is networking. These are groups of people who get together out of some common interest or background, such as gender, race, or functional area. Examples of groups formed around a functional area are an organization for people in sales across many different industries or an organization whose members are all writers from various settings, including newspapers, magazines, advertising industry, and others.

Ready-Made Networks

Three major networking and referral organizations that can point you to a chapter near you are Ali Lassen's Leads Clubs, Inc., (800) 783-3761 and http://www.leadsclub.com; Business Networking Int'l, Inc., (800) 825-8286 and http://www.BNI.com; and LeTip International, Inc., (800) 25-LETIP and http://www.letip.com.

These groups are sometimes referred to as "breakfast clubs" or might just be called "networking groups." For salespeople and entrepreneurs, they are often referred to as "leads" or "tip" groups because a main focus of their meetings is to share leads to customers or clients. One such group came in handy for Marvin, a client of mine who worked in a printing business but wanted to start his own dating service. For help in getting his business going, he joined a group of African-American entrepreneurs who met for breakfast once a month. Most of them were older and more experienced than Marvin, so he learned a great deal about how to launch and run a successful business. The group consisted of about fifteen people and wasn't listed in any kind of directory; he heard about it through word of mouth.

If you don't already belong to a networking group—either a small, informal one or one of the large, formal ones (see the Ready-Made Networks note)—but think one could be useful to you, ask your friends and colleagues to see if anyone knows of any such groups.

Professional Groups Contacts Worksheet

Professional or trade associations:

_____

_____

_____

_____

Networking groups, breakfast clubs, tip or leads groups:

_____

_____

_____

_____

Career Services Contacts

If you are working with a career consultant or job placement professional or have in the past, be sure to count that individual as part of your network. This group includes career counselors in private practice as well as ones who work in college- or community-based career development or employment centers. Also consider recruiters in employment agencies and executive search firms, as well as outplacement consultants. Some public libraries are also staffed with career resource experts. (The various types of career services professionals are also discussed and defined later in this chapter in the "Allied Forces" section.)

Think about any career services professionals you have ever worked with in the past or are dealing with currently and add them to the worksheet that follows. If you don't know of anyone to list, consider asking your friends and professional colleagues for referrals to people they have worked with.

Career Services Contacts Worksheet

Employment agencies and executive recruiters:

_____

_____

_____

_____

(continued)

(continued)

Outplacement firms:

_____

_____

_____

_____

Career counseling centers or employment offices:

_____

_____

_____

_____

Career counselors or consultants in private practice:

_____

_____

_____

_____

Career resource librarians:

_____

_____

_____

_____

Personal and Professional Services Contacts

People who provide personal and professional services are excellent sources of leads, resources, and information. People like your physician, dentist, accountant, hairdresser, or fitness trainer might be just the link you need to the right people or information because they come across a large number of people daily.

Don't forget, too, about stockbrokers and financial planners, insurance agents, real estate agents, pharmacists, mechanics, doormen, landlords, dry cleaners, tailors, housekeepers, and many others. You never know who might turn out to be a wealth of leads and information.

I never cease to be amazed by the stories I hear from clients and friends who tell me how these types of people have helped them. There was the recent college graduate, for example, who landed his first job in marketing because one of the trainers at his gym passed his resume on to a high-level marketing executive who happened to be one of the trainer's best private clients.

Then there were the two public relations executives who didn't know each other but happened to use the same stockbroker. They both talked to the broker about their interest in leaving their jobs and starting their own firm, so he put the two of them in touch with each other, and they ended up becoming partners.

Even more amazing was the young woman who went to a tailor to have her interviewing suit altered. Being a chatty type, she talked to the tailor while standing there having her hem pinned up, telling him she hoped this new suit would bring her luck, particularly with one company she had been trying to get an interview with. He said, "What a coincidence, a customer was here this morning who works for that company." The savvy job seeker then left a copy of her resume with the tailor, with a note attached, and asked the tailor to give it to the customer when he came back to pick up his clothes. He did, and the effort resulted in an interview for the job seeker.

Hard to believe, but those are all true stories! It clearly takes just a little luck and chutzpah, plus a lot of initiative, to make the most of situations like these.

Now think about the people you come across on a daily or periodic basis who provide personal or professional services not just to you, but to many others as well. List their names on the following worksheet.

Personal and Professional Services Contacts Worksheet

Physicians and other medical/health professionals:

_____

_____

_____

_____

Dentists:

_____

_____

_____

_____

Attorneys:

_____

_____

_____

_____

Accountants:

_____

_____

_____

_____

Stockbrokers and financial planners:

_____

_____

_____

_____

Bankers:

_____

_____

_____

_____

Insurance agents:

_____

_____

_____

_____

Realtors:

_____

_____

_____

_____

(continued)

(continued)

Hairdressers or barbers:

_____

_____

_____

_____

Manicurists:

_____

_____

_____

_____

Fitness trainers:

_____

_____

_____

_____

Pharmacists:

_____

_____

_____

_____

Mechanics:

_____

_____

_____

_____

Dry cleaners:

_____

_____

_____

_____

Tailors:

_____

_____

_____

_____

Landlords:

_____

_____

_____

_____

Doormen:

_____

_____

_____

_____

Housekeepers:

_____

_____

_____

_____

Multimedia Contacts

An often-overlooked source of network contacts is all around us every day—media and technology. The Internet has obviously revolutionized the way people can network with e-mail, instant messaging, and online forums such as bulletin boards, newsgroups, and chat rooms.

Besides the Internet, though, less-obvious networking opportunities exist through books, newspapers, magazines, television, and radio. Reading or hearing about people whose work interests you or whose career paths you admire is a great source of people to contact who might be willing to help. You can also use information presented in the media to contact companies and organizations that may be good sources of information and help.

Whether you are networking for a job search or for another pursuit, contacting people or places you read about is generally more effective than the less targeted approach of mass mailings to random lists of people or organizations. This is one of the ways to tap into the proverbial "hidden" job market.

Multimedia Contacts Worksheet

Internet

Online forums (bulletin boards, newsgroups, chat rooms):

_____

_____

_____

_____

_____

Web sites:

_____

_____

_____

_____

_____

My personal e-mail address list:

_____

_____

_____

_____

_____

Newspapers, Magazines, and Journals

Editors:

_____

_____

_____

_____

_____

Reporters:

_____

_____

_____

_____

[continued]

(continued)

(continued)

Writers:

_____

_____

_____

_____

People and organizations profiled or quoted in articles:

_____

_____

_____

_____

Books

Authors:

_____

_____

_____

_____

Editors:

_____

_____

_____

_____

Radio and Television

Producers and directors:

_____

_____

_____

_____

Reporters and anchors:

_____

_____

_____

_____

Guests or people profiled or mentioned:

_____

_____

_____

_____

Network Strengths and Weaknesses Checklist

Now that you have identified sources of people for your networking base, take stock of where you stand in each sphere. Use the following checklist to see how you stand in each area. Put a check in the Strength or Weakness column next to each type of contact to see where the gaps are in your network.

Network Strengths and Weaknesses Checklist

	Strength	Weakness

Personal Contacts

	Strength	Weakness
Family	_____	_____
Friends and acquaintances	_____	_____
Clubs and social organizations	_____	_____
Community groups	_____	_____
Neighbors	_____	_____
Local merchants (e.g., dry cleaner)	_____	_____
Professional service providers (e.g., accountant)	_____	_____
Sports	_____	_____
Religious organizations	_____	_____

Work Contacts

	Strength	Weakness
Co-workers (current and past)	_____	_____
Supervisors/managers (current and past)	_____	_____
Subordinates	_____	_____
Associates (e.g., clients, vendors, etc.)	_____	_____
Volunteer work colleagues	_____	_____

Career Services Contacts

	Strength	Weakness
Employment agencies and executive recruiters	_____	_____
Outplacement firms	_____	_____
Career counseling and employment offices	_____	_____
Career counselors and consultants	_____	_____
Librarians	_____	_____

	Strength	Weakness

Education Contacts

Alumni (high school, college, graduate school) _____ _____

Continuing education course classmates,
instructors, and guest speakers _____ _____

Job training program classmates, instructors,
and guest speakers _____ _____

Teachers and professors _____ _____

Advisors, deans, and coaches _____ _____

Professional Groups Contacts

Professional and trade associations _____ _____

Networking groups _____ _____

Multimedia Contacts

Internet

Newsgroups _____ _____

Web sites and e-mail lists _____ _____

Newspapers and magazines

Editors _____ _____

Reporters and writers _____ _____

People and organizations profiled in articles _____ _____

Books

Authors _____ _____

Editors _____ _____

Radio and Television

Producers and directors _____ _____

Reporters and anchors _____ _____

Guests or people profiled _____ _____

Taking a Closer Look at Your Network—The STARS System

When you take stock of your network, there is a danger in simply having a random list of names on paper or in a database. Sure, you can look at your list with pride and say, "Look how many people I know!"—but can you say with certainty that you know the right people to help with your objectives and goals?

Think about how this idea plays out in your personal life. Is there a particular person you vent your frustrations to when you have a rough day at work? Do you have others you rely on for advice about your finances or problems in your marriage or relationships? You might also have people you can call on to talk you through a computer malfunction or to recommend a good book on a particular topic. And there are always those who can be counted on to recommend the perfect restaurant or for a reliable review of the latest movies.

The people in your personal network fill a variety of roles. Some provide emotional support, some give information, and others help with strategy. Some might set a good example, serving as role models. Others are friends, family, and co-workers. Still others might be professionals like a psychotherapist or a financial advisor.

Well, the same thing happens with your professional network. Some people are the ones you turn to for help in solving problems on the job, others provide inspiration or emotional support as you make transitions, and some give you concrete leads or strategy tips for obtaining jobs, customers, or clients. Many people will provide more than one of these "services," while others might be best equipped to meet just one specific need.

To examine the roles played by the people in your network, you might use a system I've developed called STARS. The STARS system involves seeing your contacts as fitting into five basic categories: Strategists, Targets, Allied forces, Role models, and Supporters. Sorting your network into these five categories can be a great way to keep your contacts organized, and it will help you be clear about which people you should turn to in specific situations.

On the following pages, you will find descriptions of each of the STARS categories, followed by worksheets where you can list the members of your network who might fit into each category. (Remember that some people will fill more than one role, so feel free to list some of the same people on more than one worksheet.) Completing the worksheets will help you make sure that you have enough people in each of the STARS categories, which, in turn, will bring you closer to reaching your career or business goals.

Strategists

Strategists are key members of your network. They are the people who will sit down with you, roll up their sleeves, and help you hammer out a strategy for reaching your goals. They might help you devise a business plan or job search strategy or may act as career coaches helping you decide on a career focus. They can be from within the field in which you work (or in which you want to work) or might be from the outside. A salesperson in telecommunications, for example, might learn new sales techniques from a strategist who is in software sales.

Strategists generally provide advice, information, resources, and leads. In doing so, they help you solve problems, become innovative in the way you work, plan a job hunting strategy, reach your goals, and get access to needed information. In most cases, strategists should make up the majority of your network since they provide the broadest range of support.

> ## Your Network STARS
>
> **S**trategists: The people who help you plot a course toward your goals.
>
> **T**argets: The people most closely linked to your career or business goals—for example, prospective employers, customers, or clients.
>
> **A**llied forces: The professionals who provide expertise to strengthen your networking efforts.
>
> **R**ole models: The mentors or sages of your search who set a good example and offer advice and wisdom.
>
> **S**upporters: The people who provide emotional support along the way to reaching your goals.

Who Are Your Strategists?

Now that you're familiar with the concept of a strategist, think about who might serve that function for you. Who could help you plan a strategy for making a career decision, getting a job, managing your career, or developing a business? Write their names below.

_____

_____

_____

_____

_____

_____

_____

_____

_____

_____

_____

_____

Targets

The targets in your network are the people most closely linked to your goals. If you're a job seeker, for example, your targets are the prospective employers who you hope will interview you and eventually hire you. If you're trying to be more successful on your job or in your own business, your targets may be potential customers or clients. Targets are obviously an essential part of any network and are often the hardest to come by of all the categories. In fact, you're probably networking primarily to get to your targets.

Hitting the Target

To identify the targets in her network, one job seeker in the finance field relied on alumni from her alma maters. She started by contacting the career development offices of the college and graduate school she had attended and requesting that they send her a list of alumni working in finance. She asked the career offices to include both alumni working in the city where she wanted to work (Chicago) and in other cities around the country that are known as financial centers (New York, San Francisco, Atlanta, Charlotte, and others). By doing so, she could gain access to a network that would include both strategists and targets. Here's why: She was able to contact the people in the cities where she didn't want to work and ask them for advice about her strategy, using them as guinea pigs of sorts. She could discuss her concerns about the transition she was trying to make and was able to show them a rough draft of her resume for their suggestions. Since she knew that she didn't want to work in their offices, she was able to be more candid with them and let them see her as a "diamond in the rough"—something she couldn't do if they were actual targets, or people she wanted to work for. She was then able to turn to her targets—alumni working in Chicago—and present herself as a polished job candidate based on the valuable advice she got from the strategists in other cities.

Now Think of Who Your Targets Are

Your list of targets is likely to be the longest of all the STARS lists, so I don't suggest you try to list your targets here in the book. Instead, you should make lists of all prospective employers or clients in your computer or on paper.

Allied Forces

If you've ever been behind the scenes in a modeling agency or movie set, you've seen the army of people it takes to get someone ready for the camera. Makeup artists, wardrobe consultants, voice and diction coaches, physical fitness trainers, cosmetic dentists, and a host of other professionals all play a part in getting someone in "camera-ready" condition. While you don't need to go to such lengths to network effectively (and movie-star physical appearance is not a prerequisite for successful networking!), you may need to call in some outside experts for certain aspects of the process. These allied forces are people who can ensure that your networking efforts are not wasted because of some flaw in your personal presentation.

For example, you don't want to go to the trouble of making ten cold calls a day only to find that your voice isn't conveying the right degree of professionalism or enthusiasm. Or you might agonize over writing a letter to request a networking meeting, only to find that your letter could have been stronger if you had consulted a business writing expert or a job search coach. Similarly, an image consultant or public speaking seminar could come in handy if you have to represent your company at a speaking engagement.

Depending on your networking objectives and the areas where you could use some improvement, your allied forces might include

- **Image consultants.** Image consultants help you make a good first, and lasting, impression. They advise clients on wardrobe, hair, and makeup as well as on other aspects of their personal presentation, such as voice, diction, and etiquette. Some also specialize in media consulting, helping people convey the right image on television or radio appearances.

- **Voice coaches.** Voice coaches help you improve your speaking voice in such areas as diction, tone, rate of speech, and energy level. Some can help correct regional or foreign accents, and some with higher levels of training can work with speech impairments or impediments. They can help you project a more confident, professional, and engaging self on the phone, in person, or when speaking in public.

- **Career development professionals.** Within the career development profession, you'll find many different titles used, reflecting the range of services these experts offer. *Career counselors*, for example, typically have an advanced degree (master's or doctorate) in counseling or psychology and may counsel clients on career direction, job search, and career management or just on one or two of those areas. There are also professionals who provide the same services but call themselves *career consultants, career strategists,* or *career coaches.* They may or may not have degrees in counseling but often have experience in human resources or other areas in which they have helped people develop and manage their careers. Then there are *executive coaches,* also known as *career management consultants.* They usually don't work with people who are choosing careers or job hunting but instead help people be more successful, satisfied, and productive in their current jobs. (You'll find more information about executive coaches in Chapter 8.) Whatever their title and whichever specific services they offer, career development professionals are often excellent sources of advice and guidance in the networking process.

- **Business strategy consultants.** Like a career counselor for the self-employed, business strategy consultants help you make decisions about going into business for yourself and also advise you on how to make your business successful once you get it started. Some work with you one-on-one in hourly sessions, while others offer group workshops or seminars. Business strategy consultants either work independently or offer seminars through business schools and other community education centers. Advice is also offered through non-profit and government organizations specializing in resources for entrepreneurs. Some of these are listed in Appendix C for your convenience.

- **Professional organizers.** I often talk with people who are fed up with the mess of papers and files on their desk or the disaster area known as their office and find they are thrilled to learn that professional organizers exist. These are people who will come to your home or office and show you how to get rid of clutter, set up organizational systems, and stay organized. It's difficult to be an effective networker when your home and office are in disarray, so a professional organizer may be a key member of your network's allied forces.

- **Publicists.** For the serious networker, or for those who are self-employed, a publicist may be just what you need. Publicists can make you or your business more visible by planning and implementing a public relations campaign that might get you on television or radio or featured in a magazine or newspaper. Remember that much of networking is about being visible—getting people to come to you instead of you having to knock on their doors. If you're willing to spend a few bucks, publicists are a surefire way to gain that visibility and spread the word about what you know and have to offer.

- **Psychotherapists.** Some people consider a psychotherapist to be an essential member of their network for ongoing support and reflection on their daily lives. Making a career decision or managing your career, for example, can bring up all sorts of difficult questions about what you want out of life. Psychotherapy may be the right arena in which to explore such lofty issues as your values, hopes, and dreams, thus enabling you to make the more mundane decisions about your daily work life.

    Others find that they benefit from short-term counseling to help them get through a tough time, such as a job loss. A job search can bring about the need for some professional mental health treatment. I have worked with many job seekers who, unfortunately, find themselves in a true depression over the trials and tribulations of job hunting. Seeking the help of a psychotherapist (either a therapist with a master's degree in counseling or social work or a psychologist with a Ph.D.) is often just what they need to bounce back and keep going with their job searches.

> **Let Your Fingers Do the Walking**
>
> In addition to the referral sources listed in Appendix C, don't forget about your local *Yellow Pages* telephone directory as a handy source of allied forces.

Finding Allied Forces

If you're interested in adding some of the professionals described above to your own "allied forces" but you don't know where to find them, you can turn to Appendix C for suggestions. In that appendix, you'll find listings of places and people who can refer you to any of these experts.

Many of the listings are for professional associations that can also provide you with guidelines for choosing a member of their field so that you know what to look for in a so-called expert before you hand over your money and time.

Taking Stock of Your Allied Forces

The following chart lists most of the typical allied forces that are useful in networking, and it also provides spaces labeled Other where you can list additional experts. To use this chart, put check marks in the Already Utilize column next to the experts who are already a part of your network. For those who might be able to help you, but whom you don't have in your network, place check marks in the Need to Find column.

Allied Forces Chart

Professional	Already Utilize	Need to Find
Career counselor	_____	_____
Executive coach	_____	_____
Business Strategy consultant	_____	_____
Voice coach	_____	_____
Image consultant	_____	_____
Professional organizer	_____	_____
Publicist	_____	_____
Psychotherapist	_____	_____
Other: _____	_____	_____
Other: _____	_____	_____
Other: _____	_____	_____

Finding Your Allied Forces in the Not-So-Ivory Tower

Involving professional consultants in your networking efforts doesn't have to be expensive and time-consuming. Seminars and classes offered in centers of adult learning or universities' continuing education departments can be an excellent way to refine your networking techniques in a group setting without the expense of a private coach or consultant. These courses are usually taught by people who are not ivory-tower academics but are real-world consultants and experts in communications, business strategy, public relations, and many other areas. Many colleges and universities have divisions or departments with names like Adult Learning, University Extension, Adult Education, or Continuing Education. These departments typically offer an interesting array of courses that are not part of a degree program and therefore don't require a big investment of time or money and usually do not have competitive admissions.

Also, be on the lookout for learning centers in your area that have names such as The Learning Annex, The Learning Alliance, The Discovery Center, and so on. These kinds of private or nonprofit organizations offer many practical career development and life skills courses.

Role Models

These are the sages of your search—the people who serve as wise counsel for any of your professional endeavors. You might think of them as mentors or teachers who guide you through the steps of your professional development. While they are likely to be considerably more experienced than you are, they don't necessarily have to be older than you.

How to Find a Mentor

It is becoming increasingly common for large companies to have in-house mentoring programs in which junior employees are paired with more senior ones. Ask your human resources department if you're not already aware of such a program. If you are not employed in a large company, or if your company does not offer mentoring, then contact local civic organizations like the Chamber of Commerce or a Kiwanis Club to see if they can help.

In addition to being people whom you get to know well and meet with frequently or periodically, role models can also be people you don't actually know, but whose work you respect and admire. You can choose all sorts of people as your role models, including prominent people in your field, celebrities, or historical figures, even though they're not people you are likely to pick up the phone and call. They can, nevertheless, serve as remote role models. Former First Lady Hillary Clinton was subjected to a lot of ribbing by the press when they got wind of her imaginary conversations with Eleanor Roosevelt. Well, regardless of the controversy surrounding that news, the late Mrs. Roosevelt is a good example of a remote role model—someone who provides inspiration because of her accomplishments and even offers guidance indirectly by having modeled certain behavior in the past. Of course, you do want to be sure that you have some living, breathing role models to turn to for an interactive relationship as well!

Who Are Your Role Models?

Think of the people who serve as role models for you or who could serve as role models if you had a chance to develop a mentoring relationship with them. Also think of remote role models—historical figures or famous contemporary people whose careers have set good examples for you. List everyone you can think of in the spaces that follow.

_____

_____

_____

_____

_____

_____

_____

_____

(continued)

(continued)

Supporters

Unlike remote role models, supporters are people you know well and who are very much accessible, maybe even living under your own roof. They are the ones who provide emotional support when the going gets tough, encouragement when you're on the way up, and a kick in the pants when you're slacking off. They are likely to be family members or close friends, but might also be that co-worker or classmate who's always there for you.

A supporter can be someone who fits into one of the other STARS categories as well, like a strategist who can dish out not only advice but also empathy and sympathy. The allied forces are also good sources of supporters. Having a therapist or counselor in your network or being part of a support group like a job hunting club or business strategy workshop can provide valuable emotional support and the cheerleading you need to keep going. Even if you're tough as nails and highly resilient, it helps to have a few supporters in your network.

Who Are Your Supporters?

Use the spaces that follow to make a list of the supporters in your network. The supporters might be people who have helped you out in the past during difficult periods of time or challenging situations. They may also be people whose supportive nature has not been tested yet but who you believe have the qualities of a supporter.

_____

_____

_____

_____

_____

_____

_____

_____

_____

_____

Quick Summary

Having a sufficient number of the right people in your network is essential for reaching your career or business objectives and goals. In this chapter, you learned that potential contacts can be found in seven main categories:

- Personal

- Work

- Education

- Professional groups

- Career services

- Personal and professional services

- Multimedia

This chapter also introduced the concept of the STARS system, a process of classifying your contacts as strategists, targets, allied forces, role models, or supporters according to the roles each person plays in your network:

- **Strategists:** The people who help you plot a course toward your goals

- **Targets:** The people most closely linked to your career or business goals—for example, prospective employers, customers, or clients

- **Allied forces:** The professionals who provide expertise to strengthen your networking efforts

- **Role models:** The mentors or sages of your search who set a good example and offer advice and wisdom

- **Supporters:** The people who provide emotional support along the way to reaching your goals

Assembling Your Self-Marketing Toolkit

Never to talk of oneself is a form of hypocrisy.

—Friedrich Nietzsche

The networking process invariably requires that you talk about yourself a great deal. Even though true networking is a give-and-take, relationship-based process, it nonetheless involves considerable discussion of what *you* need, who *you* are, and what you want others to do for *you*. While networking is not about outright asking for a job or promotion or blatantly soliciting business, self-promotion is an inevitable component of networking. The self-promotion can and should be subtle, but it does need to be there.

If you want people to help you make a career decision, get ahead in your career, land a new job, or develop your business, you have to show them that you're worth the trouble. In this chapter, you learn how to prepare a toolkit of self-marketing materials that will help you do just that. You also learn how to construct a self-marketing sound bite—a personal pitch that is the most basic element of your toolkit. We'll also touch on how to develop resumes, bios, reference lists, portfolios, and business promotional materials. We'll begin, though, with a few preparatory steps outlined in the following section.

Preparatory Steps to Effective Self-Marketing

In order to make a good impression and get your point across when networking, you should take three steps to prepare: Know yourself, know what you want, and know your achievements. Taking these three steps will make it much easier to pick up the phone and make a cold call; converse with a stranger at a conference; or write resumes, bios, and other written tools.

Know Who You Are

Taking stock of who you are—your interests, strengths, values, personal qualities, and work style—is an essential foundation for all networking communication. Knowing yourself ensures that you can clearly convey to others what makes you uniquely you.

Networking for a job search or career advancement, for example, requires that you sell other people on your strengths and capabilities. Knowing your strengths is a first step in having a convincing self-marketing campaign. Networking to help you make a career decision also requires that you have a solid handle on who you are and what your priorities are so that as you learn about various career options, you can rule out options that don't fit and rule in the ones that do. Self-awareness also enables you to understand the way you actually go about networking. It helps you recognize your communication strengths and weaknesses and empowers you to adopt networking methods that fit your personality style.

How do you achieve this self-awareness? Some of it comes from experience. The more experience you have in your career, and life in general, the easier it is to say what you like and don't like, what you do well, and in which kinds of environments you thrive.

Although lots of experience helps, you can acquire self-awareness at any age or career level by doing some careful self-assessment. Self-assessment methods range from the informal, such as simply thinking about who you are and jotting down some thoughts, to formal testing offered by career counselors and other qualified professionals.

Many people do just fine with the more informal methods. You can sometimes gain a lot of self-awareness by sitting on the proverbial hillside contemplating the proverbial blade of grass. Keeping a journal of your thoughts and observations on your experiences can also be useful.

Other people, though, find that they need some kind of structure to guide their thoughts so they can more effectively determine their strengths and skills. Many of the books listed in the job search and career targeting, changing, managing, and researching sections of Appendix D include exercises that help you identify your personal qualities and get them down on paper in a methodical way.

If you want to be even more thorough in your self-assessment, consider formal assessment—that is, testing administered by a qualified professional. Interest inventories, skills assessments, values clarification questionnaires, and personality style measures provide an objective look at who you are. While the term *test* is commonly used among those of us who do this type of assessment, most of these are not actually tests per se in that there are no right or wrong answers. They are instead inventories of your self-expressed preferences. The most common ones have personalized reports or supplementary materials that list career fields, specific types of jobs, or work environments that match your results. While they can't provide all the answers and only rarely reveal any hidden talents that you were hoping to uncover, they can be powerful ways to find out what makes you uniquely you.

Popular Career and Personality Tests

Strong Interest Inventory (http://www.cpp.com)

Campbell Interest and Skill Survey (http://www.pearsonassessments.com)

Holland's Self-Directed Search (http://www.self-directed-search.com)

Myers-Briggs Type Indicator (http://www.cpp.com)

Career Anchors (http://www.pfeiffer.com)

(continued)

(continued)

Some of these assessment tools are available only through professionals certified to administer them, including career counselors as well as some psychologists, social workers, college career centers, and human resource departments. Only the Self-Directed Search is, you guessed it, designed as a do-it-yourself tool.

Know What You Want

Equal in importance to knowing who you are is knowing what you want. As you learned in Chapter 2, having clear goals and being able to define objectives to reach those goals is essential for effective networking. Knowing what you want also strengthens your self-marketing efforts. Let's look at an example of what can happen if you aren't clear on what you want.

Peter is a college senior trying to figure out what he wants to do with his life, so he conducts a fact-finding mission with an alumnus of his school who works in advertising. (That's one field Peter is considering). The purpose of the meeting is to get information about that field to help him determine if it's the right career for him. Here's how the conversation goes:

Alum.: "What are you looking for in a career?"

Peter: **"I don't really know. That's why I'm here."**

Alum.: "Well, I can tell you about the different types of jobs in advertising, and maybe that will help you."

(The alumnus then proceeds to talk for a while about the nature of the work, satisfactions and frustrations, typical earning potential, and skills needed for the many different specialties in advertising.)

Peter: **"So do you have any idea which area would be right for me?"**

Alum.: "I can help you make that decision if you can tell me what your main strengths are, what kinds of people you want to work with, and what kinds of work responsibilities motivate you. What's most important to you in a job?"

Peter doesn't really have an answer. He has some vague thoughts on these issues but hasn't done enough self-assessment to be able to determine if he's more suited for being in account management, media planning, production, or any of the many other areas within the diverse field of advertising. In this case, he's not expected to know exactly what career he wants because that's why he is in the meeting in the first place. He doesn't need to have his career goal perfectly formed, but he does need to be able to paint a general picture of what he is looking for.

He would have been a more effective networker if he had said, "I don't know what area of advertising is best for me, but I do know that I want to combine some creative work with a lot of client contact. I also want to use skills like persuading, negotiating, and just generally interacting with people a lot. Making money is also important to me, so I want to get on a career track in which I can advance and grow." In that case, the alumnus might have pointed Peter in the direction of an entry-level position in account management. Peter would have provided enough concrete information about himself and what he wants for the two of them to get him closer to a career focus.

Peter also would have impressed the advertising executive with his self-awareness and clear convictions about what he wants. In other words, he would have been a more convincing self-marketer. In fact, he might have impressed the advertising executive enough to have that person go from being a strategist to a target—someone who would not only give him advice but possibly a job as well, or at least leads to jobs.

Know Your Achievements

If you know anything about interviewing for jobs or developing customers for a business, you probably know that it's important to sell the prospective employer or customer on your accomplishments. It's not enough just to tell them what you could do for them—you need to talk about your past achievements to provide evidence of what you have done in similar situations in the past.

Now, if we're saying that networking is not about asking for a job or directly soliciting a customer but instead is about building relationships and seeking information that could lead to jobs or customers, then you don't need to be talking about your achievements, right? Wrong! Remember that there needs to be a subtle element of self-marketing in every networking encounter. Every time you develop a new networking relationship or revive an old one, you need to let the other person know what you have to offer so that they can feel comfortable helping you advance in your career or business. Letting them know about your achievements gives them the confidence they need to help you expand your horizons.

So, what is an achievement? It's an example from your recent or not-too-distant past that demonstrates what you have to offer. It's an example of how you can make a difference for an employer or a customer or client by using the skills, talents, personal qualities, and knowledge that you possess.

How to Communicate Your Achievements

Achievements need to be conveyed as concise stories that include three basic elements: Context, Action, and Outcome. Context refers to the situation you faced, action is what you did in that situation, and outcome is the result of your action.

Here's an example to illustrate this Context-Action-Outcome (CAO) formula: Derrick is a plant manager for a chemicals manufacturer. The situation he faced when he started in this job was that employee morale in the plant was very low and turnover was high. Employees were not satisfied with their working conditions and were leaving for better opportunities with competitors. Derrick put several innovative programs and policies in place that improved morale and reduced turnover by 27 percent in his first eighteen months on the job.

See the CAO in this example? The context is that Derrick came into a challenging situation where employee turnover was too high. The action he took was to make some significant changes that brought about the positive outcome of a reduction in the turnover rate. In a networking meeting, Derrick could describe this situation briefly and then get into more specifics about his actions and the outcome depending on how much the other person wants to discuss the details of the achievement.

Identifying Your Achievements

Thinking of achievements to talk about when networking may be a cinch for you. You may be able to come up with several off the top of your head. You might even be the organized sort who keeps an ongoing written record of your achievements as part of your own career management strategy. But what if you just can't think of anything you've accomplished? This is particularly common in people who've done work that doesn't have an obvious direct impact on an employer's bottom line in a dollars-and-cents sort of way, such as technicians or support personnel who do important work but don't always see the impact they have on their organizations. Or perhaps you've been a stay-at-home parent who feels your biggest achievement has been raising healthy, happy kids, but you don't know how to turn that into an achievement story for the business world. Don't despair—everyone has achievements that are worthy of his or her self-marketing toolkit! To find them, try asking yourself the following questions:

- Is there something I am particularly proud of (whether it was formally recognized by others or not)?

- Was I able to do more with less?

- Have I done something in a new way? Been more creative, innovative, or efficient?

- Did I save my organization money by cutting costs or other measures?

- Did I bring money into my organization? (Even if you weren't in a direct revenue generation role, did you work on projects or provide support to business development efforts that yielded a certain amount of revenue?)

- What makes you different from the people you've worked with? Are you known for a particular skill or talent? Known for doing something better, smarter, faster?

(continued)

(continued)

- Did you receive rewards or special recognition for anything? Did you get special mention in a performance review for something you did?

Achievements come in all shapes and sizes. They may contain impressive dollar amounts or major awards or honors. They may have taken place during exceptionally challenging times, or they may simply be things you did well under fairly routine circumstances. As long as it is something you are proud of and that you think showcases your skills and distinguishes you from the competition, it's a worthy achievement.

Scripting One of Your Achievements

Now think about an achievement you can discuss in your own networking. Pick a story that relates to the goals you are trying to achieve and that would therefore be relevant in your networking encounters. Use the space below to develop an achievement story you could start using right away.

Context: Briefly describe the situation, whether it was routine or an unusual challenge. Think of the conditions or circumstances surrounding your accomplishment. You might use phrases such as "during a period of major organizational restructuring," "despite challenging market conditions," "within exceptionally tight deadlines," or "accomplished as additional responsibilities while successfully maintaining regular workload." Give enough detail to set the context, but not so much detail that the story becomes too long.

_____

_____

_____

Action: Here, list the actions you took. Jot down key phrases or short sentences to describe specific actions.

_____

_____

_____

Outcome: Briefly describe the results that came about from your actions. Whenever possible, quantify the results by citing dollar amounts or percentages, such as revenue generated, costs reduced, etc. If the outcomes can't be expressed in numbers, that's fine; just be as precise as possible.

_____

_____

_____

Now that you've jotted down ideas for each of the three elements, pull them together in one story you can tell when networking. Don't try to memorize your achievement stories word-for-word. Script them only to be sure you have the story fleshed out coherently and concisely, and then practice speaking it in a way that flows naturally without reading from the script. (You might want to list key points from your script in bulleted format to help you remember what to say.)

Repeat this process until you have several achievement stories prepared. You won't necessarily talk about all of them in any given networking meeting; in fact, most networking meetings are pretty brief, so you probably wouldn't have time to cover them all. But having several prepared will enable you to select the one or two that are most appropriate for any given situation.

Describing Yourself with a Self-Marketing Sound Bite

When you've assessed who you are, what you're looking for, and what you've achieved, you should be able to construct a self-marketing sound bite. This is a personal pitch that is the cornerstone of your self-marketing efforts and of almost all communication with your network. Your sound bite is a brief statement that typically takes about thirty to sixty seconds to say. If you present it in writing, it is a brief paragraph of a few to several sentences.

The self-marketing sound bite introduces you and your situation and explains why you're worth the listener's or reader's attention. The content and length of your self-marketing sound bite will vary slightly as you use it in different situations, but its core elements should be fairly consistent.

Why You Need a Self-Marketing Sound Bite

Your self-marketing sound bite helps you convey information about yourself in a concise and effective manner. Efficiency is important when dealing with busy people who have only limited time to talk on the phone or read a letter. Concise communication is particularly vital when networking via e-mail, online chat sessions and message boards, and voice mail messages. With a thirty-second sound bite, you can get your point across succinctly and clearly without clogging someone's voice mail or inbox.

Constructing a sound bite also makes it easier for people to speak on your behalf. There are many occasions in networking when you need people to pass the word along to others that you are looking for a job, seeking a promotion, or offering a particular product or service. What often happens, unfortunately, is that your message loses something in the translation.

For example, your message might be that pet owners should use you as their dog trainer because you had twenty years of experience working in kennels and volunteering for the ASPCA before freelancing. If you convey that message in a long-winded fashion, such as listing every job you have held over twenty years and giving too much detail, the person who passes on your message to potential customers is not likely to pass the message along in an accurate and effective way. For example, she might just say to someone, "I think he'd make a great dog trainer for you because he has a lot of experience." That's not a very convincing sales pitch.

An additional reason for developing a sound bite is that it's a great time-saver for you, not just the listener or reader. Every time you have to make a cold call, respond to the popular interview opener "So, tell me about yourself," or compose a letter, you can use your sound bite as an opener. Using your sound bite as the building block for all types of communication keeps you from having to reinvent the wheel every time you face a new networking situation.

Constructing Your Self-Marketing Sound Bite

There are so many things you can say to introduce yourself to someone and to present yourself in a positive light that it can be difficult to know what to include and what to leave out. The way to choose the best information for your pitch is to think of what is relevant to the person you're communicating with, your goals, and the situation at hand. There should be four main elements to your sound bite:

1. Put yourself on the map

2. Pitch your strengths

3. Back up your claims with evidence

4. State what you're looking for

These four elements are described in the following sections.

Putting Yourself on the Map

Putting yourself on the map means establishing who you are in terms of your work or educational status, situation, and roles. What that might mean is any of the following:

- **Work role.** This includes job title, career area, functional area, and overview of your experience. Examples: "I have fifteen years of sales experience, with the past five years in sales management, most recently for AT&T," or "I'm a physical therapist at Hope Hospital," or "I interned last summer at AOL."

- **Education.** If you are a current student or recent graduate, mentioning your education will certainly be a key part of your opening lines in your sound bite, and it may replace the work role. If you are a working adult who has gone back to school for a degree or a short training program to advance in, or change, your career, you might mention education in addition to your work role. Examples: "I'll be graduating from Michigan State next spring," "I received my B.S. in business from Bentley College in 1996," "I have an M.B.A. from U.C. Berkeley," "I'm currently completing my associate's degree in administrative studies," or "I'm in a program to become a certified network engineer."

Pitching Your Strengths

Here's where you mention the positive points that will help you reach your goals. These points might cover the following categories:

- **Skills.** Examples: "I am fluent in Spanish and Russian, both written and spoken," "I am proficient in most major word-processing and database applications," or "I have strong research and writing skills."

- **Areas of expertise.** Examples: "I have a broad knowledge of human resource functions, including recruiting, training, and benefits administration" or "My interdisciplinary major exposed me to many current issues in education, politics, and sociology."

- **Personal qualities.** Examples: "I'm the kind of person who gives 110 percent when I care about something, and I care about the problems of the homeless," "My bosses have always commented on my reliability and willingness to take initiative," or "I'm a good problem-solver."

Backing Up Your Claims

You might include a very brief mention of one of your achievements as part of your self-marketing sound bite. Remember, be brief—you can always elaborate on the story later in the conversation.

- **Achievements.** Examples: "I received the customer service award at my company three years in a row," "I received a national award for my training video," "I chaired a school fundraiser that brought in over $20,000," or "I maintained a B+ average all four years of college while working 20 hours a week the whole time and serving as editor of the yearbook my senior year."

Describing What You're Looking For

A final component of your pitch is to clarify what you want or need. This includes a brief explanation of why you are talking to this person. If you're looking for a job, you would briefly state why you are on the market. If you're seeking career management advice, give a concise description of where you are in your career and why you are looking for the advice. If you're self-employed, simply state where you are in the process of starting or growing a business.

For example, "I'm hoping to expand my business into the southwestern region of the U.S.," "I need to make a decision about the kind of work I want to do after graduation," or "My position with XYZ Company was eliminated and now I'm looking for a position as a sales manager in a technology company."

A Common Mistake to Avoid

When marketing themselves and communicating who they are, people too often include information that drags down their pitch. Extraneous detail or information that can be seen as negative should always be left out. If you're a recent grad applying for jobs that are not related to your major, for example, don't mention your major, at least not right off the bat. If you're making a transition to a field you've never worked in but you have transferable skills, talk about those skills before getting into details of your work history. In other words, be strategic about how you present yourself in conversation and in writing. Information that is not directly relevant to your goals should not be offered until after you've stated the more positive, relevant aspects of your qualifications and experience. Then, when the less relevant points are raised, de-emphasize them as much as possible. It is the simple strategy of putting your best—and most relevant—foot forward.

Some Examples of Self-Marketing Sound Bites

The following samples of sound bites give you an idea of how they can, well, sound. One of the most important things about a sound bite is to include only positive information that is relevant to your objectives. The samples labeled "Spoken Sound Bites" are written as if someone were speaking them instead of being intended for written presentation. They would be adapted slightly if they were for letters, such as having shorter sentences and sounding a bit more formal. You'll see that the samples labeled "Written Sound Bites" are slightly different in tone from the spoken ones.

Remember, too, that a spoken sound bite is only part of an overall conversation. The information you see here would go along with formalities like saying hello, stating your name, mentioning how you were referred to the person, and so on. Also keep in mind that sound bites can be shorter than the samples here, particularly when being used at the start of a phone call. The samples provided here are a little longer to illustrate fully what can go into a sound bite.

Spoken Sound Bites

A pitch from an operations specialist to a potential strategist for help in making a career transition and planning a job search:

- I have over 20 years' experience in operations, most recently in the role of operations manager for a major global software developer. I am now looking to bring my expertise to a smaller start-up company where I can initiate new business practices focusing on cost reductions through process improvement measures. Throughout my career, I've always been commended for my ability to streamline processes, motivate teams, and cut costs. For example, at my current company, I've cut our division's operating costs by 15 percent over the past year by forming and overseeing teams implementing continuous process improvement techniques. Since you have such a good handle on the software industry, I was hoping I could take you to lunch and hear your ideas on which companies would be best for me to approach and to get some feedback on my self-marketing plan.

A sound bite from a college senior to a potential strategist for help in defining a career focus:

- I'm calling to see if it would be possible to meet with you to discuss careers in the not-for-profit sector. In a few months, I'll be graduating from Smith College, where I've done extensive community service, and I majored in cultural anthropology. I want to pursue a career in a nonprofit organization but am not sure if I'm best suited for fundraising, programming, or direct service. I've done a lot of research on the field and now would like to speak with you for help in making my decision. Last year I founded an organization on campus to help the homeless in our community, and it now has over one hundred student members. I'm very committed to a public service career; I'm just not sure in which area I should specialize.

A pitch to a role model (a mentor) asking for advice on how to get a promotion:

- Martha Jameson suggested I call to see if you might have the time to advise me on a career move I'm trying to make. I'm currently a systems engineer at MM&G and am hoping to move into a management position, either at my employer or elsewhere. I know I have the qualifications, and I've been taking on more management responsibilities to complement my technical work. I'm just not sure what else I should be doing to best position myself, and I would like to speak with someone knowledgeable like yourself for some advice.

Written Sound Bites

Remember that a sound bite is simply one element of a letter or e-mail, so the sample written sound bites that follow are not complete written communications. They are just the core element that would be surrounded by some introductory and closing remarks. Examples of complete written communication are provided in Chapter 6.

A sound bite in an e-mail to a target (a prospective client for a consulting business):

- Ben Weinberg suggested I contact you because he thought you might be interested in hearing about my Web site consulting services and might have some thoughts on how I could market them in the real estate industry. I have put together some very successful sites for local businesses in other industries. I learned about real estate when I handled the Lanford Realty account for WebWorks before going out on my own. I'd like to learn more about businesses like yours and see how I might help them grow through a better presence on the Web.

A sound bite in a letter to a possible strategist who can help with making a career decision:

- My interest in a health care career stems from my solid background in science, experience as a lab technician, and strong interpersonal skills. As a high school science teacher for the past several years, I have developed a commitment to educating others and have had to stay apprised of current developments in the sciences. I would now like to make a transition into a health care profession and was hoping to speak with you about career options within your field.

Assembling Self-Marketing Materials

Once you've laid the foundation for self-marketing by doing some self-assessment and constructing a personal pitch, you're ready to put together your written self-marketing materials. How you present yourself on paper is an important element in your networking success because written materials are an extension of your overall professional image.

Depending on your situation, the materials you'll need might include business cards, resumes, bios, reference lists, letters of recommendation, portfolios, and business promotional literature. Preparing these documents can be very time-consuming, so it is important to spend time on them before you start networking heavily.

There are, of course, lots of things to say about self-marketing materials. Bookstore shelves are filled to capacity with guides to writing resumes, as well as job search guides that include good advice on gathering references, putting together portfolios, and other such topics. Comprehensive guidelines for writing resumes, assembling portfolios, and the like are beyond the scope of this book. (Appendix D lists many books that provide all the details of how to put these materials together effectively.) Instead, I focus on tips related to these documents as a part of networking—not just as a part of a job search or business marketing plan.

Business Cards

If you're unemployed and looking for a job, you probably don't have a business card. You can't use the cards from your former employer, and you don't have a new job yet, so you find yourself in between cards and might assume you will have to just do without. Having a card is important, though, because it establishes you as a polished professional to be taken seriously, as opposed to a scattered job seeker who has to scribble his or her name and number on a scrap of paper when meeting someone new. Cards simply make it easier to connect with people during your networking.

They can also serve as a mini-resume. Networking business cards often have a brief blurb about your qualifications and career objective or a few bullet points showing your accomplishments, either on the front or the back of the card.

When designing your business card, keep it simple. No fancy logos, images, or design patterns are necessary. The text is what's most important, and it requires some careful thought. Some of the text is obvious: first and last name, address, phone number(s), fax number (optional), and e-mail address. If you have a Web site, include the URL. The other text you include varies from situation to situation, but there are typically two main items you want to include:

- **Functional/industry tagline.** In the place where a job title would normally be on a business card, include instead a brief tagline that gives the recipient an idea of your functional and/or industry specialty. You may choose to make it broad or narrow depending on how broad or specific your job objective is.

- **Summary of qualifications.** On either the front or back of the card (usually there's more room for this on the back), include a very short paragraph that gives an overview of your background, skills, and achievements or bullet points that do the same. Your self-marketing sound bite is a great place to pull this from.

The samples provided below give an idea of how networking business cards can look. These examples are from actual job seekers who received positive feedback on these cards and found them very useful in their searches.

Here's an example of a card with text only on the front. It contains plenty of information about areas of expertise and industry specialization, so it wasn't necessary for her to have any text printed on the reverse.

Telecommunications & Networking

Specialist in Wide Area Data/Voice Networks

Ellen Smith
Sales Engineer

1111 Walnut Street
Arcadia, CA 99999

cell 777.555.0101
fax 777.555.0111
smith@fauxmail.com

Accomplished Manager

Operations ♦ *Plant Facilities* ♦ *Team Building*

PHILLIP D. ROGERS

111 Any Street, Peachtree City, GA 33333
Phone (000) 555-1111   PDRogers@fauxmail.com

The front of this card gives the reader a quick overview of this job seeker's expertise, while the reverse of the card provides more details of his qualifications.

The text for the reverse of Phil's card was taken almost verbatim from the summary section of his resume and serves as a handy mini-resume.

Qualifications Summary

Results-driven manager with 14 years in plant operations. Solid track record of accomplishments in areas that include

- Managing engineering projects
- Implementing productivity and process improvements
- Lean manufacturing techniques
- Cost reduction and waste control management
- Empowering teams to exceed goals
- Vendor and contractor relations

Where to Get Business Cards

Having business or calling cards made up need not be expensive. Check with an office supply or copy shop to have some nice, but reasonably priced, cards made up for you or go to http://www.vistaprint.com for a great selection of free cards you can order online (you must pay shipping and handling).

If you're handy on the computer, you can also create your own cards with software templates and perforated card sheets for laser printers. The do-it-yourself version is especially useful if your address is likely to change often (which is not unusual for a student). You can print up a small number of cards at one time and then print a new batch when you need to change the information on them. (You can also print both your current address and your permanent home address on the cards. Doing so ensures that people can get in touch with you even after long periods of no contact.)

Resumes

Too often, resumes are seen simply as chronicles of one's work history and lists of credentials rather than as a marketing tool. When you buy a product at the grocery store, are you first attracted to the fine print on the back listing the ingredients or to the snazzy packaging on the front? Even if you're an avid label-reader, chances are you wouldn't even notice the product if something about the packaging didn't attract your attention.

It's the same with resumes. Some people do want to know all the details, but they also want quick answers to two basic questions: What do you have to offer me or my organization and what are you looking for? These questions are not only asked when you're applying for jobs, but they're also relevant when networking. Besides all the obvious advice about having no typos and other critical issues addressed in resume guidebooks, you'll need to take into account some special considerations when your resume will be used primarily for networking purposes.

Generally speaking, your resume will need to be more versatile than it would be for a job search. What I mean by that is that you are likely to interact with many people outside your own career field or industry while networking, so your resume needs to be relevant to all of them. For example, downplay terminology or jargon relevant only to your organization or industry and highlight more transferable skills. The following are some specific ways to make your networking resume versatile:

● Use a profile or summary statement at the top of the resume. This usually consists of a brief paragraph or a bulleted list of points that gives a concise overview of your background and qualifications. This section helps the reader quickly identify who you are and what you have to offer. You usually don't mention specific jobs in an overview statement, only transferable skills and areas of expertise. Your self-marketing sound bite is a good starting point for your resume's profile or summary statement.

The following are samples of summary or profile statements from actual resumes. These summaries are specific enough to give the reader an idea of the job seeker's qualifications, but broad enough to work well in a resume written to be used during the networking process before a specific job target and search strategy is defined.

SUMMARY OF QUALIFICATIONS

Over fifteen years of experience in diverse corporate environments with a focus on business and financial analysis. Detail-oriented and skilled at identifying and implementing processes to improve performance. An energetic team leader who communicates effectively with people of all ages and backgrounds. Works collaboratively to motivate team members and achieve organizational objectives.

QUALIFICATIONS SUMMARY

Results-oriented financial manager with 10+ years of diverse accounting and management experience. Solid track record in Lean/Six Sigma environments, with proven expertise in the following critical functional responsibilities:

Forecasting	Plant Start-up
Cost Standards	Cost Analysis
Inventory Control	Plant Closure/Asset Divestiture

SUMMARY OF QUALIFICATIONS

Accomplished network administrator with background in customer support and technician roles. Consistently demonstrates technical, interpersonal, and problem-solving skills. History of achievements in client/server development, operating system migration and enhancements, and direct client interaction.

PROFILE

Seasoned manager with expertise delivering large-scale initiatives to generate revenue in technology organizations. Proven ability to manage and develop teams in complex, changing environments. Industry and product knowledge in software, hardware, and services. Diverse skill set with accomplishments in

Change management	Enterprise transformation
Strategic alliances	Profit and loss responsibility
Marketing and sales	Project management

PROFILE

Enthusiastic senior executive with a proven track record of developing and executing strategies to build businesses. History of effectively scaling business from start-up stage through logical analysis and planning, dynamic leadership skills, and a practical goal orientation. Skilled at designing and implementing innovative business development, marketing, and sales initiatives that align with corporate capabilities and goals.

- Make sure that any job descriptions in your resume are generic enough for readers not well versed in your field to understand. Minimize the use of job-specific or industry-specific jargon (unless it would be relevant for the reader). Also, avoid describing every job duty in painstaking detail. Give people a big-picture view of your main areas of responsibility on a job rather than every task.

- Instead of having any job descriptions at all, you may want to design your resume in a functional format. A functional resume consists of three or four experience sections, each with a heading like "Management," "Research," "Project Coordination," or any other functional areas relevant to your experience. You then describe your experience and accomplishments in a bulleted list under each functional heading. Follow that with a brief employment history near the end of the resume—usually a list of job titles, employer names, and dates of employment. (More details on functional resumes and samples can be found in JIST's *The Quick Resume & Cover Letter Book, America's Top Resumes for America's Top Jobs,* and the *Gallery of Best Resumes*, as well as in other books listed in Appendix D.)

● Emphasize your achievements and successes, not just your responsibilities. Even though you're using the resume for information and leads, not for an actual job search, you still need to do some self-promotion.

Best Taste in Resumes—Resume Deli

If you want to steer clear of the poor resume advice that is all too available online or from wannabe resume writers who set up shop without adequate credentials, put your resume in the capable hands of the experts at Resume Deli (http://www.resumedeli.com). I highly recommend them as one of the best one-stop shops for resume revamps. The key lies in their team of experts who are professional career counselors skilled at assisting job seekers at every level of experience and in every major industry, as well as in their streamlined system that ensures prompt and reliable service.

Bios

A bio is a one-page overview of your experience written in the third person. It usually isn't divided into any categories like a resume, but instead is written more like a story, giving the highlights of your work experience, educational background, accomplishments, areas of expertise, and occasionally personal information.

Bios are rarely used in a job hunt except for very senior level positions, such as executive roles, but are often helpful for professional networking situations. They can be a handy way to introduce yourself to someone when you send a letter requesting an informational meeting (sending a resume could look like you're asking for a job, when in fact all you want is information). Bios might also be requested when you are to give a talk somewhere or are featured in an article or other publication.

Here are a few tips about bios:

- Make sure that your bio conveys your unique expertise, experience, and qualities. The bio should paint a picture of you. It should not be simply an account of your experience and credentials, which can sound generic. Your bio should convey who you really are and highlight the features of your background or current professional activities that you think best reflect you.

- Consider having a few variations of your bio on hand that emphasize different aspects of your background to use with different groups.

- Always have both a complete bio (usually one full page) and a very brief bio that can be used in situations where the long one is too much. A typical situation where a brief one is called for is when you're being introduced as a speaker. If you leave it up to the person who introduces you to edit the complete bio down to a 30-second introduction, you might be disappointed with what the individual chooses to leave in or take out.

- If you're not sure how to put together your own bio, ask your co-workers and other professional colleagues if you can see theirs. You can also hire a public relations consultant or publicist to help you write one. Some career counselors and executive coaches also assist with bios. (See Appendix C for more ideas of experts who could help you put together a bio.)

Sample Executive Bio

About Spencer Brooks

Spencer Brooks is an accomplished senior manager with expertise in operational leadership, project management, and strategic planning for business growth, both domestically and internationally. He is a results-driven leader with in-depth knowledge of global product supply systems, manufacturing operations, and world-class capital and initiative management processes. Skilled in motivating technical and non-technical human resources to deliver stretch objectives, Spencer brings out the best in all he works with.

Spencer's successes are enhanced by his multi-faceted background. Through his 26-year career with Smith & Barnes, he has worked throughout North and South America fulfilling roles ranging from plant engineering leader to regional executive and global program manager. He has a track record of benchmark results in ten different product lines and six countries.

Spencer is known for his ability to approach situations from a variety of perspectives, having worked in hands-on as well as executive level management roles both in the field and in regional corporate offices. As a result, senior management relies on Spencer for his no-nonsense approach and commitment to deliver beyond expectations, while operating managers and technicians trust his commitment to deliver a solid product and deal in an even-handed, people-focused manner.

A graduate of the Georgia Institute of Technology with a bachelor of science in civil engineering, Spencer is also a Certified Expert in Project Management and Capital Management. Through his international experiences he has become fluent in Spanish and conversational in Portuguese.

Spencer is a member of the Project Management Institute, the Institute of Six Sigma Professionals, the American Management Association, and the American Society for Training and Development. He has also been an active volunteer and leader in numerous civic and community organizations, including the United Way and the Multiple Sclerosis Society.

References

Having a list of bosses, professors, and clients who will recommend you for opportunities is usually required only when job hunting and applying to educational programs. Only rarely in a networking situation will you be asked for a reference list or letters of recommendation, but it doesn't hurt to have them on hand. While this is a fairly straightforward process, consider the following guidelines:

- **Ask for a letter immediately.** Try to request a letter of recommendation as soon as possible after a class, project, or job ends. You will get a better letter if you're still fresh in the instructor's, supervisor's, or client's mind.

- **Give guidelines to the writer.** Don't assume that you're going to get a great letter just because the person likes you. Provide a list of points you'd like included and remind the writer of ways you distinguished yourself from your co-workers or classmates (or competitors if you own a business).

- **Make your objectives clear.** Always let the person recommending you know what the letter is going to be used for and which personal qualities and skills you'd like the individual to emphasize so that the letter will be targeted to the goals you are striving to achieve.

- **Don't ask for recommendation letters at the last minute.** No one, not even your biggest fan, can write a good letter under time pressure. Sometimes it's unavoidable, but whenever possible, ask for a recommendation long before you actually need it.

- **Keep a "kudos" file.** Don't think of letters of recommendation as being only from former bosses or teachers. If you receive letters, notes, or e-mails for doing a job well, save them. Your manager, for example, might take the time to write a note thanking you for a project well done. A colleague might send an e-mail congratulating you on that same project. Or a client might write to thank you for a great service or product you provided. Keep all of these in a file and select the best or most relevant ones for your portfolio. (Portfolios are discussed in the next section of this chapter.)

- **Compile a reference list.** In addition to having letters on hand, you should have a list of four to six people who can be contacted (by phone or in writing) to speak on your behalf. Type up the list as you would your resume with your name and contact information at the top; then, under a "References" heading, list the names, titles, addresses, and phone numbers of each reference. If your connection to the reference is not obvious from your resume (for example, a former boss is now at a different company), add a line or two briefly stating in what capacity the person knows you or worked with you. Depending on your situation and age, the list can include just employers or a combination of employers and professors or teachers. It's also good to include people you've worked with as vendors, suppliers, customers, peers, and subordinates to give a complete 360-degree view of you, not just the view from your boss. If you're self-employed or in a job that is based on working with clients outside your organization, then all or part of your list might be made up of clients.

Portfolios

Once the sole domain of artists, designers, writers, and others who need to show tangible proof of their work, portfolios have become increasingly popular among people in all career fields. A portfolio is a collection of documents that serve as samples of your work and are testaments to your success. The materials can be put together in a three-ring binder with plastic sleeve pages that hold documents. You can also place your material in plastic sleeves but loose, inside a pocket folder with a flap that closes. Office supply stores typically have a selection of items you can use to construct a portfolio. You can include any or all of the following in your portfolio:

- Your resume

- Letters of recommendation and/or reference list

- "Kudos" (see References section)

- Writing samples (articles, business correspondence, etc.)

- Project lists, project details, client lists (when not confidential)

- Notifications or certificates of awards or honors you've received

- Academic transcripts (usually not necessary if you've been working for a while unless you've had some recent educational experience to retrain for a new career field or higher-level job)

- Copies of diplomas, licenses, or certification documents

- Samples from projects you've worked on

- Press clippings

All of the items on this list might not be relevant to your situation, so don't worry if you don't have any documents in some of the suggested categories. Just put together enough materials to paint a complete picture of your credentials.

Business Promotional Materials

If you are self-employed as a small business owner, consultant, freelancer, or professional in private practice, the literature you use to describe what you do is one of the most important elements in your success—or lack thereof. Promotional literature speaks for you when you're not around, gets people to take you seriously, and helps distinguish you from the competition. Having a brochure, information packet, flyer, client list, or other document is critical for attracting business and referrals for more business. You may have these in print, on a Web site, or both.

As with bios, one of the best ways to put these materials together is to look at what other people in your line of work are using. You can also find some useful tips in some of the books listed in the "Books for Entrepreneurs and Freelancers" section of Appendix D. To get you started, here are a few pointers to keep in mind when developing or revising your promotional literature:

- Focus on the benefits of your services or products, not the features. Tell people what you can do for them, not every detail of how you do it.

- Take the time and invest the money to put together a polished presentation because your promotional materials reflect on you and the quality of your offerings. Make sure that the paper and print quality are top-notch and that the content has been carefully proofread.

- Don't invest a lot of time or money in promotional literature until you are certain of your business objectives, services, and target clients or projects. If you're just getting started in a solo endeavor, take some time to iron out the kinks before putting together materials that you'll have to live with for a while.

- It's usually not a good idea to list prices or fees in a brochure or flyer, particularly if you print many at one time. Doing so limits your ability to change fees or prices and can also scare off customers before you get to talk to them directly. In some cases, though, you might feel that listing them is beneficial or expected, so use your best judgment and do so if warranted.

Putting Your Self-Marketing Tools to Good Use

In this chapter, you've learned how important it is to reflect on who you are and what you need and to communicate all that through a personal pitch and various written materials. Your toolkit is now assembled and you're ready to put it to good use!

Quick Summary

All networking encounters involve an element of self-marketing or self-promotion. This chapter offered guidelines for effective self-marketing.

Self-marketing is a process of presenting yourself in a favorable light and projecting an appropriate professional image through the things you say about yourself and through written materials.

Self-marketing is necessary so that people will see you as deserving of the opportunities that you seek and so that they will be more inclined to share their time and expertise with you.

The preparatory steps for effective self-marketing are these:

- Know who you are: your interests, strengths, values, personal qualities, and work style.

- Know what you want: the goals and objectives you are trying to achieve through networking.

A first tool in self-marketing is the self-marketing sound bite:

- A self-marketing sound bite is a brief spoken or written statement that identifies who you are and what you need.

- Your self-marketing sound bite is the cornerstone of all your networking communication. It can be used when speaking to people in person or by phone and in written materials such as letters and e-mail messages.

Your other self-marketing tools are these items:

- Resumes

- Bios

- References

- Portfolios

- Business promotional materials

This chapter offered tips for putting these written documents together when they are to be used primarily for networking purposes rather than for a job search.

Honing Your Communication Skills

Just know your lines and don't bump into the furniture.

—Spencer Tracy

Have you ever had a conversation with someone that felt like you were from two different planets? You were speaking the same language but didn't really understand anything the other was saying? Or perhaps there was no problem with *what* was being said—the problem was with *how* it was being said. You simply weren't connecting. The way you communicate with people can make or break your networking efforts.

This chapter offers do's and don'ts for effective communication in content, delivery, and rapport and also provides tips for communicating by telephone, through public speaking, and in writing, including e-mail. This chapter serves as a "communications primer" before you venture into the networking situations described in Chapters 7 through 9.

Content: How to Say the Right Thing

The self-marketing sound bite that you developed in Chapter 5 is a good starting point for many of the conversations you'll have with your network contacts. Remember that the sound bite enables you to convey who you are, what you need, and what you have to offer in a concise but convincing manner. It is a particularly important component of your communication when you are networking for career choice or career management. In those situations, you have to subtly but powerfully convince people that you are worth helping.

Remember, too, that networking is a two-way street. To develop solid relationships, you can't talk only about yourself and what you need; you have to demonstrate a genuine interest in the other person. You have to find out what the other person needs and then tailor a discussion of your skills, talents, products, or services to meet those needs.

When you consider the content of a conversation or written communication, keep the following in mind:

- DO present yourself in the best possible light, but never embellish so much that you're telling lies (or even half-truths).

- DO avoid controversial topics like politics or religion (unless that's the focus of the conversation).

- DO avoid using industry- or job-specific jargon and acronyms unless you're speaking to someone in your own field who will understand what you're saying.

- DON'T say anything negative about a current or former boss, colleague, teacher, or classmate—or anyone or anything else, for that matter. People like, and will respond better to, a positive person.

- DO have an agenda for the conversation in mind so that you cover everything you want to.

- DO speak with strong action verbs, saying, for example, "I communicate well with customers" instead of "I am good with customers."

Special Tips for Your Conduct at Networking Appointments

Always be on time. Being late is inconsiderate and reflects poorly on your commitment level and organizational abilities.

Don't be too early. Showing up more than ten or fifteen minutes before a scheduled appointment time is often an inconvenience for the person you're meeting and is not a good use of your time.

If you requested the meeting, come with an agenda to make the most of the time.

If the length of time for the appointment was not settled in advance, clarify it early on so you know how much time you have. Be considerate of other people's time.

Make an effort to establish rapport. Ease into your agenda after some small talk. Don't just talk about yourself—be sure to learn about the other person. In addition to appearing more personable, you are likely to get some great information.

Keep your agenda flexible so that your interaction is natural and conversational, not mechanical.

If you're in the meeting for information, gently but assertively press for specific, concrete information, not just vague ideas.

Be courteous and show appreciation.

Leave when time is up. Don't hold the other person up from other appointments or responsibilities.

Send a thank-you note or e-mail (if you initiated the meeting) within 48 hours. If the appointment was a mutual idea, thanking is not so crucial, but you do want to maintain the relationship, so follow up promptly with a note saying you enjoyed the meeting.

Delivery: How You Say What You Say

Delivery of your message is as important as—and in some ways more important than—the content of your message. You might have to make a conscious effort to keep your tone of voice positive and upbeat, especially on days when you are so tired of job hunting or struggling to make a career decision or trying to get a business off the ground that making yet another phone call is the last thing you want to do. You have to remember, though, that each person you speak with by phone or in person needs to be treated as if they're the first person you've contacted in your search. Your voice, as well as your overall physical presentation for in-person meetings, needs to be fresh and enthusiastic.

This advice isn't just for job seekers either. No matter which goal you are working toward in your networking, the style in which you deliver your "message" is critical. The tone and pace of your speech are just a couple of aspects of that delivery. To ensure a top-notch delivery, keep the following ideas in mind:

- DO be concise. Don't ramble. If what you have to say is complicated or convoluted, edit it in advance so you can convey it smoothly and efficiently.

- DO speak clearly. Don't garble your words or mumble.

- DO convey energy and enthusiasm. Avoid speaking in a monotone or tired manner.

- DON'T speak too fast or too slowly.

- DO pay attention to the volume of your speech. Make sure you're not shouting or whispering without realizing it. Project but don't scream.

- DON'T get rattled. Try to remain composed and relaxed. Pause and take a deep breath if you feel yourself getting nervous or talking too fast. Asking questions can give you a breather and help you relax a bit.

- DON'T crowd others' physical space when communicating in person. Keep a comfortable distance between you and the other person.

- DO convey a confident air, but don't be aggressive.

- DO pay attention to your overall image and self-presentation. Are you well groomed? Are you dressed appropriately for the occasion?

- DO minimize distracting body language.

  - Are you blinking a lot—or hardly at all?

  - Do you have any nervous twitches?

  - Are your arms and hands flailing wildly?

  - Are you making eye contact (but not staring the other person down)?

  - How's your body position? Slouching? Overly stiff?

Here's Looking at You, Kid

Research on social interactions has consistently shown that first impressions are formed in the first sixty seconds of meeting and actual words account for only about seven percent of that first impression. According to Gail Geary, a career transition and image consultant (http://www.gearycommunications.com), "Positive body language and voice tone are critical to creating an initial impression that says, 'I am friendly, successful, confident, and capable.' You can create this impression through erect posture, appropriate and stylish business attire, a forceful voice, and confident, energetic movements. Our research shows that most people associate forceful speech and body movements with energy and intelligence. If you want people to believe that you are friendly, successful, confident, and capable, show them before you tell them," advises Geary.

Rapport: How You Connect with People

In addition to paying attention to what you say and how you say it, it's also important to strive for a connection with the people to whom you're writing and talking. Perfecting your pitch, rehearsing conversations, developing a flawless speaking voice, and having impeccable grooming and comportment can actually have a downside: You might come across as too rehearsed—robotic, even. While good preparation is key, just being yourself is even more important.

As discussed throughout this book, networking is not just about making a good first impression, having a quick interaction with someone, and then going on your merry way. Networking is based on relationships, so the way you establish rapport with the people you meet, including coming across in a genuine manner, is directly linked to the success or failure of your overall networking effort.

Joseph learned this during an initial failed attempt to acquire a mentor for help in steering his career in the right direction. He had been attending a particular monthly meeting for people in his industry and had met a more senior member of the group there named Bill, who was very successful in his career. He had been familiar with Bill's work even before meeting him and had always viewed him as something of a remote role model. Joseph now hoped to get to know Bill and have him serve as a mentor of sorts for him. He made a point of speaking to Bill at the next month's meeting and then got up the nerve to call him and request that they get together for lunch. Even though Bill had been a bit cold to Joseph at the meetings, Joseph hoped that he would be receptive to his request. Well, he wasn't. Bill ignored his repeated attempts to contact him, and he finally had his assistant call Joseph to say that he was too busy to meet with him at any time in the foreseeable future.

What went wrong? A number of factors probably led to this failed networking attempt. Joseph may have pushed the relationship too quickly. He could have waited to get to know Bill better at the meetings before attempting to set a lunch appointment. He might also have talked too much about himself and his own career needs during their brief encounters at the meetings. The main reason, however, might simply be that they just didn't connect on some intangible level, and nothing Joseph could have done would have made a difference. If you're looking to have a mentoring relationship with someone, it's important that the chemistry be there from the start. You can't force people to like you, and you certainly can't force people to take you under their wing and help you develop your career. If the rapport is not there, no relationship exists. Joseph soon realized this and turned to other people in his role models STARS category to find a mentor.

Is That a Cell Phone in Your Pocket?

If you think that making or answering calls on your cell phone during a face-to-face networking appointment or group event makes you look important, think again. Use your mobile phone only if absolutely necessary, which boils down to when your wife is in labor, you're expecting an employer to call with the job of your dreams, or you're on the brink of a business deal that will make or break your company. If you must keep your phone on, have the ringer set to a silent alert, such as vibration, and leave the room immediately to take your call, explaining to anyone you were talking to that you have to excuse yourself for an urgent call you've been expecting.

Rapport is a factor when you network for other purposes as well. All of the networking goals—career choice, job search, business development, and career management—require that you establish solid rapport with people to enlist their help.

When you are trying to establish rapport, consider the following do's and don'ts:

- DO smile. As you talk to someone, try to notice if your face is frozen. This can happen without your realizing it. Relax your facial muscles and smile naturally. You don't have to beam incessantly as if you were on the lead float of the Rose Parade, but do try to have a generally pleasant look on your face.

- DO be courteous. Be respectful of other people's time and sensitive to others' needs and feelings. A little tact goes a long way.

- DO be down-to-earth. If there's one mistake that people most often make in career-related communication, it's coming across as overly formal.

- DO be sincere. If you don't have a genuine interest in the people you're communicating with, you have no business talking to them. Insincerity is easy to spot and is one of the quickest ways to squash rapport.

- DON'T be unfriendly. Even if you're having a bad day or are extremely busy, try to be patient and pleasant in all your dealings with people.

- DO listen to the other person. Don't tap your foot and get an impatient look on your face while the other person is talking. Trying to monopolize the conversation won't do you any good—in fact, if you're doing more than half of the talking, you're probably talking too much and not listening enough or asking enough questions. Listen attentively and don't act as if you're just waiting until it's your turn to talk.

- DON'T interrupt. Wait until a pause in the conversation to speak. And when you do resume talking, make sure that what you say is related to the preceding points. Otherwise, you give away the fact that you weren't listening to the other person.

- DO get to know the other person. Ask questions and show interest—in fact, be interested. Again, insincerity is usually easy to spot.

- DON'T rush the process of establishing rapport. Although you can establish immediate rapport by using simple techniques like smiling and being courteous, lasting rapport develops over time. So, try to be patient and don't rush it.

- DO be attuned to the chemistry (or lack thereof) between the other person and you. Be prepared to back off if the other person simply doesn't seem to want to connect with you.

Making Small Talk That's Not So Small

Talking about the weather only gets you so far before the other person's eyes glaze over. To make sure you always have something interesting to say in any sort of networking situation, make a habit of reading at least one newspaper every day, one popular magazine (relevant to your field) every week, and one professional or trade journal each month.

Communicating by Phone

As long as you're not having a videoconference, communication by telephone can be very convenient. It won't matter that you're having a bad hair day or wearing your ratty old sweatpants. Barring a case of laryngitis, phone communication seems fairly easy compared to face-to-face encounters where you have to worry about all the nonverbal and image issues. Beware, though, as that ease can lull you into a false sense of security or overconfidence. Phone communication has its own set of pitfalls to avoid and tactics to employ. The content of what you say over the phone still has to share the spotlight with your phone "presence."

Tips for Leaving Messages on Answering Machines and Voice Mail

State your name slowly and clearly, and spell it if the spelling is not obvious.

Say your phone number clearly and slowly as well. People often race through their number because they're so used to saying it and know it so well. Remember, it's new to the person you're calling, so slow down! Repeat your number at the end of the message in case the listener wasn't able to write it down the first time around.

Make it easy to reach you by giving times when you'll be available.

Briefly state your reason for calling if your call isn't expected.

Don't waste time leaving the date and time of your call if you're pretty sure you're speaking in a voice mail system, because it will automatically record the date and time. (It's okay to do so, though, if you want to be extra clear about the time you left your message.)

When you communicate by phone, remember the following:

- DO pay special attention to your tone of voice, as well as to the pitch, speed, and volume of your speech.

- DON'T litter your speech with *uh*s and *um*s. These are much more noticeable when someone is only hearing you, not hearing *and* seeing you.

- DO sound energetic and positive. Your voice is the only clue to your enthusiasm.

- DO stand up while talking on the phone if you need a quick energy boost.

- DO make sure your background is quiet—no barking dogs, screaming kids, chattering roommates, or loud music or TV.

- DON'T have an unprofessional or overly personal message on your answering machine or voice mail if you're actively networking for professional purposes.

- DON'T let a child or housekeeper answer the phone if you're doing business from home (unless they've been instructed to answer the phone in a professional manner, stating the business name rather than saying "hello").

- DO have a notepad and pen handy, as well as any materials to which you might need to refer.

- DO disable call waiting if you're going to be on an important business call.

- DO make note of the time difference when calling people in other time zones.

Public Speaking

Speaking in public is often an efficient and effective way to make contact with large numbers of people at once. It lets people get to know you and makes them aware of your particular expertise. Since being visible is an important element of successful networking, public speaking can be a useful vehicle for communication.

For our purposes here, public speaking can refer to anything from formal speeches to informal small gatherings and everything in between. For a formal speech, you might find yourself standing at a podium in front of an audience of hundreds, while an informal setting could be a workshop you conduct for a small group of people sitting in a circle of chairs. Whichever setting you find yourself in, the following are some tips that can help you do it right:

- DO carefully prepare your presentation or speech. No matter how much you know about your subject, it's not a good idea to wing it.

- DO practice how you're going to deliver your talk or conduct your seminar, but don't try to memorize your talk or lecture word for word.

- DO know your audience and make sure your presentation is relevant to them.

- DO ask questions of your audience to involve them. If people aren't readily forthcoming with answers or comments, simply ask for a show of hands as a reply to your question. Even the most shy, inhibited audiences will usually raise their hands to indicate yes or no. Asking for a show of hands is also useful when your audience is large and interaction is difficult because of its size.

- DO use visual aids like overheads, slides, or flip charts whenever possible.

- DO make your notes readable. A few main points in large print on index cards to jog your memory are much easier to follow than pages of detailed notes in small type.

- DO keep an eye on the time. In an informal situation with a small audience (perhaps about twenty-five people or less), it is not unusual for the speaker to pause and check how much time is left. Doing so is preferable to running out of time at the end or to going overtime. In more formal talks, however, or to larger groups, you should not interrupt the flow of your talk to inquire about the time. If there's no clock in sight, be sure to have a watch positioned nearby within your line of vision (not on your wrist).

- DO be as down-to-earth and informal as you can be, given the circumstances.

- DON'T talk about things you don't know anything about or don't believe in.

CEOs Say the Darndest Things

The best example I've ever seen of a speaker being down-to-earth and relating to her audience was Anita Roddick, founder and head of the enormously successful company The Body Shop. She was the third in a series of keynote speakers to appear at the opening session of a conference for leaders from community service and volunteerism. After the audience had sat through two long speeches, Ms. Roddick came onto the stage in front of nearly a thousand people, clad in a colorful sundress, and opened her talk by saying, "I know you're all probably wondering when is it time for us all to have a pee, so bear with me. [My talk] won't be long, but it'll be intense." Needless to say, the audience was a bit taken aback at first, evidenced by the nervous murmur that swept across the room for a few seconds. But then a collective laugh broke out through the crowd—not a tense, polite laugh, but a genuinely relaxed reaction to her irreverent remark. Yes, we had all been sitting in that overly air-conditioned room listening to speeches from politicians and corporate bigwigs far too long. And, yes, most of us probably could have used a restroom break at that point. She was right on target. In the film *Jerry Maguire*, the wife of Tom Cruise's character tells him, "You had me at 'hello.'" Well, Anita Roddick had us at "hello."

- DON'T open with a joke unless you can really pull it off—and only after you've tried it out on some guinea pigs. If they don't laugh, scrap it. A lame joke can kill your entire presentation.

- DON'T read from a script unless you're giving a very formal speech to a large group or in cases where accuracy of facts and figures is key. Whatever you do, do not read your talk unless you have been trained to do so. Nothing turns off an audience as fast as someone who is poor at reading a speech.

- DO keep distracting body movements to a minimum.

- DON'T wear busy, patterned clothes, particularly if your presentation will be taped or televised.

Written Communication

Many networking situations require written communication. Letters to request meetings, e-mail to check-in with people in your network, letters to promote your business, and thank-you notes all have one thing in common: They must not only be well written, but also strategically written. Here's how to do so:

- DO review your objectives for the correspondence before writing (and keep them in mind as you write).

- DO state early on in a letter why you're writing.

- DON'T start a letter with "Hello. My name is...." Who you are should be evident from your signature and typed name at the bottom or your name on the letterhead.

- DO use your personal pitch as the cornerstone of your correspondence.

- DO back up any claims you make about yourself or your business with two or three concrete examples.

- DO use a minimum of words to have maximum impact. Don't ramble or be verbose.

- DO use correct grammar, punctuation, and spelling.

- DON'T have any typos or other errors in a letter.

- DO make sure that your hard copy letter is visually appealing— balanced on the page and printed on clean, unwrinkled paper.

- DO use proper business format. (See the following sections for examples.)

Letter Formats

Most typed, professional correspondence related to your job, business, or career planning should be laid out on the page in a way that conforms to a standard business letter format. You have three basic choices of formats (they are displayed on the following pages): indented, block, and modified block. Which one you choose is up to you. Simply pick the style that you like the best or that best reflects the content of your letter.

By the way, if you are writing your letters on stationery that already has your name, address, and phone number at the top and/or bottom of the page, you don't need to repeat that information. The formats in the following examples include the sender's information for people writing on plain paper, not personalized letterhead.

Indented Style

Sender's Address
City, State, ZIP
Phone, Fax, and/or
E-mail

Date

Recipient's Name (first and last)
Job Title (if applicable)
Organization Name (if applicable)
Internal Address (for example, Suite or Floor #)
Outside Address (Street or P.O. Box)
City, State, ZIP (and country if applicable)

Dear Ms./Mr./Dr.: (Can use first name if familiar with
recipient)

   Indent the first line of each paragraph one tab from the left
margin. Continue the rest of the paragraph like this with lines
starting at the left margin.

   Skip one space between paragraphs.

Closing,

Sender's Signature
(first name only if
the recipient knows
you well; otherwise,
sign first and last
names)

Sender's Name
(typed first and last)

Encl. (Can also type "Enclosure"; use this if you send anything
with your letter.)

Block Style

Sender's Address
City, State, ZIP
Phone, Fax, and/or E-mail

Date
Recipient's Name
Job Title
Organization Name
Internal Address
Outside Address
City, State, ZIP

Dear Ms./Mr./Dr.:

Justify all lines of the paragraph flush with the left and right margins (also called justified).

Skip one line between paragraphs.

Closing,

Sender's Signature

Sender's Name Typed

Encl.

Modified Block Style

Same as regular block, but sender's information, date, and closing are on the right-hand side of the page.

Sender's Address
City, State, ZIP
Phone, Fax, and/or E-mail

Date

Recipient's Name
Job Title
Organization Name
Internal Address
Outside Address
City, State, ZIP

Dear Ms./Mr./Dr.:

Justify all lines of the paragraph flush with the left and right margins (justified).

Skip one space between paragraphs.

Closing,

Sender's Signature

Sender's Name Typed

Encl.

Sample Written Communication

The following letters, notes, and e-mail are provided as samples of written communication for various networking situations. (For examples of thank-you notes, see Chapter 13.) Only the bodies of letters are included here as samples to illustrate effective content. In reality, these letters would have the recipients' and senders' contact information as shown in the letter style guides on the preceding pages.

Requesting an Appointment to Discuss a Career Transition—Formal Example

Dear Ms. Mansour:

Dr. Susan Tyler of the neonatology department at St. Bartholomew's Hospital suggested that I contact you to discuss the field of genetic counseling. As someone with a strong background in science, an interest in bioethics, and experience as a science teacher, I think I am well suited for work as a genetic counselor. Before I make this career transition, however, I would like to speak to people already working in this area for further insight into the profession.

I have already done extensive research into the nature of genetic counseling work, outlook for the field, and educational options, so I would be coming to you with focused questions to help me make the right decision.

Dr. Tyler spoke highly of your work, so I would welcome the chance to meet with you. I realize you are busy, and I would very much appreciate any time you can spare to speak with me for a few moments. I will call you in a few days to see if we might arrange an appointment. Thank you.

Sincerely,

Signature

John Stevenson

What makes this a good letter:

- It gets to the point of what the writer wants early in the first paragraph.

- It balances sounding as if he's not fully focused on a career goal with a bit of self-promotion.

- It flatters the reader.

- It is very courteous and respectful of the reader's time.

- It shows he's already done his homework and won't waste the other person's time with very basic questions.

- He takes the initiative to follow up instead of waiting for a reply.

E-Mail Requesting an Appointment to Discuss Business Strategy—Informal

Hello Dave,

Janet Beezley, my former roommate at USC, recommended I contact you to learn more about your consulting business. She said you've been very successful and might not mind sharing some insights with me—I am launching a similar venture targeting local businesses here on the West Coast. I've been a software developer at MMM, Inc. for the two years since graduation and have been doing some freelance work on the side as well. I want to build this freelance work into a serious business and have some questions about strategy. So, if you can spare a few minutes to talk about life as a full-time consultant, I'd be much obliged. Could you let me know a good time to call you? Thanks a lot.

Monica Chu

What makes this e-mail effective:

- Has casual and friendly tone—appropriate for the situation.

- Clearly defines connection to referral source.

- Makes it clear that she's not a competitive threat to the reader's business.

- Gives a concise overview of her background so she'll be taken seriously.

- Flatters the reader.

Tips for Making Your Point with E-mail

- Make sure your e-mail address is professional. BettyBoop@, SingleDadof3@, and other silly or overly personal e-mail addresses just won't cut it. Try to have an e-mail address that contains your name or some portion of it.

- Avoid confusing e-mail addresses. Sometimes when you can't get the address you want (such as your name) because it's taken, your Internet service provider will prompt you to select your name plus some combination of numbers. Or you might switch to your initials plus some numbers. When doing this, be aware of how difficult the address will be to type. If I get e-mail from a name like llt111100018@ and for some reason have to type in the address rather than just hitting Reply, it drives me nuts! Be especially mindful of how the lowercase letter "l" and the numeral for "one" can be easily confused.

- Be specific in your e-mail subject field. Avoid generic subjects like "hello" or "advice please" or "my resume." Put your full name in the subject field and a brief phrase with a few words defining the purpose of your correspondence.

- In the body of your e-mail, don't use any special backgrounds for your text. Making the background a different color than the standard default one can be hard on the eyes, and having any sort of image like flowers can appear unprofessional (unless you're a florist).

- Similarly, don't use emoticons (those symbols that simulate smiley faces, winking faces, etc.). If you wouldn't put it in a regular typed business letter, why put it in an e-mail?

- Don't mark the e-mail as urgent or high priority unless it truly is— and then only do so if you already have a relationship with the recipient. Remember, what's high priority to you in your networking efforts may not be so high priority to the other person.

- Keep your e-mails brief. If you have more to say, wait for a reply and then say it in a follow-up e-mail or when you meet your contact in person or by phone.

- Don't send attachments unless the recipient knows you well or has requested something to be attached.

Informal Note to Check In with a Network Contact

Dear Gloria,

Saw this article on the new convention center in Albuquerque and thought of you—looks like a great facility. I still have nice memories of that wonderful conference you coordinated in the old one a few years ago.

Sorry to have been out of touch. The last few months have been hectic as I'm now managing two departments: domestic and international travel. I hope you're doing well. I'd love to see you and hear about your current projects in the world of event planning. Things should settle down for me in a few weeks, so I'm making a note to call you then to set up a lunch.

Regards,

Susan

What makes this note effective:

- Sends a relevant article as a good excuse for getting back in touch.

- Has a warm and friendly tone.

- Has informal sentence structure—a style that implies "I'm a busy professional, but I'm taking the time to write you a quick note."

- Contains some self-promotion, but does it subtly.

- Shows interest in the reader.

- Flatters the reader.

Letter as Part of a Large Mailing to Update a Network

Dear Friends and Colleagues,

As the one-year anniversary of the founding of Day-Ja News approaches, we want to thank all of you for your support. Your advice, encouragement, and referrals have enabled Day-Ja News to grow from a glimmer of an idea on a cocktail napkin to a thriving enterprise. The following are the highlights of our year:

- Acquired ten major corporate clients needing monthly newsletters and special quarterly publications.
- Expanded our staff to include three top-notch graphic designers.
- Nominated as one of three finalists for an award from the Association of Corporate Communicators.

Our plans for the coming year include expanding our electronic newsletter services and continuing to strive for being the best desktop publishing and communications consulting firm in the Chicago area. We will keep you posted on our progress. Please let us know if there's anything we can do to help you.

Best regards,

Merrill   *Jon*

Merrill Day   Jon Jacobi

What makes this a good letter:

- It's a "brag" letter, but it balances boasting with a genuine show of appreciation for the readers' role in their accomplishments.

- It is well designed, having three distinct parts with successes highlighted as bulleted points.

- It highlights specific areas of their success, and it doesn't just make general, vague claims.

- It contains an offer to help the reader.

- The salutation ("Dear Friends and Colleagues") is appropriate for a mass mailing. Each recipient does not have to be addressed by name since the content of the letter makes it obvious that the correspondence is part of a large-scale mailing. If the writers wanted to personalize the letter for some recipients, they could write a brief note on each letter to address the recipient by name.

- It is also appropriate that the senders signed only their first names, not first and last, as doing so is in keeping with the personal, friendly image they want their business to convey.

Quick Summary

Networking is all about interpersonal interaction and developing relationships, so effective communication is a key to success in networking.

This chapter focused on three key elements of communication:

- Content: What you say

- Delivery: How you say it

- Rapport: How you connect with the other person

Communication do's and don'ts include

- Prepare ahead to know what you are going to say in networking interactions but avoid sounding overly scripted.

- Make sure the content of your written communication is clear and concise.

- Convey confidence and enthusiasm in all written and spoken communication.

- Establish rapport by listening intently and showing interest in the other person rather than monopolizing the conversation or talking only about yourself.

Part 3: It's Show Time! Three Types of Networking Interactions

You've laid the foundation for effective networking in Parts 1 and 2. Now it's time to put all that you've learned and prepared into practice. This section covers the three main types of networking interactions: networking to make decisions, networking to reach your goals, and networking to develop business. Whether you're networking in person in one-on-one meetings or at large group events or networking by phone or online, most networking encounters fall into these three categories.

Chapters 7, 8, and 9 describe fact-finding missions, strategy sessions, and referral meetings and guide you through the process of setting up, conducting, and following up on these three types of networking interactions.

Fact-Finding Missions: Networking to Make Decisions

A single conversation across the table with a wise man is worth a month's study of books.

—CHINESE PROVERB

Consider some decisions you've made on your own in the past. If you had consulted other people, could you have made better choices? That's what fact-finding missions are all about: getting input from reliable sources who can help you make better decisions. Relying solely on what you read or on your own knowledge about career or business choices is simply not enough. Good choices are based on complete, accurate, and up-to-date information; even better decisions are based on all that plus experience and wisdom. That's where your network of contacts comes in. They can provide the information and experience, plus a healthy dose of wisdom, that you need to supplement what you've read or what you already know so that you can make a better decision.

What Are Fact-Finding Missions?

A *fact-finding mission* (FFM) is any interaction you have with one or more people in which you seek information in order to make a particular decision about your career or business. An FFM can be a formal meeting where you go to someone's office for a scheduled appointment, or it can be an impromptu encounter that turns into a fact-finding mission. It might also be an exchange of information by e-mail, letters, or phone. The purpose of a fact-finding mission is to collect information about options you are considering and to get input from experts on decisions you are making. By *experts,* I mean anyone who has knowledge and experience that you do not possess yourself.

Fact-finding missions are particularly useful in the career choice process, but they can also come in handy during a job search or as a career or business management tool. You don't outright ask for a job in an FFM, but the connections you make and knowledge you gain through them can be a valuable source of future job leads.

Careful Consideration Is Key

Consider the case of Martin, a menswear buyer for a major department store. Martin wanted more autonomy in his career and had an entrepreneurial drive that wasn't being satisfied by working for someone else. After several years in the retail industry, he had developed a strong sense of style and good customer relations skills and felt that he had a natural talent for advising other people about their appearance, all of which could be put to good use if he were to become a freelance image consultant. Because he was aware of the ups and downs of being one's own boss, he was reluctant to dive into self-employment without careful consideration, so he proceeded to go on fact-finding missions to get all the information he needed to make the right decision and feel comfortable with it. He met with several image consultants specializing in female clients. (He planned to specialize in male clients, so the consultants he interviewed did not view him as competition and were more forthcoming with advice and trade secrets.)

In addition, Martin met with other professionals tangentially related to image consulting, such as photographers and stylists to get their take on the work. He also talked to a few entrepreneurs in fields completely unrelated to his to get insight into the self-employed life. After all his hard work, Martin was confident that he knew what he was getting into and that the choice was a good one for him. He then set out to plan a strategy for his transition and gradually began to take action toward his new goal.

Where Fact-Finding Missions Fit in the Career Exploration Process

Too many people involved in the career decision-making process think that they can skip over fact-finding missions because they already know what a given field entails. Doing so can be a mistake, though. Martin, for example, could easily have transitioned right into self-employment since he already had a basic understanding of the work of an image consultant. Just knowing about a given career option is not enough, though. You have to know if it's right for *you*.

FFMs don't tell you things you already know. They give you an opportunity to take what you know about yourself—your strengths, priorities, and life goals—and compare that self-knowledge with what a particular career field or business opportunity has to offer. The process of talking to people and getting outside opinions on the decision you're making is a proactive approach to matching your priorities with the best option.

Fact-finding missions also serve as important reality checks. Just having an inkling of what a career option entails doesn't mean you necessarily know enough to make a significant life decision. And even if you've read everything there is to read on a particular option, you might still be lacking real-world information that can only come directly from people with experience in the field.

How Fact-Finding Missions Differ from Informational Interviews

You might be familiar with the term *informational interview*—it's a concept that has been popular for many years. The description you have read of fact-finding missions so far might sound a lot like an informational interview, but there is one critical difference. A primary goal of FFMs is to engage others actively in your decision-making process, and that's where fact-finding missions differ from informational interviews. In an informational interview, you can easily lapse into a passive stance. You sit back and soak up information and then go off to make a decision about whether to rule in or rule out that career option. Sure, you do have to take somewhat of a proactive stance to interview the person for the information you need, but it's not as active a process as engaging the person in the decision-making with you. That's where a fact-finding mission is different.

You *are* interviewing for information, but you're also putting the other person in the role of surrogate career coach and having the individual help you decide what you should do. You're on a mission to get specific information that you have identified as being key to your decision-making strategy. You are on a mission to make a decision, not simply to collect random information. In an informational interview, the emphasis is on asking open-ended questions about work responsibilities and other facts, getting an answer, and then going on to the next question. In a fact-finding mission, you ask the same type of questions, but you also describe who you are so that the two of you can evaluate whether the work fits your preferred work style, strengths, and goals. A fact-finding mission is an opportunity to test assumptions and strategically obtain answers to your questions as they directly relate to your goals.

Where to Find People for Your FFMs

You may already have people in your network who can provide the information you need to make the decisions that you're facing. Look at the people listed in your STARS categories from Chapter 4 and see who might be able to help you with your FFMs. (Strategists and role models are often the best sources.)

If the people you know in those categories are not knowledgeable about the career fields or business opportunities you're investigating, you'll need to turn to other sources to cultivate new contacts. For fact-finding missions, alumni networks of high schools, colleges, and graduate programs are among the best places to find people who are amenable to the idea of meeting with you. If you're not already part of an alumni club or in possession of an alumni directory, contact your alma mater (or current institution if you're still a student) to see what services are available.

Also ask co-workers (past and present), clients, customers, vendors, and other people you know through work to connect you with people they know in the fields you're considering. Remind them that you're not asking to be put in touch with people who can hire you, but rather those who can simply provide information and have input into your decisions. Professional and trade associations are excellent sources of new contacts as well. (See Appendix B for a list of associations.)

Be as creative and persistent as possible in tracking down people with whom you can conduct FFMs. It's easy to say, "I've thought about looking into arts administration, but I don't know anybody who does it, so I have no one to talk to." In addition to meeting people by simply attending a meeting or conference of an arts administration professional association, you can also think of someone you know who might know someone in that field.

Sometimes the connections are a bit remote. Do you know anyone who's an artist who might have applied for a grant through a nonprofit arts organization? Do you know a teacher who might have once arranged a student field trip at a museum and therefore has had contact with a museum administrator? There are an infinite number of ways to get connected to anyone in any field. You just have to do some brainstorming. Appendix A does some of the work for you, listing connections between career fields and industries. That list is only a start, though, and doesn't include individual connections, like the fact that your sister's husband's brother's podiatrist knows someone in public relations.

Don't forget about career counselors or coaches as people to have fact-finding missions with, too. Careers professionals often know a lot about various career fields and definitely should know how to guide you in reconciling who you are with what your options offer. They don't always know as much about a particular field as the people who work in it daily (and that's not really a career coach's primary role anyway), but they can help you take what you've learned from reading and from other FFMs and make a good decision.

Where and When Fact-Finding Missions Take Place

People who take an active role in managing and shaping their own careers actually hold impromptu as well as planned FFMs all the time, not just when they're facing a major decision. In today's world of work, we can all benefit from being like reporters constantly researching the next story. People who are naturally curious collect a lot of interesting, useful information as they go through life. Then, when a career turning point or crisis arises, this information can come in quite handy.

The settings and circumstances of fact-finding missions are less important than the actual exchange of information. An FFM might be an official, scheduled meeting at someone's workplace or on the phone, or it can be a brief conversation that takes place in an elevator, in an office hallway, on a train or plane, or just about anywhere else. You can also conduct FFMs by e-mail or instant message if distance prevents you from meeting with someone or if you don't want to incur long-distance phone expenses. Ideally, though, FFMs should take place in person, preferably at the workplace of the person you're meeting with. The tips in the following section focus on this method because it's the most common one.

How to Prepare for a Fact-Finding Mission

There are several bases that you must cover before you can conduct an FFM. First, determine which "facts" you need to find. Then make an effort to gather those facts through books, magazines, journals, and online sources. At that point, you can contact people for fact-finding missions, knowing that you have done adequate preparation. The following sections provide more detail on ways to prepare.

Know What You Are Looking For

The most important thing you can do to prepare for a fact-finding mission is to determine what you need to know. This only makes sense, right?

What this really means is that you have to know what data is preventing you from making a good decision. For example, you might be a recent college graduate considering entering the book publishing field as an editorial assistant. Everything you've read about the field makes it seem right for you: You like to read, write, edit, proofread, and follow developments in contemporary literature. You're also aware that publishing is a business and not just a bunch of literary people sitting around in tweed jackets reading manuscripts and going out to lunch with authors. But, while you *think* the field is right for you, you're not certain. That's where a fact-finding mission comes in. You don't need to talk to someone just to learn the basic duties and responsibilities of an editorial assistant—you need to sit down with somebody to ask pointed questions that will help you understand what publishing is *really* all about. FFMs are not only for entry-level people, either. The same fact-finding is necessary for mid-career and senior-level professionals who need to uncover the subtle nuances between career options in order to make good choices.

Do Some Research

To make the most of a fact-finding mission and to be sure you don't waste anyone's time—yours or the person's you're meeting with—be sure that you've done your homework. That means reading as much as possible about the career or business options you'll be discussing in the FFM. It's helpful to think of your research as having four main layers:

- **World of work overviews.** Books and Web sites that provide an overview of the world of work (or most of it) are a good place to start. These provide descriptions of the occupations or industries that you are considering. The Department of Labor compiles two handbooks for this purpose: the *Occupational Outlook Handbook* (known as the *OOH* and available from JIST Publishing) and the *O*NET* (only available in print form from JIST Publishing). These are accurate, objective reference books found in most public libraries and school libraries. These books are good places to start your research, but they probably won't be very satisfying for those who already have an advanced knowledge of the work world. Additional books for researching career fields are found in the bibliography of Appendix D.

Useful Online Resources for Researching Careers

Occupational Information Network (O*NET): http://online.onetcenter.org/

Occupational Outlook Handbook: http://www.bls.gov/oco/home.htm

Career Guide to Industries: http://www.bls.gov/oco/cg/home.htm

JobStar Central's Guides for Specific Careers: http://jobstar.org/tools/career/spec-car.cfm

- **Information on specific careers.** The books mentioned in the preceding bulleted item typically provide only a brief description of a given career field or occupation. To get more complete information, you should next turn to books that focus on just one career area.

Ferguson Publishing's *Career Opportunities In* series is a good example of the many career guides available in bookstores and libraries. The *Career Opportunities In* series includes titles that explore career paths in art, science, health care, food and beverage, banking and finance, law, and many more. These books, and ones like them from other publishers, describe the nature of the work, typical salaries, qualifications needed, career paths, and employment outlook for a particular career field or set of related occupations.

Many of the Web sites listed in Appendix C are also good sources of information on specific career fields. Some sites post career field or industry overviews and may also feature various occupations in chat rooms or auditorium events.

● **Insider information**. Publications of industries and professions themselves are often good sources of information about your career options. Many professional associations have information on their Web sites about career paths in their field. At the very least, the organization's membership information (such as a listing of the association's specialty divisions and special interest groups) can offer insight into what the field is all about. Also informative are the magazines, journals, or newspapers for a particular trade or profession.

● **Creative sources**. In addition to the traditional places to find occupational information, be on the lookout for less obvious sources. Popular magazines and newspapers can give insight into the inner workings of various fields. Articles that are not written for the purpose of educating readers about an occupation may nevertheless do so. Business magazines and newspapers are obvious examples. For example, reading about a merger between two corporations gives you insight into the work of investment bankers and lawyers. Articles about a new advertising campaign for a familiar product can shed light on how advertising executives and other media professionals do their jobs. Try to get in the habit of reading with two objectives in mind: reading for news and reading for useful *career* news.

When you've gone through a thorough research process, you're ready to test what you've read by talking to people for more real-life accounts of life on the job in the field you're considering. Fact-finding missions can supplement what you've read with up-to-the-minute experiential information needed to make your decisions. FFMs can also answer questions that books and Web sites can't answer—for example, how does this or that option fit with who I am and what I want?

Protocol and Strategy for Fact-Finding Missions

When you are prepared for FFMs, go ahead and begin to set them up. The following sections describe how to do so.

Requesting the Meeting

An effective FFM strategy begins with how you request the meeting. You may do so either in writing (by regular mail or e-mail) or over the phone. The pros and cons of each method are about equal, so there is no one best way. Choose the method that fits with your best communication style, the time frame you're working under, and how well you know the person you want to meet with. Sending a letter or e-mail is preferable if you don't know the person and if you're not under tight time pressure. It's also the better method for those who dread making cold calls and get a little tongue-tied talking to strangers or distant acquaintances. If you're comfortable on the phone, however, and need to schedule an FFM as soon as possible, or if you know the person fairly well, using the phone is the better approach. Whichever way you ask, make sure that your request includes the following points:

- Who you are (your name and any other relevant identifying information). You can use the short version (about twenty seconds) of your self-marketing sound bite.

- How you got the contact's name.

- Why you're calling (that is, to obtain advice, information, and help with a decision). Always make it very clear that you are not asking for a job (or soliciting their business, in the case of self-employment). You are simply asking for advice, insights, and referrals.

- Your broader objectives (that is, to make a decision about a specific career direction).

- How much time you need—usually at least 30 minutes to get anything accomplished, with 45 to 60 minutes being preferable. (Some job search experts suggest asking for only 15 to 20 minutes for this type of meeting, but that's hardly enough time to get the pleasantries out of the way.)

What to Wear

The most important guideline for your attire at an FFM is that you should dress to fit the environment. If you are going to a conservative business setting, wear an appropriate suit; to a business casual environment, dress down a notch but still look professional and well groomed. Since an FFM is not a job interview, you don't have to be as formal as you might for an actual interview, but you should show respect for the person and the organization you're visiting. Like all face-to-face encounters, a fact-finding mission is a chance to make a good first impression, so even though you're not there to apply for a job, it never hurts to look the part of a serious job candidate. If you're not sure what to wear, ask someone familiar with the career field, industry, or specific organization you'll be visiting.

By the way, you might think that you don't have to worry about what you wear when you conduct an FFM over the phone (unless it's a videoconference), but think again. Do you feel professional and confident lounging in your pajamas and fuzzy slippers or sweatpants with holes in them? Some people actually find that they come across better if they make phone calls wearing business attire—or real clothes of some sort!

Protocol During the Meeting

Whether the FFM is conducted by phone or in person, be respectful of the other person's time, sticking to the agreed-upon schedule. If no time limit was set in advance, ask how much time has been set aside for your meeting so you can be sure not to wear out your welcome.

It's okay to take notes in front of someone because an FFM is not a job interview. It's also acceptable to read from your own notes to remember questions you want to ask. Just make sure the interaction isn't too mechanical—be sure to make it conversational rather than reading from a list. If the person you're speaking with is freely forthcoming with information and talkative, try not to interrupt the flow by relying too heavily on your list of questions. Sit back and take it all in and then turn to your notes to make sure all your questions were addressed.

Avoid asking personal questions unless the person starts volunteering such information. If you're tempted to ask about salaries, ask in general terms, such as "I've read that typical base salaries in this industry for someone transitioning in at my level are in the sixty- to seventy-thousand-dollar range nationwide. Would you say that's accurate for jobs in this city?" That question is preferable to saying "How much do you make?"

Phases of Fact-Finding Missions

Generally, FFMs consist of several stages that you should plan an agenda around:

- **Greetings**. State your first and last name clearly and listen closely to the other person's name if you were uncertain about pronunciation. Convey energy, enthusiasm, and confidence. If face-to-face, give a firm handshake.

- **Gratitude**. Open the meeting by expressing your appreciation for the person's agreeing to meet with you, taking time out of his or her busy schedule, and so on.

- **Reassurance and expectations.** Remind the other person that you are not there to ask for a job; nor do you expect him or her to know of any current openings. (Or, in the case of self-employment, you are not there to hit him or her up for business.) Reiterate why you asked for this appointment—what specific information you need, what kind of decision you're trying to make, and where you are in the fact-finding process (for example, how much you know already from your prior research or other meetings).

- **Fact-finding.** Here's where you get what you really came for: the information and advice you need to be better informed about your career options.

- **Problem-solving.** This is the part that distinguishes an FFM from a traditional informational interview. Using the facts you've gathered in the preceding steps, you now engage the other person in your decision-making process. In the "Facts to Gather During a Fact-Finding Mission" section at the end of this chapter, you'll find a list of topics to cover during the fact-finding and problem-solving stages of an FFM.

- **Resources and referrals.** As you begin to wrap up the meeting, be sure to ask for names of other people to talk to, as well as any other resources you might not already be familiar with, such as Web sites, professional groups, publications, or conferences for fields you're investigating. If you have discussed such names during the meeting, you do not need to ask for them as a separate step near the end.

- **Closing and plans for follow-up.** In addition to expressing your thanks for the meeting and saying good-bye, the closing is a time to establish how future contact and activities, if any, will proceed. This is where you confirm anything the other person has agreed to do for you, like place a call to a colleague on your behalf or circulate your resume. Now is also the time to ask permission to contact the person in the future if you have any additional questions.

After your meeting, be sure to follow up promptly with a thank-you letter or e-mail, or, at minimum, with a thank-you call. Tips on thanking (and gift-giving, where appropriate) are provided in Chapter 13, along with sample thank-you notes. Try to do so within 24 to 36 hours, but if you procrastinate and miss that window of time, do still send a thank-you—it's better late than never.

Tips for Conducting FFMs in Writing

As mentioned earlier, there are times when it's not convenient or possible to meet with someone face-to-face or even to speak over the phone. In those cases, you might find yourself sending e-mail to request assistance with your career decisions and hoping for an online response. The most important strategy for this situation is to keep your requests concise and to the point. Don't make blanket requests for information or advice. You have to keep the readers' time in mind and not overwhelm them. You're not likely to get a response if you ask for the world. In other words, be as specific as possible.

I sometimes get letters or e-mail from people considering becoming a career counselor that essentially say, "Hello, I'm looking into becoming a career counselor and was wondering if you could offer any advice or assistance." Of course, the correspondence is a bit more detailed than that, but that's the way it comes across to me. Sometimes people are closer to being on the right track in that they do ask specific questions for me to answer, but those e-mails are often off-putting because they ask too many questions that I don't have time to answer or ask for basic information, revealing that they've done no initial research on the field. If you're going to use letters or e-mail for your fact-finding missions, do your homework first, limit your requests to one or two specific ones, and be very appreciative in advance, acknowledging that the reader's time is valuable.

Facts to Gather During a Fact-Finding Mission

The following topics are a sampling of the kinds of information you might need to gather for help in making your career decisions. Choose from this list and add to it according to your individual needs. Note that many of these questions work for decisions about traditional career choice or job searching as well as for those about entering self-employment.

Nature of the Work—Daily

Questions about day-to-day activities on the job should cover the following topics:

- Typical responsibilities and the percentage of time spent with each duty

- Amount of travel involved, if any

- Work environments (in office or outside, cultures, norms, level of formality, and so on)

- Satisfactions and frustrations of the field

- Typical methods of being evaluated

- Opportunities to advance

- On-the-job training opportunities

- Typical starting salaries and projected future earnings

Nature of the Work—Long-Term

Longer-term considerations should include the following:

- Typical career paths in this field

- Future outlook for the field in terms of job growth and industry developments

Qualifications Required

You should also ask whether a particular job or field has any entry requirements, such as the following:

- Educational credentials

- Specific skills and expertise

- Specialized training

- Licenses, certificates, or other registration requirements

Resources for More Information—People, Online, and Print

Some of the most important information you can gather is additional contact information:

- Other people with whom to hold FFMs

- Professional associations and other networking groups for this field

- Journals, newsletters, and other publications for the field

- Meetings and conferences to attend

- Web sites and Internet newsgroups related to the field

- Best places for education or training to prepare for the field

Problem-Solving for Your Decision

To get to the bottom line, ask the following questions:

- Based on what I've told you about my strengths, interests, and priorities, do you think this career choice would be a good fit for me?

- In what specific ways would this be a good choice for me?

- What types of people are most satisfied and successful in this field? What are the characteristics of those who are least satisfied and successful?

- Given what you know about me, do you anticipate any trouble spots or see any reasons why I would not be satisfied or successful in this field?

Quick Summary

A fact-finding mission (FFM) is any interaction in which you seek and receive information that assists you in making a decision and in which you actively engage others in your decision-making process.

FFMs are particularly useful when you make career choices. They give you a reality check on a given option and help you decide if it's the right career or business venture for you.

FFMs can take place almost anywhere—as a formal appointment in someone's office, over the phone, or as an impromptu conversation with someone you've just met.

Preparation for a fact-finding mission involves knowing what questions you need to get answered and researching a field through print and online resources. This enables you to ask more informed questions and prevents you from wasting your contacts' time asking things you should already know.

You should follow proper protocol for requesting FFMs and for conducting them as well. Guidelines include being respectful of the other person's time and making the appointment convenient for him or her, as well as not abusing the situation by asking directly for a job or making other unrealistic requests.

The agenda for a typical FFM includes greetings, chitchat, thanks, the objectives statement, fact-finding, problem-solving, a request for more resources and referrals, and the closing and plans for follow-up.

Always call or send a thank-you note promptly after a fact-finding mission.

Strategy Sessions: Networking to Reach Your Goals

The winds and waves are always on the side of the ablest navigators.

—EDWARD GIBBON

Your networking strategy is key to reaching your professional goals. It's the guiding vision that determines what you should do day-to-day, week-to-week, or month-to-month to get where you want to be in your career or business.

One of the biggest mistakes made by job seekers, professionals trying to advance in their careers, and entrepreneurs seeking business is to focus too much on the end result and not enough on the strategy needed to reach that result. Job seekers hope that a networking meeting will lead directly to a job. People managing their careers hope that a mentor will hand them a promotion on a silver platter. Entrepreneurs hope that a networking encounter will result in immediate business. These are normal desires that any of us might have. On the surface, there's nothing wrong with having these hopes. After all, isn't it good to be goal-oriented and always have your eye on the prize? Sure, but there's a downside to that—a downside that trips up far too many networkers.

The downside is that all too often networking meetings don't lead directly to a job, a promotion, or new business. Often, a job seeker must go on literally hundreds of networking meetings to land a position, and an entrepreneur might need to develop many referral sources before new business results. Looking at networking as an immediate, direct path to your goals can be detrimental to your progress, not to mention your morale.

Instead, I recommend looking at networking as a way to get input on the best strategy for reaching your goals. Remember that one key to successful networking is to interact with people who have expertise, experience, and knowledge related to your needs—the idea expressed in that tongue twister from Chapter 1, "Who knows what you need to know?" Well, in strategy sessions, you meet with the people who know what you need to know—that is, those who can help you devise a strategy for making a career choice, finding a job, managing your career, or developing a business. A good strategy is like a trusted navigational device: It tells you where you are and how you can get to where you're going.

Look at it this way: You could ask ten people if they know of a job for you and could easily come up dry because none of those ten people knows of a single job opportunity. That's ten failures. But if you have ten networking encounters in which you get advice on the best strategy for finding a job (such as referrals to people and places who might know of jobs, coaching on your resume, and advice about how to position your skills for the marketplace), then you've just had ten successes. And I can almost guarantee you that nine times out of ten those successes will end up having played some role in the job you eventually land.

What Strategy Sessions Are

Strategy sessions take over where fact-finding missions leave off. Fact-finding missions provide the information and expert advice to help you make informed decisions and set career or business goals. Strategy sessions then enable you to plot a course for reaching those goals. Fact-finding missions get you only so far. They enable you to decide what you're going to do, but they don't always tell you how you're going to get there.

During a strategy session, you speak with someone who knows what it takes to succeed at the endeavor you're about to tackle—perhaps that's searching for a job, negotiating with your boss for a raise, or launching a consulting practice. The strategy session gives you an opportunity to plan a strategy that is based on reality, not on your assumptions of how you should go about reaching your goals. It is also a chance to get valuable feedback on the tools of your search or business. Sharing your resume, cover letters, self-marketing sound bite, portfolio, Web site, or business promotional materials with someone who knows what works—and what doesn't—is an excellent way to polish your approach. You can also practice your interviewing technique, workplace communication style, or business sales pitch in a strategy session.

The sample questions in the sections that follow will give you a more specific idea of what can be discussed in a strategy session.

Questions to Ask During Job Search Strategy Sessions

Following are questions that you might need to ask if you are holding a strategy session during a job search:

- Here's how I plan to conduct my job search. Can you tell me where you think I'm on target and where I'm off base?

- How effective is networking as a way to get jobs in this field (in relation to other job search methods, such as searching online or sending out unsolicited resumes)?

- Would staffing agencies (or executive search firms) be good sources for my target job? If so, which ones do you recommend? Can you provide me with a name to contact there?

- Which other job search methods are typically effective in this career field or industry?

- On which method(s) should I concentrate most of my time and effort?

- How did you get your job when you were at my level?

- Are there newsletters or other publications that list jobs and contacts for this field?

- Which Web sites do you recommend for my job hunt?

- Do you know of any meetings, conferences, or other networking opportunities coming up soon that I could attend?

- What are the strengths and weaknesses of my resume? How can I improve it?

- If you were a prospective employer receiving this cover letter (or follow-up letter), would you be impressed by it? How could I make it more effective?

- Can you help me refine my interviewing technique?

- How do I come across in general (communication style, voice, energy level, image)? What could I do to improve?

- If this were an actual job interview, would I be dressed appropriately?

- Am I coming to this job search with any serious deficits in skills or experience? How might I bridge the gap?

- Do you know of anyone else I could speak to for further strategy advice?

- Do you know of any positions available?

- Do you know of anyone I could speak to who might know of job openings?

- Do you know of any organizations that often or occasionally have openings in my target area (whether or not you know of any current openings there)?

- How long should I expect my job search to take?

- May I stay in touch with you for help with my strategy along the way?

Questions to Ask During Career Management Strategy Sessions

The following are some typical questions people ask in strategy sessions when they are trying to manage their careers more successfully. These are offered only as basic suggestions. Career management strategies tend to vary significantly from one person to the next, so you may find that you have needs not addressed here. If so, use this list to get the basic idea and then tailor it to fit your own situation. The questions in this list are grouped into four main categories that reflect typical areas addressed in career management strategy sessions: effectiveness, communication, professional image, and career advancement.

Effectiveness

How can I be more effective on my job? Specifically, how can I…

- manage my time more efficiently?

- be more productive?

- be more creative or innovative?

- solve problems more quickly or effectively?

- deal with change in my organization?

Communication

How can I improve my communication style and interpersonal relationships in the workplace? Specifically, how can I…

- be a better team player?

- be a more effective leader?

- manage other people more skillfully?

- have more harmonious relationships with co-workers, bosses, or subordinates?

- deal with office politics more successfully?

Professional Image

How can I enhance my professional image? Specifically, how can I…

- be a more confident or polished public speaker or presenter?

- be more skilled at writing for business purposes?

- avoid making business etiquette or protocol errors?

- improve my attire or personal grooming?

- become more visible?

Career Advancement

How can I advance and grow in my career? Specifically, how can I…

- negotiate a raise?

- position myself for a promotion?

- gain more responsibility?

- move laterally to a new position for fresh challenges or a new routine?

- negotiate a different schedule or flexible working arrangement?

- plan my long-range career track?

- develop new skills?

- broaden my professional network?

Questions to Ask During Self-Employment Strategy Sessions

When conducting strategy sessions for self-employment purposes, you might have questions related to starting, promoting, and expanding or maintaining a business. The following sections contain some questions you might need to ask depending on your specific circumstances.

Starting a Business

Questions about starting a company, consulting practice, or freelance business:

- Is my business idea a viable, marketable one?

- Do I have the background and credentials to succeed in this type of business?

- Which features of my products or services are the best selling points?

- What's the most important part of a business plan for this type of endeavor?

- Could you critique the business plan I've prepared?

- What are some potential funding sources for my business?

Marketing and Promotion

Questions about promotional materials and marketing strategies:

- Are the plans I have for marketing and promotion likely to be effective?

- Are direct mail campaigns effective ways to advertise my services and products?

- Which promotional methods do you think are most effective?

- Is my Web site, brochure, information packet, flyer, ad, or direct mail piece effective? How can they be improved?

- May I practice my pitch to prospective clients and customers with you?

Expanding or Maintaining a Business

Questions about expanding or maintaining an established business:

- Is there a secret to your success?

- Could you help me troubleshoot weak areas of my business?

- Here is my plan for expanding my business. Does it sound appropriate?

- Do you know of any organizations or other resources I should be using to grow?

- Has your business ever had slow periods? How did you handle them?

- Are my business growth objectives realistic?

- May I keep in touch with you for occasional input into my business decisions?

How to Find Strategists

Anyone familiar with your career field, target job, or proposed business is an appropriate choice for a strategy session. Also appropriate are the allied forces in your network, particularly career counselors, job search coaches, and career management or executive coaches. While these people may not necessarily be experts on your field or industry, they do have expertise in the techniques that lead to success in careers or businesses in general. In other words, it is their job to help you plan a strategy for most any kind of career or business endeavor. (See Appendix C for ways to find these professionals and Chapter 4 for a description of the allied forces.)

Coaching You to Success

When plotting a strategy for managing your career, you may find an executive coach or personal coach to be a valuable ally. Coaches are experts who can help with the day-to-day management of your career and with plotting a course for your future. Found in outplacement firms and consulting firms as well as in private practice, coaches have backgrounds in business, psychology, or social work—or ideally some combination of the three. If you work for a savvy corporation, your employer might send you to an executive coach, but you can also seek out one on your own. (The "Career and Job Search Counseling" and "Coaching and Executive Coaching" sections of Appendix C list resources to help you locate and select a qualified executive coach.)

The people you select as your fellow strategists might be some of the same people with whom you had fact-finding missions. In fact, some FFMs turn into strategy sessions in the same meeting. While asking the questions listed in Chapter 7, you might also go ahead and start asking about strategy. If you didn't already get into strategy with your FFM people, you can still contact them to say that you have made a decision and would now like advice on strategy. Most people will be receptive to this request, particularly if you closed and followed up on the FFMs properly as suggested in Chapter 7—that is, following through with a nice thank-you note and asking their permission for continued communication.

In choosing strategists, be sure to select at least one or two people who are far enough along in their careers or businesses to be able to advise you from a position of authority based on substantial experience. It is also helpful to network with at least one or two people who may be close to your career level and who perhaps have just recently gone through a job search, gotten a promotion, or started a business. Their fresh perspective on the process and up-to-date contacts and resources can be invaluable as you plan your strategy. Meeting with both experienced strategists and those who have recently achieved the goals you are striving toward will give you a balanced perspective.

Where to Hold Strategy Sessions

Just as for fact-finding missions, the setting for a strategy session is less important than the exchange of information that takes place. Because a strategy session is basically a structured conversation, it can take place in person, over the phone, or by e-mail or instant messaging.

One difference between strategy sessions and FFMs, however, is that strategy sessions are often quick meetings by phone or an exchange of e-mail rather than scheduled face-to-face meetings. The reason for this is that when you are in the thick of a career transition—job searching, trying to advance in your career, or starting or expanding a business— questions undoubtedly arise as you go along. It's not always realistic to hold your questions for an appointment scheduled at a later date; you may need answers right away.

Although such "mini" strategy sessions can come in handy along the way to your goals, it is important initially to have a few strategy sessions of substantial length (thirty minutes to an hour or more) to map out a plan for reaching your goals. Then, as career crises or pressing needs emerge along the way, you can check in with your fellow strategists for input.

How to Prepare for Strategy Sessions

The first step in preparing for a strategy session is to make sure that you have carefully researched your options, made a career or business decision that you're comfortable with, and set realistic, clearly defined goals. If so, you are ready to start plotting your course. If not, you may need to go back to the research stage, including conducting fact-finding missions. In order to make the most of the strategy session, you need to be able to state your job search, career management, or business objectives clearly and without hesitation.

The second step is to put some thought into your strategy yourself before asking for input from others. Your fellow strategists are more likely to be able to help if you come to them with a rough plan in mind that they can critique. If you need help preparing for your strategy sessions, consult some of the excellent job search, career management, or business strategy books that are readily found in bookstores and libraries, as well as advice dispensed through Web sites. Many of these books are listed in Appendix D, and Web sites are found in Appendix C. By using these resources, you can develop on your own a rough strategy that can then be critiqued and refined in strategy sessions.

These resources can also help you prepare the tools that you need to reach your goals. These include resumes, cover letters, and a portfolio for job search or career management purposes or promotional materials and a business plan for a self-employment endeavor. Having at least a rough draft of the tools that are relevant to your situation is crucial for making the most of strategy sessions. If you're going to send letters and resumes for jobs, for example, why not have those materials critiqued by someone comparable to your target employers? You'll get important feedback that will help you make your search as effective as possible.

The final step in preparing for strategy sessions is to set an agenda and objectives for the strategy session itself. You don't want to waste your time or your fellow strategist's, so it's important to think through in advance what questions you have and what topics need to be addressed. The questions provided earlier in this chapter give you some idea of what might be covered in a typical strategy session.

Strategy Session Protocol

Keep in mind that, like all networking encounters, a strategy session is not a meeting at which you just show up, sit back, and passively soak up advice. You need to do your homework first to make the most of the meeting, and you also need to do your share of the work during the meeting. Don't say, for example, "How should I write a cover letter for this kind of job?" You should say instead, "Here's a rough draft of a cover letter I've written for one of my target employers. Is this a good letter for the kind of job I'm seeking? How could I improve it?" Additional tactics for a strategy session are discussed in the following sections.

Requesting the Meeting

As with fact-finding missions, you may request a strategy session by phone, e-mail, or mail. Because strategy sessions are often (but not always) held with someone you already know, you're likely to request most of them by phone or e-mail. When you ask for a meeting, consider the following:

- If you need a strategy session as part of a job search, emphasize that you're not asking for a job, but that you are simply planning a strategy before actively searching.

- Ask for permission to bring your resume, letters, business promotional materials, business plan, or other materials relevant to your situation so that you can have them critiqued. But don't inundate your strategist with documents to review. Limit your request to one or two items you want input on.

- Let your prospective strategist know what you've already done to plan your strategy so that it's clear you don't have to be spoon-fed.

- Give a minor, subtle sales pitch for yourself so that your strategist knows that you are committed to your goals and that they are realistic for you—that is, that you're worth your prospective strategist's time and effort.

What to Wear

The guidelines for strategy session attire are essentially the same as those for a fact-finding mission (see Chapter 7). Strategy sessions, however, are one step closer to an actual job interview (for those of you networking for job search purposes), so you may want to take extra care with your appearance, making sure that you look professional in a way that is appropriate for that environment. Even if you're not job seeking (you're networking for career management or business development purposes, for example), you're still one step closer to your goals when you are at the strategy session stage, so you should start to look the part. If, for example, you're strategizing about starting a business as a management consultant, you should dress for a strategy session as you would for a client. If you're meeting with someone to plan how you can get a promotion at work, dress like someone who deserves a promotion.

Protocol During the Session

As with FFMs, be mindful of the other person's time and show appreciation at both the beginning and end of the meeting. It is also acceptable to take notes and refer to your own notes (as with an FFM) because you're there for information gathering, not to be interviewed for a job.

Like FFMs, strategy sessions unfold in certain phases. These include the following:

- **Greetings.** If this is someone you haven't met before, state your first and last name clearly and listen closely to the other person's name if you are uncertain about how to pronounce it. Be sure to convey energy, enthusiasm, and confidence in order to make a strong first impression.

- **Thanks.** Early in the meeting, thank the other person for agreeing to meet with you, being generous with their time, and offering to share their expertise.

- **Reassurance and expectations.** Restate the purpose of the meeting. If you're there to discuss a job search strategy, make it particularly clear that you are not there as an official job candidate. (Don't worry—if you come across well in the strategy session, you will certainly be considered for any jobs that might happen to be open.)

- **Strategizing.** This is the main part of the session during which you map out a plan that will enable you to reach your goals. The questions provided earlier in this chapter can help you conduct this part of the meeting. Be considerate of the other person's time, however, and don't bombard him or her with every question in every category of those lists.

- **Critiquing of tools.** Here's where you ask for feedback on your resume, letters, portfolio, business plan, or any other materials you've brought with you, unless these items were already discussed during the strategizing. Again, don't overwhelm the other person with too many items to critique. Keep it manageable.

- **Requesting resources and leads.** Before closing the meeting, be sure to ask for recommendations of any resources (such as newsletters listing jobs, books on small business marketing, useful Web sites, etc.) that could help you attain your goals. This is also the time to ask for any leads to jobs, client referrals, other people to talk to, and so on, if they haven't already been discussed.

- **Closing and plans for follow-up.** As the appointment wraps up, express your thanks for the meeting and the advice, but before saying good-bye, be sure to establish the boundaries for future follow-up. Ask if it is okay to contact the person if you have further questions. At this point, you should get a sense of how available the strategist is willing to be to you in the future.

As always, follow up with a thank-you note. (Sample thank-you notes are provided in Chapter 13.) Since strategy sessions are likely to take place in bits and pieces over time instead of being just one formal meeting, you won't need to write a note after every phone call or e-mail. In those cases, you should keep track of how often you've expressed your appreciation and write thank-you notes periodically. If someone works with you over the long term, either in a professional capacity or informally as a mentor, it is common courtesy to acknowledge that individual's role in your success when you get a job, solve your workplace problems, or launch your business. A well thought-out thank-you letter or small gift is appropriate at that point and helps reinforce that person as an ongoing member of your network.

Quick Summary

Strategy sessions take over where fact-finding missions leave off. FFMs provide the information that helps you make informed decisions and set career goals. Strategy sessions help you plot a course to reach those goals.

To avoid making mistakes, you should conduct strategy sessions before you act toward any career or business goal.

Strategy sessions can be scheduled meetings in person or by phone, but they may also be brief conversations or exchanges of e-mail when you need advice along the way to your goals.

To prepare for a strategy session, make sure that you're ready for it—that is, that you've set clearly defined goals. Also, do some work first so that your fellow strategist doesn't have to start from scratch. Be sure to set objectives for the meeting.

The phases of a typical strategy session include greetings, thanks, reassurance and expectations, strategizing, critiquing of tools, requesting resources and leads, and the closing with plans for follow-up.

As always, send a thank-you note promptly after a strategy session. If you're receiving ongoing advice from someone, an occasional phone call or note will suffice. You don't need to send a formal thank-you letter after every brief encounter.

CHAPTER 9

Referral Meetings: Networking to Develop Business

Everyone lives by selling something.

—ROBERT LOUIS STEVENSON

A referral meeting is a lot like a sales call, but it's not a sales call. In a traditional sales call, you meet with someone you hope to do business with. You hope that by presenting a case for how your business' products or services can meet the other person's needs, you'll win them as a customer. A referral meeting, on the other hand, is a networking interaction in which you let others know what kinds of people or businesses they can refer to you to support your career or business.

The key difference is that your goal in a referral meeting is to win the other party as an ongoing source of customers or clients for your business. That doesn't mean you wouldn't want that other person to become an actual client or customer, but the real value in a referral meeting is having the client send you lots of business from a variety of sources in the near future.

Successful entrepreneurs, salespeople, consultants, and others whose livelihoods depend on acquiring customers, clients, or projects have always known that they can't just sit back and wait for business to roll in. To generate business, you have to generate activity, which means that you have to expend energy. Holding meetings with people who can generate some of that activity for you is a good way to expend your energy strategically. Look at it this way: You can put a lot of effort into bringing in one prospective client, which might yield one client. Or you can put effort into cultivating one referral source—someone with access to the kinds of clients you're seeking—and that effort can yield an endless stream of clients. It's obvious which approach is more efficient and helps you conserve time, energy, and resources.

Strategy sessions with key advisors and guidance from role models are one way to do that. Another way is through referral meetings in which you gain access to people and information resources that can help you do your job more effectively. I know of one human resources manager, for example, who regularly has meetings (by phone and in person) with people who can refer top-notch candidates for positions at the large corporation for which she recruits. Think about the kinds of resources you rely on to do your job well and consider holding periodic referral meetings with people who can lead you to those resources.

Referral Meetings in Action

Consider the following examples of the role that referral meetings can play in various career management or entrepreneurial situations.

Madeline, a real estate agent specializing in residential sales and rentals, took Joan, a corporate human resources executive, out to lunch. Joan's company actively recruits new employees from around the country, most of whom need a good real estate agent to help them find a new home to go with their new job. Joan's company also brings in its own employees from branch offices worldwide for short stints in the headquarters office. Madeline could arrange short-term residences for these people. This lunch meeting was a first step for Madeline to cultivate a relationship with Joan so that she would become the agent of choice when Joan's company has relocation needs.

Frank was a clinical psychologist at a large mental health clinic with a small private practice in the evenings and weekends. After several years, his client flow was steady enough to let him cut back his hours at the clinic to part-time and expand his private practice to a few days a week. Before making the transition, however, he set up a series of referral meetings over a three-month period. He made office visits to fellow psychologists and therapists, college counselors, physicians, career counselors, and others who were in a position to refer clients to him. The meetings ensured that he had a strong referral base to support the expansion of his practice.

As a sales rep for a small environmental products company, Alvaro had been selling items such as water filters and air purifying systems, mainly to individuals for household use. He began to realize that many of his company's products would be suitable for businesses as well and that commercial contracts would be more lucrative, so he set a goal of breaking into new markets. He started with a strategy session with his friend Suzanne in the purchasing department of a large corporation. She helped him develop a plan for promoting himself and his products in a way that would appeal to corporate clients. He then set up referral meetings with five people Suzanne recommended. In some respects, these were traditional sales calls in that he hoped some of the five would buy his products, but they were also referral meetings in that they opened doors to other companies. The five people had been chosen for their high visibility and involvement in their industries as a whole, not just in the companies for which they worked. They could therefore be good sources of referrals to other companies, thus substantially expanding Alvaro's network.

How to Prepare for Referral Meetings

Referral meetings are usually less structured than fact-finding missions and strategy sessions since referral meetings are more like conversations between two colleagues than the quasi-interview format of the other two types of meetings. It is all the more important, therefore, that you prepare carefully so that the interaction isn't just a social conversation with no real purpose. The following sections describe what you need to do to prepare for a referral meeting.

Know What You Have to Offer

Because you're there to promote your business or professional service, it's essential that you articulate clearly and concisely what you have to offer. Your self-marketing sound bite becomes key here. When delivering that sound bite in a referral meeting, it is particularly important to take a tip from tried-and-true advertising and marketing principles: Sell the benefits, not the features. What that means is that you might say, "As a time management consultant, I help people get their act together so they can be more productive and efficient," instead of saying, "As a time management consultant, I assess people's organizational deficits in the areas of paperwork and clutter, setting objectives, and scheduling their time." The first statement cuts right to the chase, telling people *how* you make a difference. The second description is just a litany of the things you do to make that difference. There's always time to get into the details of specifically what you do and how you do it if the other person is interested. Until then, concentrate on emphasizing the result of your work, not the means to the end.

Knowing what you have to offer is not just a task for entrepreneurs, either. Take the example again of that human resources manager who seeks referrals of qualified job candidates. In order to persuade people to make referrals to her, she has to sell the strengths of the company she recruits for. She has to show people that her company is a great place to work so that they will feel comfortable referring job candidates to her.

Support Your Claims with Relevant Examples

It's not enough to make claims about your business or your employer; you have to prove those claims with hard evidence. If your business involves making a product that you can bring to a meeting, that's great, but in most cases, it's not possible to trot out examples of your work. This is especially true for businesses based on intangible products and services. They must back up their claims with stories that provide powerful examples of their benefits. Before going to a referral meeting, think of a few examples of clients or customers you've helped or projects you've completed with much success. Recounting tales of your achievements brings an objective twist to your self-promotion; you're essentially saying to the other person, "Don't just take my word for it— here's evidence."

Know to Whom You'll Be Talking

Assessing your own strengths and preparing examples of them is not enough. If you don't consider the perspective of the person you'll be meeting with, your sales pitch might fall on deaf ears. Consider the work that the other person does and choose relevant examples of your business accomplishments. Also, consider potential needs the other person has and think about ways you might meet those needs with services or products from your own business. You might also be able to help with resources to which you can refer that person.

Prepare Your Promotional Materials

Be sure that any written materials related to your business are in good shape and that you have an ample supply of them. If all you use is a business card, bring several along so that the potential referral source you're meeting will have a few extras to hand out to people interested in your services. If you have brochures, information packets, flyers, or other print materials, take at least one of each, or more if you think they're warranted. Don't overload the other person with bulky materials, however. Bring a reasonable amount and then mail more after the meeting if the person is interested in having a supply to pass on to others.

Protocol and Agendas for Referral Meetings

Many of the strategies recommended in Chapters 7 and 8 for fact-finding missions and strategy sessions apply to referral meetings, as do the networking tips offered throughout this entire book. Meeting for the purpose of generating referrals does require some special tactics, however.

Requesting a Meeting

The key to requesting a referral meeting is subtlety. There's a real danger that your request will come across as "Let's get together so you can refer some business to me." Even if you don't think that's what coming out of your mouth, that's how it can sound to the other person. The way to avoid this is to stress two points: that you'd like to offer yourself as a resource and that you'd be getting together out of common interests. You want the meeting to sound like a collaborative, cooperative effort, not a one-sided sales pitch. Remember, a referral meeting really isn't a sales call. It's a two-way street—an effort to see how two (or more) people can be resources for each other.

During the Meeting

Subtlety is still important once the meeting is in progress. Don't bowl the other person over with an aggressive sales pitch. Take the time to establish rapport—get to know the other person's business and particular needs and interests. At the same time, though, be sure you meet your objectives for the meeting. Subtlety doesn't mean passivity. Be assertive in getting your points across—that is, the benefits and evidence of what you have to offer. That means maintaining a careful balance between talking about yourself and listening to the other person. That also means not being shy about handing over your promotional materials.

Developing Your Business on a Shoestring Through Bartering

Exchanging products or services with fellow entrepreneurs and small businesses—instead of paying fees—is a great way to keep your start-up or operating costs down and to gain visibility. In doing so, you'll be in good company, as all the advanced civilizations of the ancient world were based on bartering. In ancient Egypt, for example, onions and beans were the main currency until about 500 B.C., when coins came into use. Think of who might want your "onions and beans" and who has something you need and approach them about a possible bartering arrangement. Back to the present, bartering sites like http://www.tradeaway.com, http://www.barterco.com, and http://www.bbu.com will give you an idea of what it's all about and how to do it.

Typical Agenda for a Referral Meeting

The flow of a referral meeting is likely to be much looser than that of a fact-finding mission or strategy session. The interaction is more of a two-way conversation between peers or colleagues, so you don't necessarily need to go in with a strict agenda in mind. It is helpful, though, to have a general sense of how you want the meeting to proceed. Keeping a mental list of topics to cover and social courtesies to address can help keep you on track and ensure that your objectives are met. You can expect the following phases during a typical referral meeting:

- **Greetings and thanks.** As always, convey warmth and enthusiasm when you first meet. This is particularly important for a referral meeting, because you are a reflection of your business. If you initiated the meeting, be sure to express thanks for the other person's time and effort.

- **Getting to know each other or reestablishing rapport with an old acquaintance.** If the two of you are meeting for the first time, take some time to get to know each other. Ask questions about the other person's business or offer a compliment on something positive you've heard about him or her. If you already know the other person well, still take some time to get reacquainted and caught up on things. In referral meetings, you always want to show genuine interest in how others are doing and in any new developments in their businesses or personal lives (if appropriate).

- **Weaving your benefits and evidence into the conversation.** Try to have your subtle self-promotion flow naturally into the conversation, rather than abruptly shift gears from a two-way conversation to a one-sided sales pitch. You might say, for example, "Oh, it's interesting you should mention that problem. I've found some new ways to help my clients get around that issue. For example, I worked with someone last month who…." By linking your business' benefits directly to a concern or an interest the other person has voiced, you're sending a much more powerful and meaningful message.

- **Looking for follow-through "gems."** As the conversation progresses, be on the lookout for bits of information or resources that the other person seems to need. Sometimes these needs will be stated openly—for example, "Do you know of a good book on…?" Other times, you'll have to read between the lines to detect what might be useful. These become your follow-through gems, those clues to how you can have an excuse to stay in touch after the meeting is over and how you can be of use to the other person. You can then send a relevant article, phone number, or other bit of information to keep the relationship going after the meeting and to put yourself in the role of informational clearinghouse for that member of your network.

- **Providing your promotional materials or business cards.** If you haven't done so already, offer your materials as the meeting winds down.

- **Remembering to follow through.** If you initiated the referral meeting or if it worked primarily in your favor, then the focus of your follow-through will be to thank the other person, often in the form of a letter rather than a call or an e-mail.

If the meeting was initiated somewhat jointly for both parties' benefit, your follow-up will include thanks for the other person's time, but that should not be the main focus. You should focus instead on strengthening the relationship by stating how you enjoyed the meeting and mentioning any ways that the meeting was informative or enlightening. With someone you know well, you might send an e-mail or fax, or you might mail just a brief note. Regardless of the nature of the relationship or who initiated the meeting, the follow-up communication is the time to make use of those follow-through gems. If you have an article, a reference to a book, a referral to another person, or any other relevant information, now is the time to provide it. Sending something useful to the other person (or leaving a phone message about it) is more effective than simply sending a thank-you note.

Quick Summary

Referral meetings are important networking interactions for anyone trying to start or build a business, consulting practice, or freelance endeavor. They are also useful for people who are not self-employed but who can benefit from referrals of people or information they can use to do their jobs better.

Referral meetings are essentially conversations between two or more peers or colleagues from the same or different industries or functional areas. In these conversations, the parties involved get to know each other's business needs and determine how they can help each other.

A referral meeting is not a sales call in which you're just trying to sell your products or services to the one person with whom you are meeting. It is instead a time to cultivate a relationship with someone who can refer business to you and who may or may not partake of your products or services directly.

Touting the benefits of your business should be based on a careful assessment of your strengths and successes and should be backed up with actual examples of your business accomplishments.

The conversation in a referral meeting should be balanced and not just a one-sided sales pitch on your part. The promotion of your business should be subtle and woven into the conversation.

During a referral meeting, it is appropriate to give out your promotional materials; at the very least, you should provide several of your business cards.

After a referral meeting, you should follow up not only with a thank-you note or call, but also with any information that could be useful to the other person, such as a relevant article, book, or name of someone else to speak to.

Part 4: Up and Over: Getting Past Networking Roadblocks

Good networking advice should never take a one-size-fits-all approach, so I am particularly proud of this part of the book because it addresses issues that are unique to certain people and situations.

Chapter 10 is a must-read for anyone who plans to network or is already in the midst of it. No matter how confident you are as you venture into networking and no matter how skilled you are at navigating interpersonal relationships, you're likely to experience some blows to the ego and some setbacks to your progress. This chapter offers advice from the trenches—tips for dealing with the difficult people and sticky situations that so often crop up in networking.

Being an introvert myself, I hold Chapter 11 near and dear to my heart. I am well aware that it can be difficult for introverts or shy people to employ the techniques recommended in other chapters of this book. The techniques might sound fine in theory, but the thought of getting out and actually doing them is another story. In Chapter 11 I provide tried-and-true solutions to this dilemma—tips and insights that will actually get you to pick up that phone or get yourself out to that networking event.

Finally, students have their own set of roadblocks when it comes to networking, the first of which is simply realizing that it's not too early to start. Beyond that, less access to professional networks, not knowing how to balance schoolwork and professional networking, and a host of other obstacles can keep students from networking. In Chapter 12 I offer suggestions tailor-made for students who want and need to network.

Dealing with Difficult People and Surviving Sticky Situations

He looked at me as if I was a side dish he hadn't ordered.

—Ring Lardner, Jr.

While networking can be an enjoyable and rewarding pursuit, there will invariably be times when it brings challenges and frustrations. Networking is all about human nature in action, so it's bound to be difficult, awkward, or downright annoying at times, just like good old humans.

Networking challenges come in all shapes and sizes. For example, you might go to lots of trouble to track down the person you need to talk to, only to have him not return your calls after repeated tries. Or maybe you do get through to a key lead, but she's not able (or willing) to meet with you. Connecting with others—or trying to—can tax the limits of even the most patient souls. And the rejection the process sometimes brings can crumble the toughest cookies.

Not only are difficult people hard to avoid, so are the sticky situations you're likely to face. When interacting with large numbers of people in your professional life, the basic law of averages dictates that you are occasionally going to say the wrong thing or lose your composure. Following the communication techniques discussed in Chapter 6, as well as other tips offered throughout this book, can minimize the chances of that happening. It is important, though, to be prepared to deal with sticky situations nonetheless. In this chapter, I describe typical types of difficult people and situations and offer strategies for dealing with them. The scenarios I chose to include here are those that my clients frequently report experiencing, as well as ones that I have had to deal with myself.

Difficult People

Some people are just plain hard to connect with—either literally in that you can't get in touch with them or figuratively in that they're difficult to deal with. In this section, I give you some pointers for dealing with the most common types of difficult people in networking situations. We'll take a look at the elusive ones, the false promisers, the rejectors, and the pains in the neck.

The Elusive Ones

As you network, you will run into your fair share of people you just can't seem to get ahold of. These people don't return your calls and thus leave you in that awkward position of not knowing when and how often it is appropriate to call back. They may also be the ones you can't even leave a message for because they have the world's most impenetrable screeners between you and their direct voice mailboxes—diligent assistants or receptionists whose sole focus in life seems to be to stand between you and their boss. The elusive ones aren't just problematic in networking by phone, either. They are also skilled at ignoring your faxes, e-mails, and letters and could probably even manage to look the other way if you sent a singing telegram to their door. When it comes to some people you'd like to have in your network, you might feel you'd have an easier time calling up the dead in a séance. Trying to reach the elusive ones is one of the most frustrating, time-consuming, and perplexing aspects of networking.

Why Some People May Elude You

There are many reasons why certain people might be unresponsive to your attempts to reach them. Often, the reasons have more to do with circumstances than with personal character. They may simply be too busy to take your calls, respond to your phone messages, or reply to your e-mail or other correspondence. Aside from circumstances, however, a common reason why people are elusive is that they assume—usually wrongly—that they can't be of any help to you. Even if you're approaching them only for advice or information, they might assume that you want them to find you a job or, if you're self-employed, that you want to sell them something. If they don't have a job for you or aren't in the market for your product or service, they simply don't respond. Then there are those who do realize that you only need advice or information but are afraid that you'll take up too much of their time. And, finally, there are some people you might contact who are simply a bit shy or introverted and are reluctant to respond to people they don't know. Whatever the reasons, the strategies suggested in this chapter for dealing with elusive types can help you overcome some of these hurdles.

When dealing with the elusive types, the following tips might come in handy.

Keep Trying

A good general principle to keep in mind when trying to track down elusive types is to be more persistent than you probably think you need to be (unless you're usually very aggressive by nature). Career management experts repeatedly find that people they coach through networking and job hunting tend to give up too early. It's easy to assume you should give up if someone hasn't returned your call after you've left two or three messages. In many cases, though, it's perfectly okay to keep trying.

Remember that you're probably not a top priority for the people you're trying to reach, particularly in the case of networking for career choice or job search purposes. Depending on the occupation and lifestyle of the people you're contacting, they may be too busy to add one more item to their to-do lists, i.e., replying to you. Since they're likely to have other priorities besides you, whatever extra time they do have is probably not going to be spent calling or writing to you. It's not fair, but that's the reality. The upside, though, is that this doesn't necessarily mean they don't want to speak to you. I've worked with countless clients who are amazed to find that when they finally get through to someone who has been elusive, that person is friendly and happy to talk to them. So keep trying! As in most endeavors, persistence pays off.

Persistence Pays Off

That was the case with Sarah, a client of mine in New York who made almost thirty calls over a period of a few weeks to someone during her job search. The person she was trying to reach was a commodities trader on Wall Street. Sarah had been given his name by a mutual friend who thought he'd be an excellent contact for her. This trader did not have an assistant or voice mail. Nor did he have a direct phone line, and Sarah's friend had warned her that he was not very prompt in replying to e-mail. Sarah set out to try to reach him, but every time she called, another trader at a desk adjacent to her target's would answer the phone and suggest that she call back later. She did keep calling back, trying different times of the day and different days of the week, knowing that she would eventually catch him. Half the time she called, she left a message with whomever answered the phone, asking the trader to call her back, but other times, she did not leave a message. By not leaving a message some of the time, the ball remained in her court, making her more free to call back without feeling intrusive. She also sent him a couple of e-mails during this time.

By the time Sarah had made about her twentieth try, she started to feel uncomfortable and considered giving up. She called the friend who had given her the trader's name in the first place and asked what she should do. That person acknowledged that the trader was almost impossible to reach and suggested that Sarah keep trying. She did, and he eventually came to the phone. Sarah just about fell off her chair when she found herself actually talking to this elusive target! She was relieved to find that her persistence had not been at all inappropriate and had actually paid off. The trader apologized for being so hard to reach and thanked Sarah for her persistence. He then agreed to meet with her and to pass her resume on to some key people in his company.

Make Your Objectives Clear and Simple

In addition to lack of time or priority, some people don't respond to your attempts because it's not clear why you're contacting them. Think about it. If you're busy and get a phone message that says nothing more than to call someone you'd never heard of before, would you have much incentive to call back? Not necessarily, or at least the return call might not be at the top of your list of calls to make.

Phone messages and e-mail that make vague requests aren't likely to get results, particularly if the person doesn't recognize your name. Avoid saying things such as "I'd like to speak to you for some advice about my career" or "I'm trying to develop my business and thought you might be able to help." These wide-open requests for assistance can scare people off. They make it sound like dealing with you will be too much trouble and too time-consuming. Try instead to be more specific in your request. By putting some parameters (limits) on your request, you make it less overwhelming, and thus you are more likely to get a response.

The preceding broad statements, for example, could be made less intimidating by saying something along the lines of "I'd like to speak to you for about fifteen minutes to discuss a few specific questions I have about making a career transition from sales to marketing," or "I'm launching a new business and was hoping to get your opinion about two specific aspects of my business plan." These statements make it clear that you are coming to them well prepared and won't waste their time. When you do connect with the other person, you can always broach additional topics if they seem receptive to expanding the conversation, but start small and keep it manageable.

Dangle a Carrot

Some people need more incentive to respond to you than merely the basic desire to help others. These kinds of people need to believe that they might somehow benefit from talking to you before they'll bother. This is an unfortunate set of circumstances that presents itself occasionally, so be on the lookout for it.

Name-dropping is one useful incentive to use in this situation. If you can mention the name of someone who is already part of your network and who will impress the person you're trying to reach, by all means do so. You might say something like, "I've been talking to a number of people in your industry, including Jane Harrell at XYZ, Inc., and Steve Rodriguez over at The BCD Group. They encouraged my efforts to get into this field and suggested I talk to more people like you." These, of course, would need to be names of prominent figures in a given industry or at leading companies or at least in some way would need to be recognizable to the person you're calling. This name-dropping establishes you as something of an insider and can also imply to the person you're calling that you have valuable connections you could share with him or her.

Also, think of anything you might be able to offer the other person as a reward for helping you. This doesn't mean showering the individual with lavish gifts (see Chapter 13 for appropriate ways to show appreciation), but instead simply offering something like information, resources, or support. In the course of researching fields or industries (or potential markets in the case of self-employment), you're likely to come across a lot of interesting data that could be of use to the people you're trying to reach. Try to work such tidbits of information into the conversation when you are making a request. You might say, for example, "I'd like to discuss with you the pros and cons of my making a transition into X. I came across an interesting Web site recently that cited studies showing X as a #1 growth industry. I'd be happy to bring you a copy of the study or e-mail you the link." If the information you found was relatively obscure (don't offer information or resources that would be obvious and well known to the person), chances are that person would welcome the information. Dangling this carrot won't guarantee that the individual will respond, but it might help.

Charm the Gatekeepers

If you keep getting a gatekeeper such as an assistant, receptionist, or other co-worker every time you call, the best thing you can do is to get that person on your side. Try to remember that the gatekeeper is a fellow human being. It's easy to fall into the trap of being too impersonal or venting your frustrations on them. Try instead to remember that they're just doing their jobs and they don't have a personal vendetta against you. Being courteous and considerate with them will get you far. Also, when leaving a message, don't simply state your name; instead, introduce yourself more personally. Instead of saying, "Please have Ms. Jones call me. My name is Cliff Bowers," say, "My name's Cliff Bowers. How are you doing?" After the response, Cliff could ask, "May I have your name, please?"

The False Promisers

Sometimes you do get through to people, only to find that they don't follow through on promises they made to help you. A common example of this situation occurs in the job hunting process when someone offers to forward your resume or make a call to a colleague but doesn't get around to doing it (or at least doesn't loop back with you to let you know it's been done), so you're left in the dark. The same thing can happen in the career management or self-employment networking processes as well. Someone might offer to put you in touch with people who can help you advance in your career or your business but never get back to you with the names and numbers. Dealing with the false promisers presents challenges to networkers, particularly regarding how assertive and aggressive one should be.

In the following sections are some tips for dealing with people who promise more than they deliver.

Directors of First Impressions

Never, ever discount the importance of receptionists and other administrative personnel. They wield more power than you may think, particularly in hiring situations. Don't even think about being condescending or rude to them. Not only do they deserve your respect simply because of the hard job they do, but they can make or break your chances of success with the seemingly more powerful people they're in place to protect.

Maintain As Much Control As Possible

The best way to solve the problem of the false promisers is some preventive medicine. By taking simple steps to maintain control over these situations from the start, you can often prevent the problem from happening in the first place. Say you're having a strategy session with someone who is critiquing your resume and offering job search advice. At the end of the meeting, she says, "When you've finished revising your resume, e-mail it to me, and I'll pass it around the organization." That's a nice offer, but what often happens is that you send the resume and follow up with a call about a week later, only to find that she didn't get around to passing it on to anyone. She promises to do so soon, but knowing how busy she is, you suspect that it could slip her mind again. You're left in an awkward position of not knowing how much more you can follow through without being too pushy, and you may be hesitant to ask if you can send the resumes out yourself because that might seem to imply that you don't trust her to do it herself.

This situation might have been avoided if you had been more direct when the offer was first made. You could have said, "That's a very nice offer. Would it be possible for me to send the resumes directly to the people you suggest and mention you in the cover letter? That way, I'll save you some effort, and I won't bother you with follow-up calls to check on the status." Most people won't object to this request because it saves them time and effort.

There's one exception to this piece of advice, however. If you think that there is substantial benefit to having the person send the resumes herself because of the clout she carries and because having her introduce you would be very advantageous, then don't send them yourself, but do ask for the names of people they'll be going to. That way, you can follow up directly with the recipients, and if they haven't gotten your resume, you can send it yourself.

This tactic works for other networking situations as well. If you're already in a situation where someone is not following through and you weren't as direct as you should have been at the beginning, it's usually not too late to regain some control midstream. Just tactfully ask to take over the task for the other person.

Reevaluate Your Own Qualifications and Networking Technique

Most lack of follow-through by people in your network results from time management issues, not from a lack of desire to help you. People usually have the best of intentions but don't get around to following through because they're very busy or lose track of what they're supposed to be doing.

There are, however, occasions when their lack of assistance results from concerns about your qualifications or credentials or because something about your networking technique is not quite working. When people offer to help, they often do so with incomplete information about you. Say, for example, that you're self-employed and someone offers to refer lots of business to you. After the first customer, though, the referrals dry up and you wonder what went wrong. While there may be many simple explanations, you can't entirely rule out the least desirable explanation—that something about your work did not meet the referral source's approval. I don't mean to send you into a tailspin of self-doubt, but it never hurts to take a second (or third) objective look at the way you conduct business, your qualifications for a job, or your approach to networking in general.

Are you treating your clients or customers with impeccable service or products? Are you going after jobs that fit your background and skills, or are the projects you're taking on too much of a stretch? Are you networking with courtesy, being considerate of others' time, and showing appreciation? If you have any doubts about these issues, you can either ask for feedback directly from the false promiser or turn to one of the role models in your network for insight into the problem.

The Rejectors

Every networking effort brings an occasional bout of rejection. Like the common cold, rejection in networking is inevitable, annoying, and temporarily incapacitating, but it's usually not life-threatening. It can seem at times, however, to take on catastrophic proportions. You invariably will be putting a good deal of effort into networking, so it can be a real set-back to have someone turn down a request or be unresponsive to you. Nobody likes rejection, but it is especially difficult if you're a sensitive person who tends to take rejection personally. It can also be particularly hard to deal with if you are networking after a blow to the ego such as being terminated or quitting a job that didn't work out. Or perhaps your ego is a little fragile because you've just gone into business for yourself and you haven't built up your entrepreneurial confidence yet.

Rejection doesn't mean that it's time to quit and go home. There are ways to handle even these difficult situations.

Keep a Balanced Perspective

Realize that having someone turn down your request for assistance or your offer to go out to lunch is not the end of the world. Rarely is one member or prospective member of your network so critical that you absolutely must have that person's assistance. The old advice about other fish in the sea definitely applies to networking. If you have trouble downplaying feelings of rejection, try these tricks on yourself:

- Recall past positive networking experiences to remind yourself that they *do* work.

- Make a list of all the reasons why you deserve the attention and assistance of others. Cite your positive personal qualities, skills, and accomplishments. In addition, consider how the person who helps you will benefit from helping you.

- Think of all the things in life that are worse than rejection. It's not a terminal illness, a death in the family, or a plane crash. These may seem like morbid thoughts, but what better way to put a little rejection in proper perspective?

- Treat yourself to something pleasant. When you're feeling a little down, it often helps to give yourself a treat of some sort. That might mean buying something you've been wanting, taking the afternoon off to have fun, or just relaxing. Find whatever works for you to alleviate the rejection blues.

Don't Internalize the Rejection

After you've put the rejection in perspective, the next step is to make sure that you don't internalize it. Doing so can prevent you from forging ahead with your networking efforts. Internalizing rejection means that you take it to heart—you make it a part of you. In other words, you take it too personally. Instead, you need to view rejection as situational. It is simply something that happens sometimes. It happens when someone else, for whatever reason, does not respond to you in the way that you had hoped. This need not have anything to do with you. Rejection is not a character flaw. In fact, it can't be, because it is a situation, not a part of you. So, when you are faced with rejection, try to look at it simply as a fact of life that you will come across now and then, not as a problem within you that you carry with you.

Adopting a Sales Pose to Deal with Rejection

Ellis Chase, President of E. J. Chase Consulting (career and executive coaching) in New York City and frequent consultant to Columbia University's Executive M.B.A. program and the nationally renowned Five O'Clock Club, suggests adopting a sales pose to deal with rejection. He recommends that you "understand that people will occasionally treat you like dirt. Someone will stand you up, not return your call, or keep you waiting without an apology. You have to realize that it's not your problem. It's theirs. Adopt a sales pose and move onto the next step. Networking is partly a quantity issue."

Even though you may not see yourself as a salesperson (unless that happens to be your occupation), you are a salesperson of sorts whenever you network. If you are looking for a job, trying to advance in your career, or promoting your own business, you are selling a product, and that product is *you*. So, just as real salespeople can't take it personally and give up every time someone doesn't want to buy their product, you too should adopt this sales pose and keep plugging away. A sales pose is a frame of mind that keeps you somewhat immune to rejection. It helps you realize that rejection is a natural part of life and is not something that should be internalized.

The Pains in Your Neck

Networking at its basic level is nothing more than human nature in action. Just as there are always a few rotten eggs in the basket of the human race, there are invariably going to be people who are just plain difficult to deal with when you network. They might be rude, inconsiderate, curt, overly critical, inattentive, or downright nasty. Whatever the particular "affliction," they can make networking quite unpleasant. Fortunately, you're not likely to come across true pains in the neck all that often, but it helps to be prepared when you do.

Don't Deal with Them

Nothing says you have to welcome everyone you come across into the hallowed halls of your network. There are times when you have to say to yourself that someone isn't worth dealing with. Successful networking does not require that you subject yourself to abuse and punishment. Carefully consider whether this pain in the neck is absolutely essential to your network. Rarely is someone so critical to your network that you must put up with that person.

Flattery Will Get You Everywhere

Some people you come across are difficult because they're on some sort of power trip or because their brusque facade masks insecurity or low self-esteem. One of the best ways to deal with narcissistic or self-doubting types is to feed their fragile egos with flattery and to play into their need for power by placing them on a pedestal. Though this tactic can work, I must acknowledge that it can be a difficult one to stomach. You might find it demeaning or against your principles to cater to someone you don't respect, so I recommend doing so only if you are sure that this person absolutely stands between you and your goals and therefore you don't have much choice.

Difficult Situations

In addition to dealing with difficult people, you'll find that there are times when difficult situations arise. These can be a result of something you said or did, or they just may happen because of unfortunate circumstances. While sticky situations are uncomfortable, there are ways to deal effectively with them. This section addresses what to do when you say the wrong thing, just don't click with someone, forget the name of someone you know, or become exceptionally nervous.

Extracting That Foot from Your Mouth

Networking involves a lot of communicating, so the odds are that you are occasionally going to say the wrong thing. The consequences of doing so can range from mildly embarrassing to quite devastating. This problem is becoming more common as technology makes it easier to goof. Think about how close you've come at times to forwarding e-mail to the wrong person with a quick click of a button. Or perhaps you put a memo into the fax machine, only to find that it's on its way to someone who doesn't need to be reading it and there's no getting it back. Although you can't turn back the clock and erase something you have said or written, you can repair some of the damage by the way you handle yourself after the deed is done.

Maintain Your Composure

A lot can be said for remaining as unflustered as possible after putting your foot in your mouth. Showing excessive embarrassment and nervousness tends only to exacerbate the problem. Try instead to stay calm and composed.

Get a Second Opinion

Before jumping to the conclusion that what you've said or written is so catastrophic that your mouth should be sewn shut and your computer privileges revoked, make sure it *really* was a big mistake. Turn to the strategists, supporters, or role models in your network (anyone you don't mind being embarrassed in front of) and get their opinion about how big a gaffe it really was.

Apologize, Correct, and Move On

If you've said or written something that will probably offend someone, offer a polite apology, but don't go overboard. If your faux pas was more an erroneous statement than an offensive remark, correct yourself as clearly and concisely as possible. There's no harm in offering some sort of an excuse, such as "You'll have to forgive me, but I'm just not myself today. I received some upsetting personal news before coming here. I wouldn't have mentioned it, but clearly it's affecting my concentration." Only give excuses, however, when you've really blown it—and when the excuse is based on at least some degree of truth.

Consider the Blunder an Entrée to Improved Communication

Occasionally, saying or writing the wrong thing can open the doors to a candid discussion with someone you haven't had a good relationship with previously. This is particularly true if you've cc'd or forwarded an e-mail, fax, or memo to a group of people and included someone by mistake—someone who might be discussed negatively in the correspondence. There's often no way to pretend that you didn't really mean what you said, so sometimes the best thing to do is to get everything out in the open and say what's been on your mind.

The Past Comes Back to Haunt You (But the Ghosts Are Friendly)

One of my most pleasant-to-deal-with clients, Margaret, found that some not-so-friendly behavior in her past came back to haunt her. Margaret had been in a very senior human resources position with a major corporation. She would receive calls from time to time from executive recruiters who were hoping to find out about opportunities in her company and get her to list those positions exclusively with them. Margaret was often so busy in her important role, especially when helping her company get through a major restructuring after an acquisition, that she often had to let those calls go unanswered.

Well, Margaret soon found herself in the job hunt after her position was eliminated in the restructuring, and she began to get in touch with headhunters. She left a voice mail for a particular recruiter, whom we'll call Don. Don returned Margaret's call promptly, leaving her a voice mail message in which he rather curtly pointed out that he was returning her call even though she had never returned his calls. Margaret was mortified! We discussed how she should handle the situation—she really did want to talk to him because he could be a valuable resource in her search—and she finally mustered up the nerve to call him back. They ended up getting together and had a surprisingly pleasant and cordial meeting.

Morals of the story: Some people will be willing to give you a second chance if you goof up the first time. Don't read too much into the tone or content of voice mail messages. Be persistent even when it might be a bit uncomfortable to do so.

When You Just Don't Click

Sometimes you'll talk to or meet with people and simply not hit it off. This is to be expected and is not a great cause for alarm. It can be awkward and uncomfortable, though, and it can be frustrating if you believe that the person is a critical member of your network who can likely help you reach your goals. In phone calls or meetings, the signs of not clicking are usually fairly obvious—the other person seems distracted, bored, disagreeable, or unable to understand you. This situation can result from an age, gender, or cultural difference; conflicting values; different personalities; or just a basic lack of chemistry. There are things you can do to get through these situations as well.

Be Objective About How Bad the Situation Really Is

Before assuming that connecting with such a person is hopeless, make sure you're not misreading the situation. Ask yourself these questions: "Are my expectations too high? Did I expect us to become fast friends when in fact that's not necessary for an effective networking relationship? Am I being overly sensitive and presuming that this person doesn't like me? Could I be subconsciously looking for an excuse in case the meeting doesn't turn out well for other reasons?" Also, think about whether you're the kind of person who can usually hit it off with almost anyone. If so, and you find a particular encounter is not going well, there really may be some problem.

Pump Up the Volume

Think of steps you can take to jazz things up a bit. Is your energy level low? Are you not conveying enthusiasm and commitment? You don't have to start tap dancing to grab someone's attention, but you may need to put in a bit more effort. Remember, networking encounters are a two-way street. You have to do your part to make an interaction engaging and stimulating for the other person. This is especially important when you're in the midst of a job search that's dragging on endlessly or you're having trouble getting a business off the ground. The demoralized (or even bitter) state you've gotten in could be coming across in your networking.

When You Forget a Name

Almost everyone knows that sinking feeling. Someone approaches you with outstretched hand calling you by name and you can't think of their name. You then go through that awkward dance of conveying warmth and familiarity without using the person's name and you pray that no one else will join you who needs to be introduced to this now nameless person.

Assess How Bad It Is That You've Forgotten

You can't be expected to remember everyone's name, so in some cases it's okay to forget. If the person is a remote acquaintance or someone you haven't seen in a long time, there's nothing wrong with politely saying, "I'm so sorry, but your name is on the tip of my tongue...." Most people will graciously offer their names at that point and not take offense. Remember that everyone has forgotten a name now and again, so most people will relate to your doing so.

Prompt Others into Saying Their Names

A popular technique to use in this awkward situation is to offer your name first if the other person or persons are individuals you haven't seen in a while and hope that they will say theirs. Another ploy is to encourage them to offer their names by enlisting the help of a third party. If you are at some gathering, immediately scan the area around you for someone you know. We'll call that person Janet Smith. Call Janet over to join you and the nameless persons and say to them, "Do you know Janet Smith?" Doing so should prompt each nameless person to introduce himself or herself to Janet.

When You are Exceptionally Nervous

Sweaty palms, cotton mouth, fumbling over your words—these are just a few of those annoying telltale signs that you're not exactly relaxed. Being visibly nervous is a frequent problem in job interviews, but it can happen in any networking encounter. Following the strategies suggested throughout this book, particularly the communication do's and don'ts of Chapter 6, can give you the confidence that's needed to minimize the nerves factor. Following are some additional tips for dealing with a case of nerves.

Acknowledge the Truth

If you're talking with somebody and fear that you're really about to blow the whole meeting because of your obvious nervousness, the best thing to do might be to openly acknowledge that you are nervous. Trying to hide it will only make you more anxious. Say something like, "I don't know why I'm nervous. I usually stay relaxed in most situations." Only do this, though, if you really think that your nervousness is so obvious that it's having a seriously adverse effect on the interaction and it's better to call attention to it honestly than to keep trying to hide it.

Try Physical Relaxation Techniques

Make sure you're breathing! Most people actually hold their breath, or take very short breaths, when they're nervous. Pay attention to how you're taking in air and try to take a couple of slow, deep breaths before continuing to talk. If you're not face-to-face with someone (and not in the view of others who may be present), you can even force a yawn to bring about relaxation. Also, take note of what you're doing with your body. Are your muscles constricted? Are your hands clenched in fists? Try to loosen your grip and relax your muscles from head to toe. The physical change should bring about a mental one.

Prevent Nervousness from Happening in the First Place

To keep your nerves from taking over at the next networking encounter, make sure you are prepared and feel confident. Having a solid handle on your strengths, goals, and objectives is an important first step. Also, be sure to do whatever research is necessary to feel knowledgeable. And, most importantly, remember that you're only going to be talking to a fellow human being!

Quick Summary

Networking is all about human nature in action, so it is inevitable that it will be difficult, awkward, or annoying at times.

You may encounter the following kinds of difficult people, and there are strategies for dealing with each of them:

- **The Elusive Ones.** These people are hard to reach. Remember that you probably need to be more persistent than you had planned to be when trying to connect with them.

- **The False Promisers.** These folks don't follow through when they promise to help you out. Try to keep the ball in your court as much as possible by offering to go straight to the people the false promiser is referring you to rather than relying on the false promiser to be your go-between.

- **The Rejectors.** These people turn down your requests for networking meetings or otherwise throw a wrench in your efforts. Don't internalize the rejection. Realize that it's a normal part of the process and move on.

- **The Pains in Your Neck.** These people are simply obnoxious, rude, or otherwise difficult to take. Either choose to ignore them if they aren't critical players in your network or resign yourself to the fact that you have to overlook their unpleasant personalities and simply get what you need from them.

Here are some difficult situations you may encounter along with tips for handling them:

- **When you put your foot in your mouth.** Emerge from these awkward moments with poise and don't imagine that you've done more damage than you actually have.

- **When you just don't click.** Don't let self-doubt get in the way here. Don't assume that the other person doesn't like you—he or she just might not be the warm and fuzzy or enthusiastic type, but that doesn't mean you aren't coming across well.

- **When you forget a name.** Either own up to the fact that you can't remember or employ creative strategies for getting other people to say their name.

- **When you are exceptionally nervous.** If nervousness is really obvious and is getting in the way, acknowledge it openly and apologize briefly. If not, use the tips offered for calming your nerves before or after they strike.

Networking for Introverts: 25 Painless Tips

One can acquire everything in solitude but character.

—Stendhal

Hello, my name is Michelle and I am a recovering introvert. If there were a twelve-step group for introverts, I'd be a lifetime member! Most people who know me through my professional life think of me as outgoing because I manage to masquerade as an extrovert. I can mix and mingle at gatherings, make small talk in one-on-one situations, speak to large groups without any visible trembling, make sales presentations that get the sale, and even chat on live television talk shows with apparent ease. But do I enjoy it? Not really. Does all that come easily for me? Not at all. It's a struggle every time. But I've learned to be outgoing when I have to be because that comes with the territory of carving out a successful career, particularly during the years when I was primarily self-employed. And yes, it does get easier with practice.

When I set out to write a book on networking, I knew that I wanted to devote an entire chapter to the networking concerns of shy people and introverted types. Through my counseling sessions with clients and networking seminars I've conducted over two decades, I have frequently come across people who admit to feeling uneasy about networking because of their tendency to be a bit reserved, introspective, or downright shy.

What's an Introvert Doing Writing a Book on Networking?!

I asked myself the same question before taking on this task. After years of struggling to incorporate networking comfortably into my professional life, I have learned that networking is a skill that can be learned. It's a skill I have developed, and I enjoy showing others how they can develop it, too. That's why I wanted to write this book. I wanted to show introverts that they can be successful networkers. It just takes a little determination, a willingness to move past the boundaries of your comfort zone, and an understanding of effective networking strategies. I also wanted to write this book for extroverts who may find networking to be such a second nature to them that they never slow down, step back, and reassess their networking technique. Because I have had to acquire networking skills rather than possess them innately, I have had to examine the networking process closely to see what works and what doesn't. This book gives me an opportunity to pass that information along to both introverts and extroverts.

If you're reading this chapter because you are something of a loner, too, or you're reserved when in groups, then you probably know what I'm talking about. It's the anxiety that creeps in when you have to make a phone call to someone you don't know or the discomfort you feel when walking into a room full of strangers. It's those sweaty palms you get when having to speak in public or the awkwardness of trying to make small talk with someone you don't know very well.

There may also be some of you who don't necessarily get nervous when interacting with other people, but who simply prefer to keep to yourself. You may feel fairly confident in social interactions, but your preference is for more independent, solitary activities. Being in the thick of things with other people is simply not a priority for you. You'd rather focus on doing your work—maybe even teamwork—rather than having to acquire a broad range of acquaintances and maintain those relationships just for the sake of "connecting." That's what true introversion is all about; being introverted does not necessarily mean you are shy. You may enjoy the camaraderie of colleagues at work and may value teamwork, but for you true enjoyment lies not with the interpersonal interaction, but with the task itself.

In the 1920s and '30s, the Swiss psychologist Carl Jung wrote extensively about personality differences among people and developed a system for psychological types, which is the basis for much modern-day personality testing, career counseling, and psychotherapy. (See Appendix D for a description of the Myers-Briggs Type Indicator, a popular personality test based on Jungian concepts.) Among the psychological types are the introverts, who according to Jung have a basic preference for focusing their attention inwardly on their thoughts and impressions. Introverts prefer to be reflective and are usually happiest when they are occupied with projects that let them be alone much of the time. They get their energy in life from focusing inward rather than outward and on tasks rather than on people. Extroverts, on the other hand, prefer to focus their attention outwardly on the people and activities around them. They get their energy from human interaction. Introverts are not necessarily shy by definition; nor are extroverts necessarily the life of the party. The two types of people simply have a different orientation to the world. Introverts are therefore much less likely to be inclined toward networking. If someone not only has this introverted orientation to the world but also happens to be shy, timid, or reserved, networking is going to be that much harder.

Unfortunately for introverts, it's very difficult to succeed professionally without developing a broad range of connections to other people. There simply is no such thing as a job or career field in which you can be rewarded entirely for what you know and how well you do your work. Who you know and who knows you (that visibility idea mentioned in Chapter 1) is often just as important.

The WRONG Attitude Toward Networking

"I'm Nobody! Who are you?
Are you—Nobody—Too?
Then there's a pair of us?
Don't tell! they'd advertise—you know!
How dreary—to be—Somebody!
How public—like a Frog—
To tell one's name—the livelong June—
To an admiring Bog!"

—EMILY DICKINSON, CA. 1861

This is especially true if you are self-employed. Word-of-mouth referrals and publicity are key to just about any type of small business or consulting practice. Remember, it's not only what you know that counts, it's who knows that you know what you know.

All of this can be a real pain in the you-know-what for introverts who would rather focus on their work than on their relationships at work. And it can be downright painful for shy types who cringe at the thought of self-promotion. The bad news is that networking as a means of career or business survival is here to stay. The good news is that networking is most definitely a skill that can be learned.

25 Networking Tips for Introverts

Using the techniques advocated throughout this book is one way to learn the art of networking. Sometimes, though, all the best strategies in the world are not enough if seeking connections with others and promoting yourself just plain goes against your grain. Believe me, I know. It's a constant struggle for me to practice what I preach. In theory I know how to network, but in reality I have to force myself to do it. In the process, I've developed some coping mechanisms that I hope you'll find helpful.

I've singled out 25 tips especially for introverts that should help you network in ways that are comfortable for you and that fit your preferred way of communicating with the world. I'm not asking you to transform yourself magically into an extrovert. Networking works best when it's conducted in a way that fits your personality. This approach is particularly relevant for introverts or shy types. So many people don't even attempt networking because it seems like an alien way of being and thus a task that's impossible to fit into their daily lives. That's unfortunate because the process can be quite rewarding, and occasionally even fun, once you get the hang of it.

On the following pages, I provide tips to make networking a little less painful. You'll recognize some of these as being very similar to techniques I've recommended elsewhere in the book. I don't claim that each of these tips is unique to introverts. What I do in this tip list, however, is show how you, as an introvert, can put a unique twist on the same techniques that extroverts might use. These are ways to employ tried-and-true networking principles in a manner that fits your own personality style. Pick the ones that feel right to you and make them your coping mechanisms.

1. **Take baby steps.** Don't try to become a master networker overnight. A common mistake introverts make is to wake up one day and announce to themselves, "Today I'm going to become an avid networker!" Such proclamations are all too common when you find yourself in a blind panic over when you're going to get a job or start making some money from your new business. Unfortunately, these declarations are about as likely to succeed as the ones announcing that you're going to lose weight or quit smoking once and for all. If networking has not been a regular part of your life and if it is not a comfortable process for you, then you need to take it slowly. If you try to tackle too much at once, you're likely to get discouraged or burn out and give up. Try instead to take baby steps and let your confidence build slowly with each positive experience. You're more likely to succeed that way.

The Danger of Taking On Too Many Networking Activities

I frequently work with introverted or shy clients who try to take on too many networking activities and end up getting overwhelmed by the process. One such client was Roger, who worked on the technical help desk for a large insurance company and was completing his bachelor's degree in computer science at night. Roger had two more semesters of classes to complete for his degree and then hoped to get a job as a programmer, either with his current employer or elsewhere. He came to me to plan a strategy for making the career transition. In our first appointment, I encouraged him to start networking long before he needed a job. We discussed all the ways that networking could facilitate his career transition and position him for a good job. He left that appointment with a list of networking activities I recommended for him. These included having strategy sessions with classmates, professors, and alumni; joining associations for computer professionals, attending their meetings and conferences, and reading their publications; and getting to know more people in the IT department of his company. I warned Roger, however, that he did not need to do all of these things at once or in a short period of time, especially considering he had told me that networking was hard for him and that he had never really done much of it. Even though I stressed that he should try only a few of the recommendations on the list at first rather than try to tackle them all, Roger was a doer who was eager to get going and wanted to do as much as possible as quickly as possible.

Roger was scheduled to return to my office three weeks later to discuss his progress and plan the next steps. When he came in, he was embarrassed to admit that he had accomplished very little since his last meeting with me. Even though I had suggested that he see networking as a slow process and that he take only a few steps to get started, he had nevertheless tried to do too much and ended up feeling overwhelmed. After a week of making cold calls to try to set up meetings, he began to feel burned out and gave up. I discussed with Roger that his reaction was normal and reminded him that change—that is, becoming a skilled networker—is a process that takes time. We then worked out a modified action plan for him that included a manageable number of networking activities per week. He soon became more motivated and came back to subsequent appointments with impressive progress reports.

2. **Don't assume you're being a pest.** Introverts tend to assume that they'll be bothering others if they contact them. Before making phone calls or approaching people in group settings, introverts often worry that they'll be seen as pests. While this perception is almost always wrong, it's understandable that introverts might feel this way.

   When assuming that they're bothering people, introverts might be projecting their own feelings onto others. We introverts often prefer to be left alone—to do our work without interruptions and not have our "own little world" invaded. As a result, we erroneously assume that other people feel the same way. I know I fall into this trap frequently. If I'm sitting at my desk engrossed in a solitary project that involves thought and concentration, I don't particularly welcome a ringing telephone or other interruption. As a result, I tend to project those same feelings onto others. When I need to make a phone call, for example, I often hesitate to pick up the phone because I wrongly assume that the person I've thought of calling won't want to hear from me—they won't want to be interrupted. When I actually do make the call, though, I find that my concerns usually could not have been further from the truth.

   So, before you assume you're going to be a pest if you try to make contact with someone, think twice. Most people will be glad to hear from you. According to research that has been conducted on personality types, approximately 75 percent of the American population is estimated to be extroverted, so chances are high that most people you reach out to will welcome the contact.

3. **Rely on your supporters.** Of all the STARS in your network, the supporters are especially important for keeping you motivated and positive as you attempt to network. If you find that networking is something of a struggle for you because it is not second nature, you might be particularly susceptible to feelings of rejection or discouragement. As discussed in Chapter 10, the networking process invariably brings challenges that can elicit less-than-positive feelings. This may be even more true for introverts or shy types. If you already feel as though you're coming into the networking game with something of a handicap (because you are not naturally outgoing or people-oriented),

it may be particularly difficult to ride out the rough times. In those cases, you need to have supporters to turn to for encouragement and empathy along the way.

4. **Get the competitive juices flowing.** Try to remember that lots of people who aren't half as capable, qualified, talented, and nice as you are getting ahead simply because they connect with others and make themselves visible. This is the case for many clients I work with who lament the fact that they have been passed over for promotions or raises or haven't been able to get a business off the ground. They usually are aware that the people who are getting ahead of them aren't necessarily any better qualified but simply are more visible or better connected. What they aren't usually aware of, however, is that they can turn this negative fact into a positive result. What I mean by this is that they need to stop complaining about the injustice in that situation and start using it to get their competitive juices flowing.

Even people who don't consider themselves to be all that competitive by nature can usually muster up some competitive drive when they see how unfair it is that less-qualified colleagues are getting ahead.

5. **Rest on your laurels.** Always have in the forefront of your mind a repertoire of situations in which you excelled at an activity that wasn't a solitary one. Remember the times you've been successful in group endeavors or one-on-one interactions with others and keep these in mind to propel you confidently into the future.

I have to use this trick all the time to boost my confidence before I go into certain situations. Even though I have spoken in public thousands of times, for example, I still have to remind myself each time that I will do okay. I have led workshops for groups of a few people, taught classes to twenty or thirty students or job seekers, and given formal speeches in front of audiences of several hundred, but each time I approach a new group situation, I still have some of the same fears I had the first time I ever did any of that. Sure, some of the concerns go away with time. I no longer worry that I'll make a fool of myself, forget what I'm supposed to say, or trip on my way to the podium. Instead, the fears that linger are those that most any introvert has: How will I connect with the people in this group? What will they think of me? Will I be entertaining enough? I also still have some of these same concerns when I anticipate one-on-one interactions, as might you.

So how do I counter these fears—and how can you? I remind myself how I have felt in the past after a rewarding individual or group encounter. I try to remember that high I feel after a really successful class I've taught or after a great conversation with someone at a professional conference. I try to remember times when I have connected successfully with people and felt how rewarding it is to do so. These recollections then give me the courage—and encouragement—to face the next networking situation.

6. **Be a leader.** Introverts don't always seek leadership roles because these positions inevitably require such dreaded tasks as committee meetings and team projects. While that may be true, it *is* possible to find more behind-the-scenes leadership roles such as being a newsletter editor or the secretary or treasurer for a professional association. These positions can play to your strengths—organizational or writing abilities, perhaps, or number-crunching skills—while not requiring you to be too outgoing or political.

Another advantage of a leadership role is that it gives you a built-in excuse for connecting with people. It's one thing to be merely a member of a professional organization and call up someone you don't know on the membership roster to request a networking meeting; it's another thing to be able to call that person and say, "Hi, I'm the new Program Committee Chairperson for the XYZ Association." Having to contact people because of your official responsibilities enables you to establish relationships with people you might otherwise never have met.

If your schedule or workload precludes your taking a leadership role, consider other ways to be involved on an official level but with less of a long-term commitment. You might join a committee to help plan one particular event or serve as a host at an event. You could volunteer, for example, to be the person checking in attendees and handing out name tags at the front table of a networking meeting. It's often easier to meet and greet than to meet and mingle!

7. **Don't go it alone.** If you have to attend a group meeting or large conference, try to take a friend or colleague with you. Strength in numbers can make the experience less intimidating. Be sure, though, that you don't spend all your time talking to your companion and not making new contacts. It's ideal if your companion is a good mixture of introvert and extrovert—too much introversion and neither of you will meet anyone; too much extroversion and you'll be left in the dust while your friend is off schmoozing.

A little networking trick I suggest for these situations is to make a pact with your friend that you will separate from each other for a certain period of time—maybe half an hour or an hour, depending on the total length of the event—and agree to get back together at a specified time. You can make this something of a contest by seeing who can meet the most new people during that time. (Yes, I know I've said throughout this book that networking is not entirely a numbers game, but when you're getting your feet wet in the networking process, this sort of contest can be a valuable exercise. Having to introduce yourself to a lot of people can be a good way to throw yourself headlong into the networking process.) If you would prefer to take a more in-depth approach to your networking encounters at that particular event, the objective of the contest could be to see who can make one meaningful connection during the specified period of time.

While these exercises can be valuable ways to get a feel for networking, remember that they are only exercises. At some point, you'll need to venture into group settings without the security blanket of a familiar companion.

8. **Enlist a spokesperson.** As an introvert or shy person, you might have names of potentially valuable contacts languishing on your contact list or business cards sloshing around in your briefcase. Even though you know it would be in your best interest to call these people, something keeps you from doing so. Perhaps it's the "I'll be seen as a pest" factor described in Tip #2. Or, maybe you just don't know what to say to them. Whatever the reason, you need to find a way to make contact with people rather than miss out on valuable opportunities.

If you're hesitant to contact someone you don't know, consider having another person act as a go-between for you. If someone in your network has given you the name of a colleague, ask your contact to call or e-mail the person first to "warn them" that you'll be calling. Most people are willing to do this.

9. **Don't underestimate the power of listening.** Networking can seem at times as if it's all about talking. As an introvert, you might worry that you'll never be a successful networker because you don't have the gift of gab. Don't despair. Listening is just as important as talking when it comes to establishing relationships with others. Introverts often make good listeners, and there's nothing extroverts like better than having someone listen to them talk. So don't feel you have to keep up the conversation as much as the other person. Listening well is a valuable and appreciated talent.

10. **Don't sweat the small stuff (in this case, the small talk).** Small talk is just what it sounds like: small. Most people don't expect you to come up with incredibly witty or profound comments when you first meet them. A sense of humor or clever insight is nice, but there's nothing wrong with a mundane comment to break the ice like "Large turnout, isn't it?" or "This is great dip." Asking a question is also a great way to initiate a conversation. You might ask someone a question about the speaker you're about to hear, or after a lecture or meeting, you can ask what someone thought of the event. Opening with a question is a great way to draw out the other person and get a conversation going.

11. **Like birds of a feather, flock together.** If you truly find group interactions excruciating, survey the group for other people who look as if they are also uncomfortable and approach them. It's a lot easier to get into the networking game when you start by mingling with other introverts rather than with the intimidating man in the red tie holding court in the center of the room. Don't get stuck with the introverts all night, though. At some point you do have to leave the nest.

12. **Make the most of what you know.** Remember that even though who you know is mostly the name of the game in networking, what you know is an important element of successful networking as well. This fact comes in particularly handy for introverts. Unlike extroverts, we're likely to be the ones who did take the time to read that industry newsletter cover-to-cover. We're the ones who consider a quiet afternoon researching on the Internet to be anything but boring. In short, introverts like to know stuff. (Extroverts like to know things too, of course, but they're more likely to keep up with people than with information.)

    Rather than fight your introverted tendencies, look at them as trump cards in the game of networking. Let people get to know you as the person they can call for the latest information on whatever is relevant to your field. Also, take the initiative to pick up the phone or send a quick e-mail to share your findings with others. E-mailing a valuable tidbit of information may be more comfortable for you than calling someone just to chitchat. So if you worry that you're not going to dazzle people with your outgoing personality, at least you can dazzle them with your knowledge.

13. **Rehearse, rehearse, rehearse.** If your phone calls are littered with uhs and ums or if you tend to be tongue-tied when meeting someone new, try planning and practicing what you're going to say. It's likely that you'll find yourself having the same sort of conversations over and over with members of your network or with new people you are approaching. You might be trying to convey information about your business or request fact-finding missions or strategy sessions. Whatever the nature of your conversations tends to be, it is helpful to streamline what you say. Your self-marketing sound bite (see Chapter 5) is one way to do that. You may also need to plan more extensive conversations.

    By suggesting that you rehearse conversations—or your side of a conversation, at least—I don't mean to imply that conversations are perfectly predictable. You never know what the other person is going to say to you. You can, however, think through in advance what you plan to say and be prepared to make adjustments when you get into the real situation.

You also don't need to memorize word-for-word scripts of what you will say, because that's likely to make you even more nervous. You also don't want to come across as sounding too rehearsed or robotic. It is helpful, nonetheless, to practice your side of typical conversations— perhaps with the help of a friend to simulate a two-way interaction. Doing so will help you be less tongue-tied when the real occasion arises.

14. **Peel your eyes from that computer screen!** It's easy to get stuck at the computer and never make it out into the world to meet people. Even though you learned in Tip #12 that your knowledge can be an asset in networking, try to resist the temptation to spend too much time reading and researching and thus isolate yourself too much. You're only delaying the inevitable. You have to get out there eventually.

15. **Leave a brief message at the tone.** There's nothing like having to leave a voice mail or answering machine message to bring out the insecurities in an introvert. If you find that you freeze up or ramble when leaving messages, get in the habit of taking some time to plan what you'll say if the person doesn't answer. Don't write out a script or your message might come across as sounding unnatural. Do, though, list the main points you need to cover in the message. It's also helpful to jot down key phrases next to certain points if you want to remember to say something in a particular way.

16. **Don't keep it to yourself.** Introverts are champions at keeping things to themselves. It's not that we mean to be secretive or selfish; we just tend to be somewhat self-sufficient when it comes to dealing with most issues of daily life. If you have some news or a problem to solve, try picking up the phone and telling someone about it instead of mulling it over indefinitely by yourself.

    Introverts tend to contact people only over the big things, like when they need some urgent information or advice about a major issue. Only when they see that a situation is too big or too difficult to handle on their own do they reach out for help. The same is true for announcing news. As an introvert, you might be more likely to pick up the phone and tell a colleague that you have a new job or that you're getting married than you are to call and tell someone about the interesting meeting you recently attended or to pass on some minor but interesting news. Again, the psychology behind this is that introverts worry that they will bother people, so we tend to reach out to others only when we are really worried or excited about something. Try, instead, to get in the habit of connecting with people over the small things, too—not just the big ones. Doing so enables you to develop better ongoing relationships and ensures that your contacts are there for you when you do need help with the big stuff.

17. **Attend events that have a purpose.** If you're likely to be uncomfortable or nervous at events that are solely networking opportunities, then try instead to attend events that have a purpose, such as educational or cultural seminars. Interactive classes and workshops are especially good bets because they often have a built-in agenda that involves structured networking. Plus, as an introvert, you naturally enjoy the world of ideas and thought, so educational settings are likely to be comfortable for you.

18. **Don't forget to write!** If you can't get yourself to pick up the phone and make a cold call, or even a cool call, consider writing. As discussed in Chapter 6, written communication is often an effective way to connect with others. Sending an e-mail or letter of introduction first can make the follow-up phone call less nerve-racking.

    While you will eventually need to stretch past your comfort zone and get used to calling people more than you are naturally inclined to do, there's nothing wrong with making the most of written communication. As I discussed in Tip #12 ("Make the most of what you know"), playing to your strengths is important. As an introvert, you might be so reluctant to call people that you never contact them at all. In that case, written communication is better than no communication at all. And it might even be better than phone contact if you express yourself more articulately and convincingly in writing. So if you have a preference for writing, make the most of that tendency. Just don't let it keep you from having telephone and face-to-face contact as well. Once you've broken the ice by writing, you then have to maintain a relationship through direct contact.

19. **Get out amongst them.** Do you tend to hole up in your office or other workplace? This tendency is particularly problematic for home-based workers, people who sit at a desk most of the time, and anyone with a busy schedule that keeps them working long hours. No matter how much work you have to do, it helps to get out of the house or office occasionally and go out among people—any people. Walk around the block, take a stroll through the park, or do anything that brings a change of scenery and a reminder that you're not alone. Although walking isn't directly networking, it does propel you out of your own little world and brings about a powerful mindset change that can lead you into networking activity.

20. **Be positive.** It's easy to become pessimistic and assume that your networking efforts will be fruitless. This is actually a defense mechanism that keeps us from being disappointed if, in fact, we do fail. Before you declare that it's not going to be worth your time to talk to Joe Shmoe or to attend a particular event, stop and think. Do you have any rational proof that the prospects are dim or are you just afraid of failure? Be honest with yourself, and if you think a networking encounter could truly be valuable, stretch past your comfort zone and give it a shot. Almost all encounters are worthwhile for the practice if for no other reason.

    If you *do* experience some encounters that are less than positive, try not to let the negative experience get to you. As you learned in Tip #1, networking sometimes involves taking baby steps. It is a process that evolves over time. It's easy to let one negative encounter turn you off of networking for good, but don't let it. Take it one step at a time and try to stay positive.

21. **Consider seeking professional help.** If you think your shyness or introversion is more than a mild nuisance, you might need to consult a psychologist, psychotherapist, or other mental health counselor. Extreme shyness that seriously hinders your social interactions (also known as social anxiety) can keep you from doing what you need to do, and you may benefit from professional treatment. Appendix C lists resources for finding someone who can help.

Online Resources for Shy Types

The Shyness Home Page, sponsored by the Shyness Institute: http://www.shyness.com

A shyness and social anxiety discussion board: http://www.socialfitnessforum.com

22. **Be comfortable in your own skin.** Sometimes reluctance to network results from insecurity about your appearance. The problem might be with your wardrobe, an accent you're embarrassed by, or something about your physical appearance. While physical attractiveness is by no means a prerequisite for being a successful networker, the package you present to others is important. If something about your outward image is dragging down your confidence, consider fixing what's fixable and learn to make the most of what's not. Appendix C tells you how to find image consultants and other types of professionals, including psychotherapists, who can help you be more comfortable with how you come across. Remember also that your true image comes from the inside, so being comfortable in your own skin is really about being comfortable with who you are, not how you look.

23. **Remember that networking is as much a skill as it is an innate talent.** As you get started networking or change the way you're networking now, keep in mind that effective techniques can be learned. Introverts are often overly hard on themselves, saying things like "This should come more easily to me. It shouldn't be such a struggle." Don't expect miracles—at least not right away! Learning anything new takes time and practice, especially when you're learning a new way of thinking and acting. Be patient and pat yourself on the back with each forward step you take.

24. **Networking is like air.** A funny thing happens when introverts get involved in networking. They find that networking is as natural as the air around us. They find that it's been happening around them among people from all walks of life with all sorts of objectives. We introverts just tend not to notice until we watch for it. When you reach that point of recognition, you find that some of the mystery is gone. Networking seems like an ordinary part of daily life rather than something you have to think about constantly. That outlook may seem quite remote if you're just getting started, but all I ask is that you have a little faith that it's true.

One Introvert's Success Story

For several years I followed the progress of Tom, one of my favorite former clients, who happens to be extremely introverted. Tom is an accountant who had been with a large firm that folded because of financial difficulties and disagreements among the partners. Tom had always enjoyed his work as an accountant but had never liked the politics of working in a large organization—he never really felt that he fit in. He wanted more autonomy and independence in his career, so he decided to strike out on his own and start an accounting practice rather than go back to another firm. He did so with considerable trepidation, however, because he knew that running his own business would require a great deal of selling. With the exception of a few long-standing clients who would follow him from his old job into his practice, he knew that clients would not be pouring through the door without some effort on his part. He would have to be a more active networker to spread the word about his services.

Tom did end up establishing his business, and about a year and a half into it, he was pleased to report to me that he felt he had actually mastered the skill of networking. He said that he knows it will always be a bit of a struggle and will never be his favorite professional activity, but once he realized that networking is a skill that can be developed and refined with effort and practice, he found that there was hope. He told me how he saw progress in himself from month to month. Each month he would stretch just a bit more into unfamiliar territory (the territory of extroverts), and each successful attempt gave him the impetus to stretch a bit further the next time. He was gradually having more referral meetings, making more cold calls to potential clients, and attending more meetings. He had also published an article in a professional journal and spoken at a conference. I was proud of Tom's accomplishments and inspired by them as well.

25. **Just do it.** Keep in mind the serendipity factor that has been discussed in other chapters. You never know where a job, a business lead, or some good advice is going to turn up. Sure, networking can be difficult, anxiety-provoking, and a plain old pain in the neck, but at some point you have to abandon all the excuses, take a deep breath, and just do it.

Quick Summary

If you're an introvert, you are not alone in finding networking difficult or uncomfortable. Introverts have a preference for being self-sufficient and independent and not being relationship-oriented, all of which can lead to a reluctance to network or an awkward networking style.

Not all introverts are shy. Introversion is merely a preference for focusing inward rather than outward. Introverts might be shy, quiet, or reserved, but they aren't always. They simply have more of a need for being alone than do extroverts and more of a tendency to live in their own world instead of seeking social opportunities. Most introverts aren't afraid of people or unwilling to socialize; they simply need time alone to regain their energy after being around a lot of people.

Just like death and taxes, there's no escaping networking. Unfortunately for introverts, there is no such thing as a job, career field, or entrepreneurial endeavor in which you are rewarded solely for what you know and how well you do your work. Networking is an inescapable fact of life. You will be better off if you embrace it and do it as well as you can.

Networking is a learned skill. Even if you aren't naturally endowed with the gift of gab and a tendency to reach out and connect with others, you can still become an effective networker. The techniques suggested throughout this book can be useful for introverts, but putting them into practice requires coping mechanisms to "masquerade" as an extrovert. This chapter listed 25 tips that can serve as those coping mechanisms.

12

It's Never Too Early to Start: 25 Networking Tips for Students

Education is not the filling of a pail, but the lighting of a fire.

—WILLIAM BUTLER YEATS

Whether you're in high school, college, or graduate school, chances are you haven't given much thought to networking. School has a wonderful way of shielding us from the real world. There are exams to cram for, papers to crank out, classes to sleep through, and fun to be had. Who has time for networking? You'd better! It may not seem like you do, but carving out time to start making valuable connections and learning the skill of networking is crucial to your future success. Consider these real-life examples that demonstrate the importance of starting to network early.

Jim was a high school senior whose transcript groaned with top grades and stellar test scores. He was certain that after all his hard work, he'd get accepted to at least one of the highly selective colleges to which he had applied. But did he? Unfortunately, he didn't get into any of his top choices. The reason? He had no extracurricular activities and had only lukewarm recommendations from faculty and advisors. Jim had spent all his time in the library, hadn't bothered to get involved in campus activities, and hadn't developed relationships with key people at school. In other words, he had not networked, and it cost him.

Heather was determined to get into a top-notch MBA program, but her undergraduate grades and GMAT scores were near the minimum cutoff for most of the better schools. However, she had a few years of excellent work experience, wrote strong application essays, and presented herself well in the admissions interview, all of which at least put her on the waiting list. How did she distinguish herself from the other candidates and move from waiting list to acceptance? She did so by networking. Heather got up the nerve to call an alumnus of the business school whose name she had been given several months before by an acquaintance. He was impressed with the case she presented for why his alma mater was the right fit for her career and educational goals. She also demonstrated her ability to do the work by citing some of her past accomplishments. He then offered to put in a good word for her with the admissions office. He did, and soon she was accepted.

Patricia was a thirty-eight-year-old mother of two. She had returned to college to complete the bachelor's degree she had started many years earlier. Patricia was convinced that the degree would be her one-way, nonstop ticket to a good job. After years of being denied the jobs she wanted, she was certain that a bachelor's degree was the only barrier between her and her career goals. She was determined to finish her degree as quickly as possible and concentrated on getting the highest grades she could. While those goals are certainly commendable, they turned out not to be enough when it came time to get a job. After graduating, Patricia was dismayed to find that other students her age with lower grade-point averages landed the kinds of jobs she wanted, while she could barely get any interviews. The problem? One prospective employer told her that he would rather see internships and part-time jobs on her resume than straight A's in English and history. In other words, she could have taken a lighter course load and taken a little longer to get her degree in order to have time to gain valuable work experience. The degree alone was not the answer to her career problems. Had she been networking effectively, she might have found this out before pinning all her hopes on the degree and grades.

But School Is a Time to Learn, Not to Schmooze, Right?

High school and college are primarily times to develop intellectually, socially, physically, creatively, and spiritually, but they are also excellent places to learn and practice valuable networking skills for a future career. The school years offer a prime opportunity to begin cultivating a circle of contacts. Even during graduate school, which is a time to specialize in an academic discipline and develop a professional knowledge base, attention must be paid to planning for the future. While impressive, those initials after your name probably won't be enough to get you to your goals.

It's easy to say you're too young, busy, or inexperienced to network. No matter what your age or past experience, it's tempting to assume that networking is not relevant to your life as a student. It's never too early to start, though, and it's essential for success in your post-student life. The following sections list some of the many reasons you should network while you are in high school, college, or graduate school.

Network to Get a Cool Job or Plum Internship

The world of work has changed dramatically in the last several years. It's no longer enough to simply have a degree and the knowledge that comes with it. To get a good job (or at least a job that doesn't require you to wear a paper hat and operate a deep fryer), you will undoubtedly have to network. Connecting with others through fact-finding missions, strategy sessions, shadowing, internships, and other methods that are described throughout this book enables you to develop relationships with people who can help you get jobs.

When you get out in the world, grades and test scores are not always important (which should come as a relief to those of you who'd like to bury your transcripts several hundred feet below ground). What does count is your ability to convey to others that you are focused, motivated, and capable of doing the job. It's a lot easier to do that when you have a network of people helping you strategize ways to get a job and perhaps even intervening on your behalf with prospective employers.

Network to Make a Good Career Choice

Most students come out of college saying, "I guess I have some skills, but I have no idea what they are. I have so many different interests, I don't know which one to turn into a career." While there are a few exceptions, most schools do not incorporate career development classes into the curriculum. Thus, most people don't learn how to choose a career in college.

The emphasis in college—on the part of both students and advisors—is on getting internships and postgraduate jobs. You may learn how to land interesting internships, write a killer resume, and interview like a pro, but rarely do you learn the steps involved in exploring and deciding which career field you should choose. Even if your college career center offers workshops on choosing a career, or even offers individual counseling, you may not take advantage of it. It's likely that you've said, "I don't have time for any of this soul searching or vague self-assessment stuff. I'm about to graduate and I need a job," or "I'm just a sophomore; I don't have to worry about all that yet."

Every job search expert knows that one of the keys to getting a job is to know what you want. The more focused you are about who you are and the more you know about the career field in which you're interviewing, the more you'll impress prospective employers. How do you get that focus? By networking, of course! As you've seen in previous chapters, talking to people about what they do and trying out career options through experiential opportunities can help you weed out the jobs you wouldn't want to do in a million years and zero in on the ones that could make you happy as a clam.

Networking for a career choice isn't just for undergrads, either. You might have gone to graduate school because you have already identified at least a general career goal. While the graduate degree will get you closer to that goal, the graduate school process often opens up new worlds that you didn't even know existed within a given field. This can leave you confused about your career focus. It's particularly important in that case to connect with alumni of your program to evaluate the pros and cons of the various options.

Network to Learn About Yourself

Unless you're going to be a perennial student or have a career as a scholar, you'll eventually be leaving the ivory tower behind. It's therefore important to start seeing your identity as other than that of student. Networking enables you to take a look at who you are outside the classroom and prepares you for the change of identity that comes as you cross the border to the real world. By getting involved in campus organizations, for example, you have the chance to test your leadership skills and learn about teamwork. By visiting people at their workplaces during fact-finding missions, you experience different work environments. You also learn about the various types of people you are likely to encounter there. You might even learn something about your own personality, work style, and values. All of these experiences help you gain the self-awareness necessary for making good career decisions and for doing the self-promotion that's necessary for getting jobs (or getting into the next degree program).

Network to Learn How to Be Proactive in Shaping Your Career

School has a tendency to make people passive. Think about it: High school and college have built-in networks and structures to guide you through the educational process. Advisors help you plan your course of study. Teachers and professors tell you what to study and when to study it. Classmates or roommates study with you and maybe even keep tabs on your emotional state.

In grad school, you're a bit more autonomous, but you still may have networking opportunities practically handed to you on a silver platter. Professors involve you in their research projects, for example, and advisors take an active role in helping you obtain internships or fieldwork experience.

All of this can lead to a disease I call SES, or Student Entitlement Syndrome. It's easy to catch, but there is a cure. There's a danger in growing accustomed to the somewhat nurturing structure of the academic environment and expecting to find that same structure when you set out to land a job or manage your career. You won't get far in the real world with SES, though. The belief that one can sit back and wait for the job offers and promotions to pour in is a trap into which even the most mature, unselfish grad can unwittingly fall. Developing networking skills while still in school, however, can equip you with a sense of self-reliance and an ability to hold your own in that real world. When reality bites, you'll know how to bite back.

Real-World Skills You're Learning in School That Come in Handy While Networking

- Research
- Writing
- Oral presentation
- Leadership
- Teamwork
- Global thinking
- Diversity awareness

25 Networking Tips for Students

The following list contains lots of ideas for ways you can begin to practice one of the most important skills you may ever learn: networking.

1. **Get involved.** Look for ways to explore your interests, develop your skills, and satisfy your values by joining organizations that do something you care about. It really doesn't matter if you join campus clubs or off-campus organizations; the exact focus is not as important as the fact that you are getting involved. Also look into joining the student

chapters of professional associations for career fields that you are considering entering. While not all associations have student divisions, many offer membership at reduced rates for students. Be sure to see Appendix B for groups you might want to join.

How Getting Involved Pays Off

Tricia was a college junior majoring in psychology with an interest in a future career in human resources. When she expressed this interest to a counselor in the campus career center, he told her that her college used to have a student chapter of a national human resources professional association but that the chapter had been defunct for several years. The counselor said that he would gladly help her revive the chapter and serve as its advisor if Tricia would consider being its president. She readily took on the leadership role and found that it proved extremely valuable in getting her postgraduate career launched. Through her involvement with the club during her junior and senior years, Tricia was able to meet hundreds of human resources professionals who turned out to be valuable contacts when it came time to secure a job after graduation. She also gained visibility in the profession while still a student by speaking at a national conference, publishing an article in the association's journal, and being featured in the newsletter. As a student interacting in professional arenas, she was something of a novelty, making these opportunities for networking and visibility easier to come by than they would be after graduation.

2. **Attend professional conferences.** Whether you join professional associations or not, it's a good idea to attend national or regional conferences to learn more about a particular career field and to make valuable contacts. These meetings usually have reduced student rates (the regular registration fees are often pretty steep). Sometimes there are special events and job fairs for student attendees. Ask your professors which conferences would be worthwhile for you to attend, or contact organizations in Appendix B that interest you to find out about their scheduled meetings.

3. **Be a leader.** Instead of sitting on the sidelines, consider taking a leadership role of some sort in your school. Not everyone can be president of student government (nor does everyone want to be), but there are plenty of other ways to test out your leadership abilities and gain visibility.

4. **Make classes count.** Be on the lookout for ways to give your class projects a real-world twist. Consider, for example, designing a project or writing a paper that involves interviewing people in the business world or examining a policy that affects your community. The idea is to have an excuse to connect with the outside world in some way. These kinds of projects have been known to lead to summer internships or jobs after graduation based on relationships established during the project.

5. **Connect upward.** A typical high school, college, or graduate school campus is filled with a wealth of resources. Faculty members, deans, advisors, administrators, and coaches can be valuable sources of advice, guidance, and contacts. Too often, though, it's easy as a student to be hesitant about bridging the gap between you, the "lowly student," and the "almighty THEM." Or you might be too caught up in your daily routine as a student to step back and look at how these key people can get to know you as a person and maybe even as a peer, not just as someone who shows up to class and turns in homework. Think about what you can do to change this situation. Now is the time to start learning to cultivate professional relationships.

Forging a Path from Campus to Career

As a high school senior, Ryan wrote a term paper for his government class on the role of corporate America in politics. By interviewing numerous business executives and government officials to research his topic and by keeping in touch with them after he finished his project, Ryan developed a large network of powerful people who came in handy later in his college career. Through these contacts, he was able to obtain a college scholarship as well as prestigious summer internships in both government and business.

6. **Get to know alumni.** Just as the people on campus are valuable contacts, those who've already left the hallowed halls of your school can be important members of your network as well. They can help you make career decisions and reach your goals through fact-finding missions and strategy sessions (see Chapters 7 and 8 for an explanation of what those are and how to conduct them). They can often provide leads to internships or jobs and might even be in a position to hire you. Check with your institution's career development office, guidance counselor, or alumni relations department to see how you can get in touch with alumni who do work that interests you.

When dealing with alumni, keep the following tips in mind:

- Be respectful of their time.

- Don't expect them to do everything for you.

- Be prepared with questions and clear objectives.

- Be courteous.

- Thank them promptly.

7. **Use your campus career center or guidance office.** Never again will it be so easy and convenient (and free!) to get good advice about your career as when you're a student. Your campus career center or guidance office should be an important part of your networking efforts. Think about it. The professionals in these offices come across jobs, internships, and educational opportunities and interact with large numbers of people daily. You need to get to know these counselors!

Tracking Down Alumni

What should you do if you attend a school that does not have an active alumni network or any official system in place for referring you to alumni? Don't despair, helpful alumni are out there! They just might not be listed in some handy directory or database, so you have to do a little sleuthing to find them. Ask professors in relevant departments if they've kept up with alumni doing work that interests you. Also, ask your school's administrators or anyone else who is likely to keep up with alumni.

8. **Shadow.** As discussed in Chapter 7, observing someone at work for a day or even part of a day is a great way to get the information you need to make career decisions and cultivate contacts. As a student, shadowing opportunities are often easy to come by as more and more high schools and colleges are establishing shadowing programs. Often held over winter or spring break, these programs match students with alumni working in careers they'd like to learn more about. If your school doesn't have an official shadowing program, ask professors or career counselors if they can help you find someone to observe.

Shadowing Suggestions

As coordinator of a shadowing program when I was a career counselor, I saw how valuable the shadowing experience could be for students. I also saw some mishaps and missed opportunities, however, so I want to offer a few pointers to help you make the most of the experience:

- Always show up for your shadowing day unless you have a very good reason not to. The person you're shadowing has probably arranged his or her schedule around you and may have planned some special activities, so be sure to take the appointment seriously and make every effort to be there. Also, make sure that you are there on time. If you can't make it for some unavoidable reason, make sure you call to cancel or reschedule.

- Dress appropriately for the environment you'll be visiting. Since "appropriate" can vary widely, ask someone who knows what's right. If all else fails, you can ask the person you're shadowing. He or she will appreciate the fact that you want to wear something that's appropriate. In any case, make sure that what you wear is comfortable (particularly the shoes). If in doubt, it is always better to dress "up" than to dress "down," so if you can't find out what is appropriate, take the better dress option. This conveys respect for the organization that you are visiting.

- Once there, be very courteous and considerate of the person whom you're observing. Be on the lookout for areas of his or her work that might be confidential and offer to excuse yourself from the room if you think he or she could use some privacy for a meeting or phone conversation.

- Whenever you're introduced to anyone, give a firm handshake, say your name, and express enthusiasm for being there. It's helpful to ask for the business cards of everyone you meet so that you can contact them in the future.

- Prepare specific questions to ask on your shadowing day. You'll ask some of them outright, and you'll keep others to yourself and find answers to them through observation. These questions are similar to the objectives for a fact-finding mission (as discussed in Chapter 7). You're there for a reality check to find out if this type of workplace fits with who you are and what you want out of a career. The shadowing experience may also be a strategy session of sorts if you already know you want to enter that field and just need to figure out how to do so. (See Chapter 8 for a description of strategy sessions.)

- Following up with a thank-you note is particularly important when someone has been willing to squire you around a workplace. Also be sure to thank all the people you meet in addition to your main "shadowee." (That's another reason for collecting business cards throughout the day.) It doesn't hurt to follow up with anyone involved in coordinating your shadowing day as well, both at your school and in the workplace (someone in the organization's human resources department, for example, might have arranged for you to shadow someone else in the company). Doing so not only is considerate, but also helps you create allies in your network for the future.

Whom to Contact If You Need Help Getting into the School of Your Choice

If you're a high school student applying to college, or a college student applying to graduate school, you might need more assistance than your school's guidance counselor has the time or resources to provide. If so, you can contact the Independent Educational Consultant's Association (IECA) at (703) 591-4850 or http://www.educationalconsulting.org for a referral to an experienced consultant in your area. They can't wave a magic wand to get you into the school of your dreams, but they can be valuable members of your network. Educational consultants provide top-notch advice and support (for a fee) as you go through the school selection and application process.

9. **Be an intern.** Having internships while in school has become a necessity in order to keep up with the competition when it comes time to look for a job. A resume without internships (or paid part-time jobs) won't get you nearly as far as one with more mundane, unrelated work experience, even if your academic record is stellar.

   Aside from the direct job-hunting benefits, however, internships are also valuable networking opportunities. Whether you're interning for a few weeks over winter break or for several months during the academic year, internships expose you to many people who could become important members of your network. Since you're actually doing work as an intern and not just observing or interviewing, the people with whom you work have a chance to get to know you as a professional. This situation is fertile ground for cultivating the relationships that are the key to a strong network. So, while interning, be sure to make an extra effort to introduce yourself to people at the workplace beyond your immediate supervisor and co-workers. Also, be open to projects or duties that would team you up with a wide variety of people.

Cooperate with Co-ops

In addition to internships, be on the lookout for "co-op" (cooperative) programs that your school and local businesses might jointly sponsor. In some cases, co-ops are simply internships by another name, but co-ops are often more structured and therefore more like real-world work experience. They can open a lot of doors for you from a networking standpoint. They also usually pay pretty well and include academic credit.

10. **Help out in your community.** Like shadowing and internships, community service lets you test career fields that you're considering. It's also a way to gain valuable experience that can open doors that might otherwise be closed to you. Of course, true community service is done because you want to help in some way. There's no denying, however, that it can also be an excellent way to meet people who could be valuable strategists, targets, allied forces, role models, or supporters in your networking efforts. (See Chapter 4 if you need a reminder of the STARS concept of networking.)

11. **Go on fact-finding missions.** Fact-finding missions are a particularly important feature of your networking efforts as a student. You should be conducting lots of FFMs to get information about the career fields you're considering and to establish relationships with people in the "real world." Remember, there's much more to the work world than what you learn in class, so look for ways to talk with people who can give you a needed reality check. For a full description of FFMs and how to handle them, see Chapter 7.

12. **Conduct strategy sessions.** As with FFMs, strategy sessions are essential for bridging the gap between what you know as a student and what you need to know to transition into a career. They help you get your job search tools in order (such as resumes, letters, and interviewing techniques), and they help you map out an effective strategy for getting a job. They also have an added benefit in that during the process of having a strategy session, you are developing a valuable contact. You are not only getting useful advice, but also giving someone the chance to get to know you, see how you think, and observe you "at work" in a sense. Strategy sessions are therefore one of the most important parts of your networking as a student. (Refer to Chapter 8 for ideas of how strategy sessions fit into the job search process.)

13. **Broaden your horizons.** When you graduate from high school, college, or graduate school, you'll be entering a world that is likely to be filled with a broad range of people from diverse backgrounds. To learn to appreciate all types of people and learn to deal appropriately and respectfully with them, consider ways to broaden your horizons. If you tend to hang around in one clique of friends, why not make an effort to get to know someone with whom you wouldn't naturally associate? Also think about organizations you could join or social events you could attend that could introduce you to a wider circle. If studying abroad is an option (or even being an exchange student at another school or college within the U.S.), that too is a great way to expand your horizons and learn valuable networking skills.

14. **Diversify.** Similar to the last point, broadening your horizons within your own scope of activities, not just people, is important as well. In other words, look for ways to make yourself a well-rounded person.

As you saw in the examples at the start of this chapter, a sole focus on schoolwork is not a sufficient foundation on which to build a career. Having a diverse range of interests and experiences will not only help you get a job or into your next academic program, but also, like Tip #13, teach you important skills for dealing with a complex world.

Why It's Important to Be Well Rounded

When you get out of college or graduate school and try to enter the job market, you may be surprised at how much importance prospective employers place on your being well rounded. Of course, their main concern is that you have the knowledge and experience necessary to do the job you're being hired for. But they also want to know that they are hiring people who are made up of more than grade-point averages and summer jobs listed on a resume. When prospective employers see that you have been on sports teams, belonged to academic clubs, enjoyed art and music, or volunteered in your community, they know they're dealing with someone who is adaptable, flexible, team- or leadership-oriented, naturally curious, and simply an interesting person. And, just as importantly, you've learned how to get along with a wide range of types of people—an essential skill for the networking you'll be doing later in your career. To be well rounded, you don't have to be a dabbler, getting involved on a superficial level in anything and everything. Just make sure that you venture into a few arenas with enough depth to expand your horizons.

15. **Start a job search club.** In addition to relying on your campus career counselors and other professionals for help, consider starting a job search club with your friends and classmates. You don't need to be experts in job search strategy to do so. The process of getting together with peers to discuss the ups and downs of your searches and share leads and resources is a good start. You can also use one of the books on job hunting recommended in Appendix D to guide your discussions.

16. **Don't hesitate to enlist the assistance of relatives.** You might be reluctant to let Aunt Gladys get you a job, but remember that when you're a student, relatives likely make up the majority of your

network. You probably haven't had much of a chance to cultivate professional contacts yet. While you shouldn't expect family members to hand you a job, it is okay to let a relative pave the way. Remember that when you do get the job, it's up to you to keep it and to grow in it. Your relative can help you get started, but after that, it's you who earns your keep. Having the assistance of a relative is nothing to be ashamed of.

17. **Use the Internet.** As a student, you're probably very Internet savvy and can find plenty of opportunities to start networking online. Networking online is key for students because the Internet is the great equalizer. It doesn't matter if you're a high school sophomore or president of a large company; everyone has equal access to the same people and places on the information superhighway.

18. **Have a resume whether you think you need it or not.** If you're not actively looking for a job or if you're young and don't have much work experience, it's easy to assume that you don't need to have a resume. Ah, but you do! A resume is a snapshot of who you are, so even if you don't have a lot to put on it, it's helpful to have one on hand as a way of introducing yourself. Having one also shows that you take a professional, organized approach to things. Several good books on resumes are listed in the bibliography in Appendix D.

19. **Have a business card.** If you thought a resume wasn't necessary to have, you probably think that having a business card is an even sillier idea. It's not, though. Think about how it could come in handy. What do you do when someone asks for your name and number? It's time-consuming and unprofessional to have to fish for a scrap of paper and write down the information. Wouldn't it be much easier to pull out a card that has your name, address, e-mail address, and phone number on it? You don't need to put a job title or company name since you're not employed full-time; just your basic contact information will do. Doing this can really set you apart from other students. (See Chapter 5 for suggestions on inexpensive, fast ways to produce business cards.)

20. **Find role models.** As discussed in Chapter 3, role models are an important component of any network, but they are particularly valuable for students. As a student, whether you're 18 or 48, you're likely to feel that you're starting at square one when it comes to a career. Having people who can guide you along the way and provide a good example is all the more important for you as a student. Be on the lookout for people who can fill this role and start developing relationships with them.

21. **Take advantage of public speaking opportunities.** You don't have to start your own cable TV show or go on a worldwide speaking tour, but you can look for less ambitious ways to get in front of groups to say a few words. Some classes require oral reports as part of your assignments. If none of your classes requires this, look for opportunities to speak before groups, such as introducing speakers at an assembly, giving a speech to campaign for a classmate running for student government, or accompanying a professor to present a paper at a conference. Whatever the occasion, public speaking is an important skill to acquire. It is also a great way to gain visibility, which can lead to opportunities down the road. If the thought of all of this terrifies you, consult some of the books on public speaking that are listed in Appendix D.

22. **Publish an article.** As with public speaking, gaining visibility and establishing yourself as a professional can also be accomplished by getting something you have written published. If you're in high school or college, a published article might be a piece in your school newspaper or a letter to the editor of your local paper. In college and graduate school, however, you might also have the opportunity to publish an essay or research report in a professional journal, particularly if you collaborate with a professor on a project. However you do it, published writing is a great way to get a strong portfolio started. (See Tip #25 for a discussion of portfolios.)

Getting Your Name in Print

If you have a knack for writing, don't assume that your publishing opportunities are limited only to the school newspaper. Keisha, now a journalism major at a large university, had applied to college with an impressive portfolio of writing samples. During high school she was a staff writer for her school paper, but she frequently wrote letters to the editor of her city's daily newspaper as well. An editor there began to notice that her perspective as a student and a teenager would be a nice addition to his paper, so he invited her to contribute occasional editorials on issues that were particularly relevant to her generation. When it came time to apply to colleges with competitive journalism departments, these published articles helped to distinguish Keisha's application from all the other students who had only school-based publications in their portfolios.

23. **Learn and practice good time management habits.** As you may have gathered from the rest of this book, networking can be time-consuming. That's why it's important to start acquiring good habits regarding time and organization early in your networking life. Now is the time to learn how to get to appointments promptly, schedule assignments and meetings in an appointment book or electronic planner, and keep neat and tidy files of information you collect.

24. **Get in the habit of writing thank-you notes.** Another good habit is writing notes to let people know you appreciated something they've done for you. It's usually obvious that you should write a thank-you note after a fact-finding mission or an interview, but did you think of writing notes to people you worked with during an internship? How about to a professor for a great class? (Write the note *after* you get the grade so it doesn't look as if you're just kissing up for an A!) Acknowledging people who do you a favor, provide an opportunity, or inspire you is not only a nice thing to do, it's also a way to keep them as active members of your network.

25. **Start a portfolio.** As described in Chapter 5, portfolios are folders or notebooks containing information that documents your accomplishments and provides evidence of your skills. Portfolios usually include letters of recommendation, writing samples, and other documents that show relevant work you've done. The portfolio is something you take to interviews, internships, or educational programs to which you're applying. Your portfolio is a supplement to your resume and other self-promotion materials. While it's not a requirement that you have a portfolio, portfolios are becoming more common. In order to keep up with your competition, consider creating and maintaining your own portfolio while you're still in school.

If you're an artist or designer of some sort, a portfolio contains samples of your work and takes on a whole new meaning. Instructors and people who work in the arts can advise you on how to assemble an art-based portfolio.

Quick Summary

It's never too early to begin to network. In today's world, a degree alone won't get you a good job. You have to start developing contacts early, both to help you explore your career options and to get leads to employment opportunities.

Use the 25 ideas presented in this chapter to help you begin networking while you are still a student.

Part 5: Making Networking Work for Life

● ●

Like so many endeavors in life, your follow-through in networking is
just as important as the initial networking activities themselves. All
throughout this book I've spoken of networking as an ongoing process
of building relationships, not just a flash-in-the-pan activity that you do
only when you need something from others.

Chapter 13 expands on the idea of networking as a two-way street—as
the building of relationships to offer mutual support. On a practical
note, Chapter 13 gets into the nitty-gritty of writing thank-you notes
and other ways to show appreciation and give back to those who've
helped you—and even those who haven't yet helped.

In Chapter 14, you ensure thorough follow-through by developing a
simple action plan that will help you find the time to network and map
out the steps for doing it.

Chapter 15 concludes the book by offering valuable tips for making
networking a seamless, ongoing part of your life. It addresses such issues
as how to keep your network from drying up, how to balance periodic
or persistent follow-through without being a pest, and how to prevent
networking burnout.

13

Doing Unto Others: The Art and Science of Giving Back

Thanksgiving comes before Christmas.

—PETER KREEFT

"May I have a few minutes of your time?"

"Would you mind giving me the names of other people I should talk to?"

"Do you have any suggestions for how I can improve my resume?"

"Can you advise me on how I might expand my business?"

Networking can seem at times to be a very self-centered activity. You might start to feel like all you're ever really saying is, "How can you help ME?" In fact, it is not all about you. The needs of the people who help you should be as much on your mind as your own needs. People in your network deserve your thanks, and they might need some assistance themselves. After all, most of them have careers and businesses, too.

It's important, therefore, not only to show your appreciation through thank-you notes or small gifts, but also to return a favor when the opportunity arises. The "Ways to Show Your Appreciation" section of this chapter discusses specific methods of thanking and giving back to people in your network.

Always remember that networking is based on cultivating and nurturing relationships, not on one-time interactions, so consider small (or sometimes large) ways you can do nice things for people in your network—often for no particular reason. The "Performing Random Acts of Kindness" section of this chapter provides some ideas of ways to do this. Such acts might include calling someone when you come across an article that would be of interest to that individual or volunteering to help out at the person's favorite charity. Not only are these nice things to do, but they also have indirect benefits to you in that they strengthen relationships and keep you visible.

The final aspect of giving discussed in this chapter is that of developing other people. Whether you are established in your career or just getting started, it's likely that you have something to offer someone else. Serving as a mentor or just giving occasional advice is an important responsibility that we all have. Chances are you wouldn't be where you are without the help of others, so why not give something back by helping out someone who's a few steps behind you in his or her career, job search, or business?

In the remainder of this chapter, we take a look at the art and science of giving back in detail.

Ways to Show Your Appreciation

Thanking people who give you advice, leads, or any kind of assistance is not just a nice thing to do, it's an absolute necessity. When people take time out of their busy schedules or go out on a limb for you, the least you can do is take a few minutes to write a quick note or call to say thanks. You might even spend a few bucks on a small gift.

There are many ways to show your appreciation, depending on the size of the favor done for you, the nature of your relationship with the person you're thanking, and your budget. The following are typical ways of giving thanks, with tips on how to know which networking situations each is appropriate for.

Thank-You Letters

The most common way to express appreciation in networking, thank-you notes should be sent promptly after every fact-finding mission, strategy session, referral meeting, job interview, phone conversation, or other encounter in which you receive advice, guidance, support, or leads. Showing appreciation by a thank-you note (sent by e-mail or snail mail) is not only a common courtesy but also an opportunity to remind someone of your career goals and objectives or, if you're self-employed, your services and products. (Pros and cons of electronic versus paper thank-you notes are discussed later in this chapter.) Because this piece of correspondence should contain more than an expression of thanks, it's helpful to be familiar with the following six components of a networking thank-you letter.

1. **Thank the person**. Your letters should, of course, thank the recipients for their time, sharing of expertise, and anything else given. Thanks are usually stated in the first sentence or two to make it clear that the purpose of the letter is to show appreciation. You might say, for example, "Dear Bob, You were more than generous with your time on the phone yesterday, and I truly appreciate it." Or, "Dear Harriette, I want to thank you for meeting with me on Monday. Knowing how busy your schedule is, I particularly appreciated your fitting me in on short notice and taking the time to share your wisdom with a newcomer to the world of entrepreneurship."

2. **Acknowledge what was helpful**. In addition to thanking someone for help, it is important to acknowledge which specific information or assistance was particularly useful and why. For example, the letter begun to Harriette in Tip #1 could continue with, "I found your comments on the marketing strategy portion of my business plan

especially useful. As I told you, I had been concerned about how best to survey the competition without giving away the unique ideas for my business, but your suggestions will help me get around that problem."

3. **State how you'll follow through on suggestions**. People who give advice like to know that you'll follow through on at least some of what they suggest. Otherwise, what was the point of sharing experience, knowledge, and insight with you? It is considerate to let people know that you took what they said seriously and plan to follow through (or have already followed through). The Harriette letter could go on to say, "I have started researching those Web sites you suggested and can already see that they will be very useful as I develop my marketing plan."

4. **Promote yourself.** A thank-you note can also be a place to remind the recipient of your career or business goals and why you deserve to reach those goals. Remember that every networking interaction offers the chance to promote yourself subtly but effectively so that others see you as a worthy candidate for the assistance and opportunities you seek.

5. **Remind the reader of his or her offer for further assistance**. If the recipient offered to act on your behalf in some way, such as forwarding your resume to colleagues or sending you names and numbers of other people to talk to, now is the time to gently remind them of those promises. (Here's where you can take a first step in preventing the problem of the "false promisers" as discussed in the "Difficult People" section of Chapter 10.)

For example, a job seeker might say, "I appreciated your offer to pass my resume along to your company's Director of Operations and to your friend in logistics at Acme Consumer Products Corp."

After a strategy session, you might write, "Thanks also for offering to look over a revised draft of my resume. I expect to finish it over the weekend and will e-mail it to you early next week."

By couching these reminders in statements of appreciation, they remain subtle, but by clearly restating the complete promise for further action, you gently nudge the reader to take that action.

6. **Conclude and state follow-up plans.** In addition to reiterating your appreciation from earlier in the letter, the closing is the place to clarify the next steps in your networking relationship. Here is where you offer to keep the reader apprised of your plans and progress or ask for permission to stay in touch. After a fact-finding mission for help with a career decision, a closing might go something like this: "Thank you again for your time and valuable input. I will let you know which direction I decide to head." Other letters might close with, "While you certainly answered all of my questions during our meeting, I will probably take you up on your offer to call as other questions come up. In any case, I thank you again for your time and will keep you posted on my progress."

Not every letter will need to include all six components, so adapt these guidelines to your own situations, being sure to keep your letter to less than one page.

Presentation of a Hard Copy Letter

When sending a letter via regular mail, or "snail mail," rather than e-mailing or faxing, the overall presentation of a thank-you letter is almost as important as its content. The way a letter looks reflects your professionalism, your attention to detail, and the amount of effort you put into it. Be sure that your letter has no typos or messy corrections and is centered on the page with adequate margins (or neatly spaced and legible if handwritten).

The main decision to make regarding format is whether to handwrite or type the note. While most professional correspondence should be typed, there are times when a handwritten thank-you note is acceptable or even preferable. These include

- When writing to an established member of your network (that is, a colleague whom you know well) with an informal thank-you for a favor or referral.

- When writing to someone you know personally, but have dealt with in a professional capacity. A typical example of this is a family friend who gave you some career advice in an informal setting like your home. (Even with personal acquaintances or relatives, though, a typed letter is often more appropriate if you need to reinforce the professional nature of this particular interaction—for example, getting Uncle Joe to take you seriously since he thinks of you as the little girl in pigtails even though you're pushing fifty.)

- When writing to someone who would probably appreciate the lost art of an elegantly handwritten letter or card.

Another Use for Your Business Card

If you do choose to write a more informal handwritten thank-you note because the circumstances call for it, consider including your business card (or "job-seeking card") in the envelope. This will bump the correspondence up a notch from social to business and remind the reader that you mean business.

Most other situations call for a letter typed in appropriate business format. (Examples of business correspondence formats are provided in Chapter 6.) This is particularly true for most communication in a job search. Letters following fact-finding missions, strategy sessions, and job interviews should almost always be typed. The general rule is that the more formal the situation and the less well you know the recipient, the more likely you should type the letter.

Choosing Paper

For a traditional business letter, choose a paper of substantial weight (24- to 32-pound) in a conservative color—white, ivory, or pale gray. If, however, the person or the organization you're writing to is very informal or creative, you can take some liberties with the color and texture of the paper. Recycled selections with bits of "debris" or subtle patterns have an interesting texture and can jazz up the look of your letter while still sticking to traditional colors. If you're tempted to go for wilder colors or styles of paper, get a second opinion from someone who knows the intended recipient's field before getting too far out.

For a handwritten note, use either the same type of paper or a smaller sheet of stationery (usually called Monarch size) or write on a nice note card. Choose a stiff card or fold-over note card. Stationery and office supply stores usually have a good selection of plain note cards in nice, subtle colors or ones with a simple design, such as a border. Try not to get the ones that say "Thank You" on the outside. You should be able to express that sentiment clearly enough on the inside! Sometimes greeting cards are appropriate, particularly the kind that are blank with no message on the inside and some kind of appealing (and relevant to the reader) scene on the front—maybe flowers, a work of art, a cityscape, or a nature scene—whatever fits the situation and the recipient.

Sending Your Letter

Most of the advice up to this point has been for a regular letter or note card sent through the mail. There may be times, however, when a more expedient or high-tech method, such as faxing or e-mailing, is appropriate. Sometimes it is important that your letter be received right away, perhaps because you'll be speaking to the person again within a few days or you need to remind the individual of action to be taken very soon. In those cases, e-mail or fax your note. Also, if you're dealing with someone in a technology field or you know that the person is a fan of e-mail, sending your letter by e-mail is completely appropriate. E-mailed or faxed follow-up notes are a less formal way to show appreciation and make for a less polished presentation, but they are widely accepted and very commonly used methods these days.

The following samples will give you an idea of how thank-you letters and notes should read.

Sample Thank-You Letter

Here's an example of a detailed follow-up letter written after a strategy session in which the recipient had advised the writer about how to make a career transition from law to finance.

Jose Hernandez
75 Allstate Road, Apt. 7
Chicago, IL 11111

Ms. Mary M. Seibert
CHS Capital Group
1111 40th Avenue, Ste. 2500
Chicago, IL 11111

December 1, 2004

Dear Mary,

I really appreciated your taking the time to meet with me last week. I hope that you had a nice Thanksgiving since we spoke.

I took advantage of the holiday weekend to begin acting on some of the useful suggestions you provided. Your ideas for revising my resume to make it more finance-oriented and less specific to the practice of law were right on target. I've added a profile and accomplishment statements and can already see that it is now a much stronger marketing tool.

The Web sites that you recommended to get me up to speed on structured finance proved to be most useful, and I've also ordered the books you recommended.

In addition to the valuable advice and resources, I want to thank you for being supportive of my plans to make this transition. I am confident that I bring a valuable combination of skills and experience with my five years of bankruptcy law practice as well as my prior work in economics as an undergrad. It was encouraging to hear your enthusiasm for the marketability of my background.

I look forward to staying in touch with you and will probably take you up on your offer to critique my revised resume. I should have something ready to e-mail you in the next couple of days and will call to see when you might have a few minutes to discuss it by phone. Thank you again for all your assistance.

Best Regards,

Jose Hernandez

Jose Hernandez

Sample Handwritten Thank-You Note

The following note is an example of a typical note a self-employed person might write to a network contact who has referred business to him. In this case, a real estate agent has referred a prospective client to a landscape designer. The designer is writing a short note to acknowledge that the prospective client has called to inquire about his services. If the inquiry were to turn into an actual contract, the landscape designer should type up a more formal thank-you letter or perhaps send a gift to the real estate agent. (Gift-giving is discussed later in this chapter.)

Elson Landscapes, Inc.

Dear Harry,

Just a quick note to let you know that I got a call from Allyson Epstein of Maplewood Properties to discuss the possibility of my doing the landscaping for their new development in Watertown. She said you had raved about the quality of my work, so I really appreciate the referral and the glowing recommendation. I'll keep you posted.

When we both get some breathing room, let's get together for breakfast again. Thanks so much for your support!

Regards,

Jim Elson

Thank-You Calls

Putting your appreciation in writing is usually the best way to thank someone because it shows that you put more effort into the thank-you and it is a bit more professional than other ways. There are times, however, when a phone call will suffice or might even be more effective. The best way to decide is to ask yourself two questions:

- How well do I know this person?

- Could I benefit by having a two-way communication over the phone rather than the one-sided communication of a letter?

If you know the person well, a letter or note might be an overly formal, and somewhat impersonal, way to show your appreciation. Just as you're more likely to pick up the phone and call a friend in personal situations rather than write a letter, professional situations with people you know well or fairly well often dictate a phone call rather than written communication. This is also true if you have frequent contact with someone. With people you find yourself thanking frequently, writing letters can become somewhat repetitive. If you have people who are helping you continually, you might prefer to call them each time you need to thank them instead of writing the same kind of note over and over or at least alternate calls, e-mails, and mailed notes.

Another benefit to calling someone (and actually having a conversation, not just leaving a message) is that you might have a chance to exchange valuable information. Sending a letter is one-sided. You say what you have to say and stick it in the mail or fax it, and the communication is over. With a phone call, however, you have an opportunity to gain further visibility; remind the other person of your career goals or business objectives; and, most importantly, get feedback and strengthen the rapport with that contact.

When I was operating a career counseling private practice, there were many times when I came close to writing thank-you notes to people who had referred clients to me, but I decided to call to thank them instead. I invariably found that calling paid off. They said something like, "I'm so glad you called. I need more copies of your brochure, but keep forgetting to ask you." Or, "I'm so glad you called. I think I have another client for you but wasn't sure if you offer what this person needs. Let me tell you about him and see if he'd be right for you."

For the self-employed, phone calls often serve as valuable memory joggers for the people you call, giving you the chance to answer questions they've had about you, provide information and resources, and just generally keep you fresh in their mind. That doesn't always happen with a letter that gets read quickly and filed or tossed.

Also, for those who are networking for career planning or advancement purposes, a phone call may have the same benefits. It reminds people of who you are and what you're looking for. One note of caution, however: Most traditional job search meetings, such as strategy sessions and job interviews, call for a formal thank-you letter or e-mail rather than a phone call. A call can be viewed as somewhat intrusive and as breaking the traditional job search "rules."

Gift-Giving to Show Appreciation

A gift can be a thoughtful way to say thank you to someone in your network who has been particularly helpful, but it also can be a major faux pas. Knowing when to send gifts, what to choose, and how much to spend is an essential skill for any savvy networker. You don't want to send a box of steaks to a vegetarian, a case of wine to a teetotaler, or a cheap paperweight to a heavyweight business executive. Many of the books listed in the "Books on Business Etiquette and Protocol" section of Appendix D offer excellent advice on the issues of professional gift giving. In addition to those sources, here are some tips on the subject.

When a Gift Is Appropriate

In some industries and career fields, gift giving is the norm, so you might already be aware of when it is appropriate and what to choose. If you're not sure, ask for advice from someone in your network who knows the field you're dealing with. Some companies have policies prohibiting their employees from receiving gifts from anyone who does (or would like to) do business with them. These rules evolve from ethical concerns over preferential treatment and obligations that inevitably come with receiving a present. In other words, no one wants to look as if they're accepting a bribe.

For most networkers, however, gift giving is a perfectly acceptable, innocent activity. If someone has been particularly helpful with your career plans or job search, there is no harm in sending a small token of your thanks.

This is also true for self-employed people who want to thank those who have supported their businesses in a significant way. When I was a self-employed career counselor, for example, every December I sent holiday gifts to the individuals who had referred clients to me. I also often sent a small gift to someone who referred a client to me for the first time as a sort of introductory show of appreciation and to encourage future referrals. I also received gifts at the end of the year from fellow career counselors and other professionals to whom I had referred business. It's important in these situations that the gifts exchanged not be extravagant lest it look like you're putting undue influence on the recipient. Business should be earned by the quality of your work, not by the size or frequency of the gifts you send.

What to Give

Like any kind of gift giving, choosing a present in professional networking is easiest when you know the recipient well. If that's the case, choose something that the person is likely to enjoy and appreciate, not something that only *you* like. If you don't know much about the recipient's personal tastes and interests—which is usually the case—then it's best to select something fairly neutral that most anyone would like.

The following are popular, and usually appropriate, business gifts:

- Flowers and plants

- Food items such as fruit or baked goods

- Champagne or wine (if you are sure that the recipient won't be offended by receiving alcohol)

- Gift baskets

- Gourmet tea or coffee

- Desk items like letter openers, attractive paperweights, and so on

- Books or bookstore gift cards

- Gift certificates to a day spa, store, or restaurant

- Stationery or nice writing instruments

- Sports or cultural event tickets

It is generally best to stay away from overly personal items unless you know the person well. In addition to stores in your neighborhood that might be good sources of gifts, be sure to check mail-order and online catalogs for convenient ways to order and ship gifts. Also, some department stores and other businesses have handy personal shopping services that can help you select professional gifts and arrange for wrapping and delivery.

Recommended Mail-Order and Online Sources for Professional Gifts

Calyx & Corolla (888) 882-2599 or http://www.calyxandcorolla.com: Elegant, fresh flower arrangements with prompt delivery.

Gift Velocity (866) 451-CARD (2273) or http://www.cardvelocity.com: Uniquely packaged gift baskets, including elegant corporate gift baskets. Featured in Oprah's *O* magazine.

Harry & David (877) 322-1200 or http://www.harryanddavid.com: Delicious fruits, sweets, and baked goods with friendly service.

Home and Office Bargains http://www.homeandofficebargains.com: Great selection of gourmet gift baskets and other items. Featured in Oprah's *O* magazine.

Horchow (877) 944-9888 or http://horchow.com: A sophisticated selection of office and household decorative and practical items at a range of prices.

Levenger (800) 667-8034 or http://www.levenger.com: Calling their products "Tools for Serious Readers," Levenger offers elegant items like leather portfolios and notepads, fountain pens, wood desk items, and other nice business gifts.

Nonnie's Traditional Southern (800) 664-0919 or http://www. nonniestraditional.com: Featured in *Town & Country* and *Real Simple* magazines, this site offers exquisitely packaged made-from-scratch pound cakes, creatively topped with a nosegay of fresh flowers and packaged in a luxurious fabric-covered hatbox.

Omaha Steaks (800) 960-8400 or http://www.omahasteaks.com: Known for quality, succulent steaks, but they also have other great foods for the non-carnivores on your list.

The Popcorn Factory (800) 541-2676 or http://www.thepopcornfactory. com: Colorful tins of flavored and plain popcorn make for fun gifts, particularly for a whole office. The Popcorn Factory even has a helpful corporate gift department.

Red Envelope (877) 733-3683 or http://www.redenvelope.com: Offers an extensive selection of original and imaginative gifts with a focus on making gift-giving fun and easy.

Ross-Simons (800) 835-1343 or http://www.ross-simons.com: Top-quality silver, crystal, and housewares at discount prices.

Tiffany & Co. (800) 843-3269 or http://www.tiffany.com: The epitome of taste and understated elegance for silver and crystal items and other gifts, including their Tiffany for Business items.

More Tips for Gift Giving

- DO make sure the recipient is in town and that someone is at the office (or home) to receive your gift when sending a perishable item like food or flowers.

- DO make sure your full name and address are clearly visible to the recipient so the gift is not a mystery.

- DO enclose a note or gift card so the recipient knows the purpose of the present.

- DON'T go overboard on what you spend.

- DON'T send something that requires assembly, is extremely large, requires special care (such as a fragile, exotic plant), or would in some other way be troublesome for the recipient.

- DON'T expect a response. Most people will acknowledge your gift so you can rest assured it was received, but since your gift was a thank-you to them, they aren't necessarily obligated to perpetuate the thanking cycle by sending you a formal reply.

Performing Random Acts of Kindness

Another way to give back to people in your network is through simple, considerate actions that are not necessarily a response to something they've done for you. In other words, you don't have to wait until it's time to thank someone to do something nice. Networking is based on relationships that are cultivated over time, so random acts of kindness should be a natural part of that process. Sometimes just picking up the phone to say hello (and not to ask for anything!) is all you need to do to brighten someone's day. Take a look at the many ways you can be considerate and show appreciation on an ongoing basis:

- **Birthdays and holidays.** Try to keep track of the birth dates of people in your database and send a card (or a gift if you know the person well) to acknowledge them. Also consider sending cards for holidays other than Christmas and Hanukkah. Thanksgiving, New Year's, and Independence Day are among some of the "safe" holidays that most Americans celebrate regardless of their religious affiliation. If you do know of people who celebrate certain religious holidays, it can be nice to send acknowledgments of those, but be sure you know they do participate in a particular holiday and don't make assumptions about their religious or ethnic background based on incomplete information.

- **Doing favors.** It's nice to get in the habit of asking people if you can do anything for them. Remember that networking is a two-way street. It's not all about you; other people have needs, too. The following are typical ways to give of your time or resources for people in your network:

  - Speak on a panel that someone is coordinating.

  - Volunteer for, or contribute money to, a charity they're involved with.

  - Send clippings from magazines or newspapers or online articles that would be of interest.

  - Notify them of events they might want to attend.

  - Share your discovery of valuable resources, such as a new book.

  - Give a professional courtesy discount, offering your products or services at a reduced rate or no charge.

  - If you're not sure how you could help someone, ask!

A Special Note for Students and Beginning Networkers

You might feel that you have little to offer someone who is older or more advanced in a career than you, but that's not necessarily true. As a student or recent graduate, you have access to valuable resources that are often out of reach of more experienced people. Is there something you've learned in a class, or an interesting book you've come across, that could be informative for someone who's been away from academia for a while? Are you friendly with a professor who could be a good contact for someone you've met? Also, if you're involved in an entry-level job search, you might come across interesting information as you research industries, career fields, and companies. People with busy jobs don't often have time to do online research, go to the library, or keep up with magazine and journal reading as you can during a search.

- **Give acknowledgments**. Acknowledging and congratulating people are not only ways for you to stay visible, but are also just nice things to do. If you hear that someone has been promoted, completed a big project, received an award, started a business, or achieved some other accomplishment, consider giving that individual a call or sending a congratulatory note.

  It's gratifying to know that one's accomplishments are recognized. This can also be a great way to expand your network since you can write to people you've never met who are visible and whose work you admire. If someone has written a book or article you enjoyed or found helpful or was profiled for a particular achievement, let that person know what you think.

Developing Others

Another important way to give back is to help others develop in their jobs and professional lives. As with random acts of kindness, developing others is not always directed at those who have done something nice for you. You can have a positive effect on the professional life of someone who is not an active member of your network and who is not in a position to repay the favor, at least not directly. Most people realize that the accomplishments in their careers can be traced in part to the help of other considerate people. It's that idea of what goes around comes around.

Maybe you landed a job with the assistance of a particularly helpful strategist who gave advice and leads or you reached a high level in your field because of the guidance of a role model. While you can repay these debts directly to the strategists and the role models by thanking them and doing whatever favors they might need, chances are you feel as if you can never repay them fully. Because you have been fortunate, one way to satisfy your need to repay is to give of yourself to help develop the careers of people who are where you once were. It's not a direct gift to the people who helped you get your start or grow, but it's a valid and valued way to give back. As I discussed in Chapter 1, networking isn't made up only of direct give and take between two people. That proverbial straight line between two points might take a few detours and pick up some other people along the way.

Service Organizations That Let You Do Good *and* Network

Kiwanis International (317) 875-8755 or http://www.kiwanis.org

Lions Club (630) 571-5466 or http://www.lionsclubs.org

Optimists International (800) 500-8130 or http://www.optimist.org

Rotary International (847) 866-3000 or http://www.rotary.org

The following are specific ways you can develop others:

- Look for people in your workplace to mentor formally or advise informally.

- Hire an intern or volunteer whom you can teach.

- Take part in a community-based program like Big Brothers/Big Sisters.

- See if your professional association has a mentoring program in which you can take part. Many do.

- Offer shadowing opportunities and grant fact-finding missions to students or others exploring your field.

- Speak at career days or on panels at schools and colleges to inform students about opportunities and career paths in your field.

The "New Career": A More Altruistic Endeavor

In *The Career Is Dead* (San Francisco: Jossey-Bass Publishers, 1996), Douglas Hall writes, "...in the new career, notions of care-giving, mentoring, caring and respect, connection, and colearning (that is, learning through relationship with others), especially colearning with others whom one regards as different, provide clues to growth and success."

Quick Summary

Networking can start to seem like a very self-centered activity, so it's important to remember that other people have needs that you may be able to help with.

It's also important to show your appreciation to people who help you and to do so in appropriate ways.

The following are ways to show your appreciation:

- Thank-you notes and letters

- Thank-you calls

- Gifts

- Random acts of kindness

- Developing others

In addition to thanking and giving back to the immediate people in your network, it is also a good idea to assist others who might not be in a position to help you directly. Developing others by serving as a mentor, hiring an intern, and granting fact-finding missions or strategy sessions perpetuates the concept of "what goes around comes around."

Your Action Plan: The Key to Networking Success

They are able who think they are able.

—*Virgil*

So it's taken thirteen chapters to get to this point—not exactly rushing you into action, am I? That's because I don't advocate taking action until you're really ready to do so. Before you take action, you need to establish career or business goals, learn and practice the best communication techniques, prepare top-notch written materials, organize your contacts, learn how to conduct one-to-one meetings, get comfortable making yourself visible at big gatherings, and master the art of showing appreciation. When you've done all that (or at least most of those things), you're ready to tackle actual networking. Whew!

Every networking encounter is precious because it has the potential to get you one step closer to your goals. If you blow it, you could be one step farther from your goals and you could lose a valuable ally. It would be a shame to have your efforts lead to dead ends only because of some minor problems that could have been avoided. A poorly written resume, sloppy business brochure or Web site, monotone voice, or outdated contact database may be all that's standing between you and successful networking, so it makes sense to take time to prepare thoroughly before entering the fray.

That said, there comes a time when you have to say that enough is enough. "I've prepared, planned, primed, primped, and planted seeds long enough. Now is the time to get on with it." If you're at that point, then this chapter is for you. The following pages will guide you through establishing and executing an action plan—one that not only gets you started but also helps you make networking an ongoing part of your life.

The rationale behind getting your action steps down on paper is that even the best-laid plans of mice and men can go awry—especially if they're just vague ideas floating around in your head. An action plan needs to be specific, doable, measurable, and, most importantly, *on paper* (or in your computer). If you've read this book from cover to cover, you might have occasionally said to yourself, "Oh, that's a useful idea. I'll have to try it." (At least, I hope you've said that!) It's easy, though, for those ideas to be forgotten when it comes time to take action, so the worksheets and checklists on the following pages summarize points made throughout the book to help you keep sight of your objectives.

The other main point of this chapter is to have you create an action plan that is specific. It's not enough to say things like, "Well, my plan is to meet more people," or "I'm going to network more." Goals need to be broken down into concrete objectives, and those objectives should each have specific action steps. As a student, for example, you might choose five activities from the 25 Networking Tips for Students list as priorities for the coming semester. As an entrepreneur, you might have a plan that includes a commitment to making ten calls a day to potential clients and attending one event per week. Whatever your situation, taking action is more likely to pay off if the action is part of a well-thought-out plan that includes clear objectives.

Setting Goals

To plan the actions that will lead to networking success, use the following sections to help you identify the questions that you need to answer.

Define General Goals

In order to define a plan, you need to start with goals. Do you want to

- Make a satisfying career choice?

- Find a job?

- Manage your career more effectively?

- Start or expand a business?

Establish Your Priorities

If you identified more than one goal, which area is your first priority? List it first, followed by the other goals if applicable. Make an actual list like the following one, customizing your goals to fit your situation:

- First priority: *Make a satisfying career choice*

- Second priority: *Find a new job*

- Third priority:

- Fourth priority:

What Makes a Goal Achievable?

It's specific—not vague.

It's based on what you want—not what others want for you.

It's consistent with your values.

It's a dream, not a fantasy. Dreams more easily become reality.

It's measurable—you can track your progress through identifiable milestones.

Defining Objectives

Now it's time to develop your specific objectives, which involves taking the goals you identified in the previous section and breaking them down into specific milestones that you can identify and accomplish. Create a table (on paper or electronically) containing two columns: one column for the overall goals and one for the objectives that lead to and define those goals. For example, someone who has a goal of increased career success might have specific objectives of negotiating a raise within the next six months, improving a relationship with a particular co-worker, and managing time more effectively. That table might look like the following:

Goals	Objectives
Be more successful in my career.	Negotiate a raise within the next six months.
	Improve working relationship with Joe Co-worker.
	Manage time more effectively: Specifically, stop having to work so late; spend more time on priority projects and less on busy work.

Designing an Action Plan

After outlining goals and objectives, your next step is to plan action steps to reach them. Throughout this book, I have suggested many specific things you can do to meet your objectives and reach your career or business goals. To increase the likelihood that you will actually act on some of these suggestions, I've put together the following chart. You'll see that this chart lists many activities that may or may not be relevant to your own needs and goals. To create your action plan, I suggest that you consider the extent to which each of these activities will help you build a stronger network of contacts and be more effective and efficient in your networking efforts. Mark each activity as a high, medium, or low priority or as not applicable (N/A) to your goals and objectives.

Activity	High Priority	Medium Priority	Low Priority	N/A
Assemble or expand a professional portfolio	___	___	___	___
Assess my personality style as related to networking	___	___	___	___
Assess my strengths and skills	___	___	___	___
Attend conferences	___	___	___	___
Be more open to the serendipity factor	___	___	___	___
Be more positive in my attitude toward networking	___	___	___	___
Consult a voice coach	___	___	___	___
Consult an image consultant	___	___	___	___
Contact former teachers, professors, and advisors	___	___	___	___
Contact people I've known through classes or seminars	___	___	___	___
Contact people I haven't spoken with in a long time	___	___	___	___
Develop relationships with executive recruiters	___	___	___	___
Do more research at the library	___	___	___	___
Expand my network	___	___	___	___
Find and use relevant Web sites	___	___	___	___
Find more allied forces	___	___	___	___
Find more role models	___	___	___	___
Find more strategists	___	___	___	___
Find more supporters	___	___	___	___
Find more targets	___	___	___	___

(continued)

(continued)

Activity	High Priority	Medium Priority	Low Priority	N/A
Find out about career and job fairs	___	___	___	___
Find someone to mentor	___	___	___	___
Get a listing of alumni from my school(s)	___	___	___	___
Get more Internet savvy	___	___	___	___
Get more involved in a religious organization	___	___	___	___
Get more involved in associations to which I already belong	___	___	___	___
Get more involved in community and civic activities	___	___	___	___
Get more involved in group sports and recreation	___	___	___	___
Get out more socially	___	___	___	___
Get public speaking training	___	___	___	___
Get to know my neighbors	___	___	___	___
Hire an intern	___	___	___	___
Hold fact-finding missions	___	___	___	___
Hold strategy sessions	___	___	___	___
Improve my speaking voice and style	___	___	___	___
Improve my writing skills	___	___	___	___
Intern at a business or organization in which I am interested	___	___	___	___
Join a gym (or go more often to the one to which I belong)	___	___	___	___
Join a networking group or leads club	___	___	___	___
Join Internet newsgroups	___	___	___	___

Activity	High Priority	Medium Priority	Low Priority	N/A
Join professional or trade associations	____	____	____	____
Keep in touch with my network more regularly	____	____	____	____
Look for potential contacts in magazines, newspapers, and books	____	____	____	____
Look up distant or "forgotten" relatives	____	____	____	____
Look up former bosses, co-workers, and clients	____	____	____	____
Make more friends	____	____	____	____
Make my thank-you and follow-up notes more powerful	____	____	____	____
Make myself known to more recruiters	____	____	____	____
Meet with a business strategy advisor	____	____	____	____
Meet with a career counselor	____	____	____	____
Meet with an executive coach	____	____	____	____
Obtain and read books listed in the bibliography of this book	____	____	____	____
Offer a shadowing opportunity to someone	____	____	____	____
Order business cards	____	____	____	____
Perform more random acts of kindness	____	____	____	____
Polish my image (wardrobe, appearance, etc.)	____	____	____	____
Prepare or revise my bio	____	____	____	____
Prepare or revise my business promotional materials	____	____	____	____
Prepare or revise my resume	____	____	____	____

(continued)

(continued)

Activity	High Priority	Medium Priority	Low Priority	N/A
Reorganize or update an existing contact database	——	——	——	——
Set up a contacts database	——	——	——	——
Set up more breakfast, lunch, or dinner meetings	——	——	——	——
Shadow someone in a career that interests me	——	——	——	——
Sign up with an employment/staffing agency	——	——	——	——
Take a continuing education/training course	——	——	——	——
Take an inventory of my network STARS	——	——	——	——
Try new methods of dealing with difficult people	——	——	——	——
Try new methods of dealing with difficult situations	——	——	——	——
Work on my interpersonal skills	——	——	——	——
Write overdue thank-you notes (or make calls or send gifts)	——	——	——	——

Do First Things First

Now look back over the chart and find the items that you identified as high priority. Choose the four most pressing activities and list them here:

1. _____

2. _____

3. _____

4. _____

When Is First?

Don't write the answer to this question here! Go to your appointment book, calendar, electronic planner, or other time management system and schedule specific times (or at least indicate blocks of time or particular days) when you'll get to work on these top-priority tasks.

Identify the Secondary Action Steps

Which activities will you get to after the first four are under way? (Review your remaining high-priority items from the objectives worksheet or go to the medium-priority ones if necessary.) It's okay if you don't identify a large number of additional tasks, but you do need to make sure that you have a number of to-do items in the pipeline to help you reach your goals. Don't focus solely on the top-tier action items.

Turn to your appointment book or other time management system again and schedule these secondary-priority tasks. If you can't give something a specific day or time slot, at least indicate the week (or even month) you'll take care of it.

Make a Back-Burner List

Make a list of any remaining activities that don't have to be done any time soon. Keep the list handy to refer to whenever your schedule lightens up and you can get to the back-burner projects. Whether your schedule loosens up or not, check the list periodically (maybe once or twice a month) to see if you can move anything off the list and onto your calendar.

Finding the Time to Network

You've now read about ways to keep track of who you know, what you know, and what you've done, and I wouldn't be surprised if you're saying, "Nice systems, but I want to know *how I am going to get it all done!*"

That's a normal concern because there *is* a lot to do in networking. It requires not only time spent meeting with people and attending events, but also lots of preparation and follow-through. All of these activities can be quite time-consuming. This can be especially difficult if you work full-time or have other significant demands on your time.

One of the best ways to solve this time dilemma between adequate networking and an already full life is to realize that you don't have to get it *all* done. You just have to do the things that are important to you, are critical for your job security or success, and will help you reach your goals.

So, how do you do even just those things? Well, like filing systems, the overall issue of dealing with time is a *biiiiiggg* topic best left to the time management books recommended in Appendix D and the experts found in Appendix C. That said, though, there are a few simple things you can do to start being more productive. In the following sections are some suggestions that you can use to make sure that you network as efficiently and effectively as possible.

Use a Frequency-of-Contact System

It's easy to fall into the trap of calling or having lunch with the same people over and over, but what about all those other names buried deep in your contact management system? Are there people you've forgotten about whom you ought to get in touch with? To make sure that you're not forgetting anyone important and to ensure that you spend the right amount of time with the right people, it is helpful to use a system of prioritizing that I call the frequency-of-contact system.

This system involves sorting your contacts into four basic categories—frequent, moderate, occasional, and periodic—based on how often you need to be in touch with them. Exactly how you define each of these terms will vary according to the nature of your work and the size of your network. If you're in public relations, for example, frequent contact might mean checking in with a particular media source or client every other day. If you're a student, frequent could mean once a semester.

Frequent contacts are those people you should speak to regularly (for you that might mean every day, once a week, or twice a month) because they are an active part of your professional life as strategists, targets, referral sources, resources, or perhaps just friends you enjoy speaking with. *Moderate* and *occasional* contacts are, of course, those people you need to stay in touch with a little less often than those in the frequent category. The *periodic* category includes those people you have no reason to communicate with regularly, but don't want to forget about or be forgotten by. They might be on a mailing list you keep so that you can update them periodically (every six months, once a year, or even less frequently) about events or happenings in your professional life or your business.

If you have your contacts in a database or spreadsheet, consider adding a field for the four categories and label each person as either frequent, moderate, occasional, or periodic. Then you can easily sort people according to their priority. For example, say you designate the first Thursday of every month as your "occasional follow-up day." (Fridays, by the way, are often a difficult day to reach people since it's the day of the week they're most likely to take off. Mondays aren't so hot either since people are likely to be extra busy then or just kind of grouchy.) When one of those Thursdays arrives, you simply type "occasional" into the appropriate search field of your database, click "find" or "search" (depending on how your system works), and get a list of the people you need to call, write, or e-mail that day. If you're using an index card method of keeping your contacts, simply arrange them in the card box by dividers labeled with each of the four categories or keep a separate list of the people in each category.

Establish a To-Be-Contacted System

The frequency-of-contact system described in the preceding section is primarily useful for long-range networking in that it enables you to keep track of people over time. There are times, though, when you need to get in touch with someone within the next week or so, regardless of whether that person is a frequent, moderate, occasional, or periodic contact. Say you're talking on the phone to someone we'll call Tim to request some information and Tim suggests that you contact Brad, a mutual acquaintance, to get the information you need. You agree to do so but know that you won't have time to call Brad in the next few days, and it's not really an urgent matter anyway. In that case, you just need some way to make a note to yourself to give Brad a call sometime in the near future. That's where the to-be-contacted system comes in.

If you keep your contact list in a computer database and/or your PDA, you may already have a feature that links contacts to your calendar, alerting you of people to call or write on certain days. If so, you already have a built-in to-be-contacted system. If not, you can easily develop your own. One way is simply to keep a running list of people to contact. Start with a sheet of paper on a clipboard and make three columns labeled "To Call," "To Write," and "To E-mail." It's a primitive system in this high-tech age, but it works, and it doesn't require that you turn on your computer to see it. Then, at the start of each day, pull some names off the list and write them on the daily to-do pages of your appointment book or on your task list in a computer program like Microsoft Outlook. That way, they don't just languish on a list; you actually get ahold of them because they're scheduled on the calendar. Of course, you can often just put a name directly in your appointment book if you need to contact the person in the next day or so—no need to put it on the list first. The list is most useful for people you don't need to contact right away, but should contact in the near future. If they're on the to-be-contacted list, you're less likely to forget about them.

Keep a Research-To-Do List

As you go about your daily routine, you might think of information you need on a particular topic or hear of a book or Web site you want to look up. It's easy to forget about these things if they're not written down. Invariably you'll be online sending e-mail or visiting a site and then sign off, only to find that you forgot to look up that neat Web site you read about in a magazine the day before. Or you find yourself stopping in a bookstore to pass some time between appointments and can't remember what book it was that you'd been wanting to get. To keep this from happening, start a research-to-do list.

Stay Alert

A great way to stay on top of new books that would interest you is through a convenient service at Amazon.com, the online bookstore at http://www.amazon.com. You can register with their Amazon Alerts service and indicate topics that are of interest to you. Amazon.com will send you an e-mail every time a new book is released on those topics. You can then go to the site and order it or make a note of it on your research-to-do list for future purchase or perusal.

You can use the paper-on-a-clipboard method, or you might want to use a page in an appointment book so you have the list with you while you're out. Divide the page into categories such as "Online" for Web sites to look up next time you're online, "Books" for books to skim through or buy next time you're in a bookstore, and "Info needed" for miscellaneous topics you need to find out about. Those are only examples; use whichever headings make sense for your needs. However you do it, keeping a list like this handy can make it much easier to keep on top of information that can enrich your professional life. This system also puts you one step closer to being the information clearinghouse that makes you valuable to members of your network.

Schedule Daily, Weekly, and Monthly Tasks

Scheduling things in your appointment book is a very simple but enormously powerful action. We tend to schedule things like meetings, classes, project deadlines, and social dates, as well as significant days like birthdays or anniversaries. What we don't often schedule are things like the day each month that you check in with your occasional contacts, the days or week each year that you take a "working vacation" at your job or in your business to concentrate on reorganizing your office and work life in general, or the time of day on certain days of the week that you make calls to the frequent contacts listed in your contact database.

Again, those are only examples. Think about the things you need to be doing to make networking an integral part of your life and block out time for them. If you don't think that you have the time, think again. Do you really not have the time, or are you just not placing priority on these tasks so you're not finding the time? Time is a stand-alone entity. It's there no matter what. We're all allotted the same amount of time every day, every month, and every year. What you decide to do with your time makes the difference.

Maximize the Return on Your Efforts

Have you ever had a day go by when you felt as if you had done a lot, but you had nothing to show for it? Sometimes you get this feeling about not just a day but a month or even a whole year that seemed busy but unproductive. This feeling often results from doing too many things that don't get you any closer to where you want to be. As you learned in Chapter 2, setting clear goals and breaking them down into manageable objectives, or steps, is essential for making career decisions, finding jobs, managing your career, or developing a business.

From a time management perspective, defining your goals and objectives is the key to answering such questions as "What should I do next today?" "Should I call this person or that one?" "Should I go to that meeting next week?" "Should I head my business in this direction or that one this year?" "Should I take this promotion at work or look for a new job elsewhere?" If you've defined what you want out of life in general and then set some specific goals for the coming months and years, you can answer these questions more easily. So, in addition to the more specific, tangible time management systems recommended on previous pages, also keep in mind that one of the best ways to be a time-wise networker is simply to keep your goals in the forefront of your mind.

Keeping the End in Sight

"Each part of your life—today's behavior, tomorrow's behavior, next week's behavior, next month's behavior—can be examined in the context of the whole, of what really matters most to you. By keeping that end clearly in mind, you can make certain that whatever you do on any particular day does not violate criteria you have defined as supremely important, and that each day of your life contributes in a meaningful way to the vision you have of your life as a whole."

Source: *The Seven Habits of Highly Effective People* by Stephen Covey (Simon & Schuster, 1990).

Quick Summary

To help you find the time to network, five systems and practices were suggested:

- **Frequency-of-contact system.** Classifying the priority of people in your network as frequent, moderate, occasional, or periodic helps you keep track of how often you should be in touch with people.

- **To-be-contacted system.** To keep from losing track of people you need to get in touch with, use a to-be-contacted system. This is either a running list of people or a system in your computer that alerts you to which people you need to contact on which days.

- **Research-to-do list.** To keep you from losing track of information you need to obtain, this list enables you to list all the research you plan to do in one place.

- **Schedule tasks.** This tip discussed the importance of scheduling specific times or blocks of time when you will get things done rather than just keeping a list of things to do.

- **Keep your goals in sight.** A final suggestion for making effective use of time was to keep your goals in sight at all times. Remembering the goals and objectives you established in Chapter 2 helps you make decisions about how to spend your time day to day or minute to minute.

Final Tips for Lifelong Networking Success

What we call the beginning is often the end. And to make an end is to make a beginning. The end is where we start from.

—T. S. ELIOT, "FOUR QUARTETS"

Chapter 1 began with examples of ways that networking is a natural, normal part of everyday life. As we wrap up this journey through networking, I'd like you to remember that important fact. Networking, ideally, should not be something you do only when you need a job, have a critical decision to make, reach a snag in your career, or are trying to get a business off the ground. Networking needs to be incorporated into your daily life as a regular activity—in fact, not even as an activity, but rather as a way of life.

Making Networking an Ongoing Part of Your Life

I know that it can seem easier said than done to think of networking as something that you do all the time. I am well aware of the realities that get in the way. You might have periods in your life when you're so busy at work that you can't imagine finding the time to get out to professional association meetings or set up networking lunches. There might be other times when your personal life is very much on the front burner and professional networking has to take a backseat. And there are those of you—such as the introverts among us—who can get burned out by too much networking and have to take breaks from it from time to time.

These are all valid reasons to scale back on networking at various times in life. All I ask, though, is that you don't let it sit on the back burner for too long. Making a little effort on a regular basis to build and nurture relationships and to keep yourself "in the know" will save you a lot of effort when it comes time to make a career or business move. In the following sections, I answer some questions that typically come up as people make this ongoing effort to have networking be a lifelong pursuit.

How Much Follow-Through with Contacts Is Too Much, and How Much Is Not Enough?

As a general rule, you need to keep in touch with your contacts more than you probably think you need to. People have surprisingly short memories, especially when they're busy—and who isn't busy? There have been many times when I have had aspiring career counselors hold a fact-finding mission with me to learn about the profession, inquire about possible internships, or ask about available jobs in career counseling. I may listen to them with rapt attention, be very impressed, and even receive a thank-you note a few days later. But what happens a couple months later when I hear about a job or internship opportunity in my field? I might not be able to think of anyone who fits the bill. Is this because the person who met with me wasn't a good candidate? No, it's more likely that I just don't remember that person. If people are out of sight, they're likely to be out of mind as well. So, whether you want people to keep you in mind for jobs, referrals, or other business, it is crucial to stay in touch so that your contacts will think of you when such opportunities arise.

That said, you might worry that you'll become a pest if you keep in touch too much. If done with courtesy and purpose, keeping in touch with contacts is typically not bothersome to them. It is possible, though, to become a pest if you push too hard. Stay alert to subtle (or not-so-subtle!) cues that someone really doesn't want you to be part of their active network. Their reasons often have nothing to do with you as a person—your contact just might not feel that the two of you share enough in common to make it worthwhile to stay in touch.

A colleague of mine, for example, once complained to me that she had been receiving calls once a month (like clockwork) from someone she had met about a year prior at a conference. She had had lunch with this person a couple of times after the conference. The two of them were in totally different businesses, which ordinarily would be great because knowing people in other arenas can expand your own network significantly. In this case, however, it was clear to her that the chances of them being useful to each other were fairly remote. My friend wouldn't have minded keeping up with this person through an occasional phone call, mailings about her business, or even lunch from time to time. But she was so turned off by the frequency with which the person kept calling to ask that they get together for lunch that she no longer wanted to deal with her at all. My friend got the feeling that this persistent networker had a list of people to call once a month and that she was just a name to be checked off that list.

Remember that professional relationships are like any other relationship you may have. You have to establish a basis of mutual respect, understanding, and shared interests and needs before moving to a level at which you spend time with each other regularly. Some busy people have trouble finding the time to have lunch with even their closest friends regularly, so they aren't much interested in devoting one precious lunch a month, every month, to a distant professional acquaintance.

So, when determining how much to follow up with a newly established contact or how often to stay in touch with an existing one, use some common sense. Make sure that you establish a solid, mutually beneficial relationship before expecting to occupy too much of someone's time. On the other hand, though, don't go to the opposite extreme and let people forget that you exist. As you saw in the example of my forgetting about people I've met briefly in fact-finding missions, it is important to stay fresh in people's minds. An occasional phone call, note, or e-mail may be all it takes to do so.

Closing the Loop

In addition to routine, ongoing follow-up with your network, be sure to loop back with people who helped you during an intense period of networking, such as when you were looking for a job or attempting to start a business. When you do land that job or get your business off the ground, be sure to send a letter or e-mail to everyone—I mean everyone—who helped you during that time to let them know how things have worked out for you. Not only is this a considerate thing to do, it will help you keep building those relationships in case you need to call upon them again in the future. And it reminds them that you wish to be of service to them whenever they might need something.

As I Know People in My Network in More Depth, Won't I Cross the Boundary Between a Professional Relationship and a Personal Friendship?

Not necessarily. Most people find that they can develop long-term professional relationships without crossing over into the realm of personal relationships. If you're an active networker with a busy career, you might sometimes feel that you spend more time with certain professional colleagues than with your own family or close friends, but that doesn't mean your professional relationships have become personal ones. It is really a question of type of contact rather than frequency or duration.

You don't have to invite these professional acquaintances to your son's bar mitzvah, your sister's wedding, or dinner every Friday night. A sort of unspoken code of behavior in the professional world is that people can become very close to each other in their work lives while respecting the privacy of each other's personal lives.

This doesn't mean that you can't inquire about the general well-being of the other person's family or talk about how much fun your latest vacation was. It's common courtesy to show an interest in professional colleagues' personal lives after you get to know them well. It is also normal to want to talk about events in your own life, especially significant ones like a marriage, the birth of a child, or purchasing a home. Strong professional relationships are friendships of a sort.

Remember, we're all human beings, and just because we're interacting in a professional arena doesn't mean that we lose our humanity.

Occasionally, a professional relationship does cross over the line and becomes a true personal friendship. There's nothing wrong with that if the feelings are mutual. Just be careful not to push it. Simply having lunch with someone you seem to click with on Wednesday doesn't mean she wants to double-date with you and your significant other on Friday.

Managing Cross-Cultural Networking Relationships

There are major cultural differences around the world regarding the issue of how personal you can get in business interactions. In some cultures, for example, it is considered extremely rude to ask a businessman about his wife, while in others it's impolite *not* to inquire about someone's family. Some of the books listed in the "Books for Cross-Cultural Networking" section of Appendix D can help you learn what's appropriate where.

How Can I Keep Expanding My Network of Contacts?

It is important to keep your network growing. Doing so ensures that you'll never get that uncomfortable feeling of "overusing" your contacts. You want to have enough people to turn to for advice, leads, or support that you don't have to worry about relying too heavily on any one person. Expanding your circle also infuses your network with fresh ideas, strategies, and insights, and it brings new adventures to keep you interested and motivated, making it more likely that networking will remain an ongoing part of your life. The following are some ways to expand your contacts:

- **Identify some new STARS.** Review the description of the STARS categories in Chapter 4 and think about where your network is lacking. Could you use more strategists to help with new issues that have arisen in your career? Are you worried that you're becoming a burden on the people who have been providing emotional support? Maybe you could use some professional help from the allied forces category. Should you reach out to more friends who could be in the supporter role? Be sure that the people in your network are well distributed across the STARS categories.

- **Go back to the basic sources of contacts.** To make sure you're covering all bases, have a look at Chapter 4 again to be certain you've cultivated contacts from all possible sources—personal, work-related, educational, professional groups, and multimedia. Which sources remain untapped? Go after them.

- **Rediscover your interests.** Make sure you've thought of all your personal and professional interests and the activities or groups that those could lead you to. When you first begin networking, it's tempting to say, "Sure, I have an interest in x, but I don't have time now to attend lectures on it. I need to do the kind of networking that has more immediate benefits." After you've been networking a while, though, those more remote activities might be just the thing you need to revive and expand your network.

- **Get more involved.** Among those professional associations or networking groups to which you already belong, take an honest look at how involved you've been. A common trap is to say, "I belonged to three professional groups this year, and they haven't done anything for me." Well, have you attended meetings regularly? Did you go to any national or regional conferences? Did you volunteer for a committee or some other leadership role? Just reading the monthly newsletter and listing the affiliation on your resume won't necessarily get your phone ringing with offers, leads, and ideas.

How Do I Keep a Positive Attitude Toward Networking?

As you saw in Chapter 10 and elsewhere throughout this book, networking inevitably brings some challenges. People who are difficult to deal with, situations that you may not have handled so well, and goals that seem unattainable can easily foster a negative attitude. To keep a positive outlook on networking, some advice I have offered before bears repeating here. That is to use positive reinforcements. Each time you make positive strides toward your networking goals, take the time to reflect on your accomplishments. It's easy to get caught up in the process and not stop to see how far you've come. Give yourself a pat on the back and maybe even a reward of some sort.

What Can I Do When Networking Seems Too Overwhelming?

Take a break occasionally. Just as you need to reward yourself from time to time, it can also be helpful and rejuvenating to take an occasional break from your networking efforts. If you're doing intense networking (particularly networking associated with a job search or launching a business), the process can become quite wearing. Although you might not have the luxury of sparing days or weeks from your networking efforts, try to take at least a brief break, whether that's a day off here and there or just part of a day. Doing so can bring new vitality to your search or business development.

If your networking is a more gradual, ongoing process—perhaps as part of managing your career or maintaining an existing business—your break can probably be a little longer. If you're a freelancer or consultant, for example, you might feel that you spend all your time looking for the next assignment or project. It's easy to get burned out in that process, so consider taking cyclical breaks.

Every business has cycles dictated by various factors. There might, for example, be times of the year when the professional associations or individuals you typically deal with are less active. This often occurs during the summer, but your own slow time might be some other part of the year. Whenever it occurs, avoid being so in the habit of networking that you forget you can take a time-out. Every business owner, consultant, or freelancer (as well as those who are not self-employed) needs a break occasionally—that time of year when a person can fall out of touch with people, maybe for a few weeks or a month or two. These breaks are an excellent time to focus on your actual work, such as improving your products or services, or reorganize your office or business procedures.

Some Final Tips

I've covered a lot of ground in this book, so I now want to highlight for you what I consider to be the most salient points from among all these pages. My intention is for these final tips to serve as a quick, handy reference to guide your actions, both now and in the future.

20 Common Networking Mistakes to Avoid

As you execute your networking plan, make sure to avoid the following common pitfalls:

1. Networking nonstrategically—that is, haphazardly and without clearly defined objectives and a self-marketing plan.

2. Losing sight of your ultimate goals.

3. Not doing adequate preparation (e.g., research, scripting a self-marketing sound bite, planning agendas for networking meetings, etc.).

4. Having a hidden agenda—not being up-front and honest with others (e.g., claiming you're not there to ask for a job but just to do some fact finding and then asking for a job outright).

5. Being too clingy, needy, or pessimistic. Nobody likes a whiner!

6. Expecting too much of others. Ultimately, only you can help yourself.

7. Being impatient. Results will come when you least expect them.

8. Mixing business and pleasure too overtly.

9. Being insensitive to cultural differences.

10. Not following through when you're given leads.

11. Contacting people only when you need something.

12. Not showing your appreciation in a timely and appropriate manner.

13. Being passive.

14. Going for quantity over quality in your relationships.

15. Having poor-quality self-marketing materials (resumes, letters, promotional literature, etc.).

16. Trying to do too much and getting spread too thin.

17. Being hesitant to contact people you haven't spoken to in a long time. It's never too late!

18. Having poor oral or written communication skills.

19. Trying to network in a way that doesn't fit your personality style.

20. Not doing enough of it!

20 Quick Tips for Successful Networking

Now that you have seen what *not* to do, the following list tells you what you should do:

1. Always be specific about what you need.

2. Know your strengths and achievements.

3. Network even when you think you don't need to.

4. Don't wait for people to come to you. Be proactive. Get visible!

5. Be more persistent than you think you need to be.

6. Don't internalize rejection.

7. Don't speak negatively about anyone or any organization or company.

8. Be friendly and down-to-earth.

9. Be helpful to others even if there's no obvious direct benefit to you.

10. Stay in touch with people regularly.

11. Never leave home without business cards (or resumes).

12. Occasionally call people just to say hello.

13. Get known as an "information clearinghouse"—a valuable resource for others.

14. Sit next to strangers at events rather than alone or only with people you already know.

15. Focus on names when you meet people.

16. Learn and follow basic rules of business and social etiquette.

17. Don't be afraid to ask others for help.

18. Keep your goals in sight.

19. Take a break occasionally—don't get overexposed or burned out.

20. Keep a positive attitude.

Keeping It All in Perspective

Having made it this far in *Networking for Job Search and Career Success*, you may feel relieved that you've already been doing most of what this book recommends—or you may be overwhelmed at all the things you *should* be doing. Well, if you're relieved that you're on the right track, keep up the good work.

If you're like many people, however, you worry that you're not doing enough networking and can't imagine how you'll ever catch up. Don't despair. Keep it all in perspective. You don't have to become a manic networker, following every single suggestion in this book to the letter. Even though networking is essential for professional success and security, there is something to be said for simply doing your job and doing it well. As long as you supplement that good work with at least some of the strategies recommended here and don't become complacent, you'll do just fine.

Make a Date to Rejuvenate

Don't forget the suggestion in Chapter 2 to get out your appointment book or online calendar and schedule a specific date about six months from now to pick this book back up and read it again—or at least skim through the relevant parts for you. Didn't do that back in Chapter 2? Please do it now! Why? You might get all cozy in your new job or business and forget about what you should be doing in the way of long-term networking. Or you might not yet be settled at that point—you may still be working toward your goals— and you might start to feel a little burned out from networking and stumped for creative ways to jump-start your networking efforts. Making a date to pull this book off the shelf could be just the catalyst you need to rejuvenate your networking. And, hey, if nothing else, it'll remind you to get the book back from the person you loaned it to!

Networking should not be a chore. Yes, it takes effort, persistence, and a positive attitude in the face of occasional rejection and frustration, but it should also be fun and rewarding. If you lay a solid foundation for your networking efforts using the preparation and strategy techniques offered throughout this book, you've done the hard part. Networking at that point should be integrated into your daily life in a way that makes it an almost routine, effortless activity rather than a burden.

Keeping your expectations realistic also helps keep networking from becoming a chore. Don't expect miracles overnight. Networking is a learned skill that takes time to master. I'm still working on it myself! Even when you do feel you've mastered it, patience is still necessary. Relationships need time to develop, and it can sometimes take weeks, months, or even years for results to come from seeds you plant.

So keep your goals clearly in sight and be persistent, positive, and patient. If you do that, and if you invite other people along on the journey with you, you'll be on the short road to your dreams. Now, go off and take that first step toward achieving all that you desire. You can do it! As an old Saudi Arabian proverb says:

> *If the camel once gets his nose in a tent, his body will soon follow.*

The No Excuses List: You *Can* Track Down Anyone in Any Field

Say you need to contact someone who does a particular type of work or is in a certain industry or line of business, but you don't know anyone who fits the bill. You're out of luck, right? Wrong. You are probably connected to more people than you think. The following table covers more than 100 career fields, industries, and interest areas with examples of the types of people who might know someone in different fields. This list will help you brainstorm people you might approach to link you to contacts in a given field. When you get the hang of how this works, you can add your own ideas to this list and tailor it to your specific interests.

If you need contacts in...	Track them down through...
Accounting	Auditors, bookkeepers, insurance agents, tax attorneys, estate planners, personal financial planners, stockbrokers, mortgage brokers, corporate finance executives, management consultants
Acting	Agents, talent scouts, directors, producers, publicists, singers, musicians, theater workers, voice coaches, advertising professionals

If you need contacts in...	Track them down through...
Actuarial Science	Accountants, auditors, insurance agents, tax attorneys, estate planners, personal financial planners, stockbrokers, mortgage brokers, corporate finance executives, computer programmers, mathematicians, statisticians, bankers, insurance underwriters, management consultants, risk management experts
Advertising	Public relations specialists, corporate communications departments, freelance writers and artists, graphic designers, media executives, photographers, market researchers, corporate marketing executives, fashion stylists, magazine personnel, songwriters
Aerospace	Engineers, biologists, chemists, physicists, other scientists, government officials, astronauts, computer technicians
Animal-Related Fields	Veterinarians, veterinarian's aides, breeders, trainers, blacksmiths, kennels, show judges, groomers, pet sitters, zookeepers, zoologists, farmers
Animation	Computer programmers, software designers, producers, voice-over specialists, artists, graphic designers, actors
Anthropology	Archaeologists, geologists, environmental scientists, linguists, translators, writers, editors, sociologists, urban planners, museum curators and administrators, demographers, professors, graduate students
Antiques and Collectibles	Interior decorators/designers, art historians, historic preservationists, auction house employees, furniture restorers, lighting designers and restorers, art dealers, rare book/manuscript experts, coin and stamp dealers, upholsterers
Archaeology	Anthropologists, geographers, geologists, architects, environmental scientists, linguists, translators, writers,

editors, social scientists, urban planners, museum curators and administrators, classicists, theologians, chemists, historians, historic preservationists, graduate students, professors

Architecture   Engineers, draftsmen, interior designers, interior decorators, space planners, historic preservationists, construction workers, contractors, real estate agents, developers, landscape architects, landscapers and lawn maintenance workers, painters, wallpaper hangers, lighting designers, handymen/women, urban planners, landlords, property managers

Art Dealing and Consulting   Fine artists, photographers, gallery owners, museum curators and administrators, art critics, art historians, corporate purchasing, facilities management departments, interior decorators and designers, architects, event planners, set designers, art appraisers

Arts Administration   Performing artists, fine artists, photographers, fundraising consultants, producers, other nonprofit organizations

Auditing   Accountants, insurance agents, tax attorneys, estate planners, personal financial planners, stockbrokers, mortgage brokers, corporate finance executives, bookkeepers, state and federal government officials, management consultants

Aviation   Pilots, air traffic controllers, FAA officials, flight attendants, military personnel

Benefits   Human resources personnel, compensation analysts, benefits and pension consultants, actuaries

Bioethics   Hospital and HMO administrators, physicians, lawyers, social workers, genetic counselors, nurses

Biology   Chemists, environmental scientists, ecologists, research and development (R and D) departments in manufacturing companies, statisticians, professors

If you need contacts in...	Track them down through...
Biotechnology	Patent attorneys, biologists, medical professionals, professors, laboratory scientists, corporate R and D departments, biotech firms
Buying	Inventory control workers, manufacturers reps, market researchers, retail salespeople and managers, anyone who works in department stores, purchasing departments, facilities managers, operations departments, office administrators, fashion designers
Career Counseling	Psychologists, psychotherapists, educational consultants, outplacement specialists, school guidance counselors, executive search recruiters, employment agencies, resume writers, job search coaches, executive coaches, corporate trainers, human resources personnel
Carpentry	Architects, construction managers, interior designers and decorators, plumbers, electricians, historic preservationists, contractors, real estate developers, property managers, real estate agents, landlords
Catering	Restaurateurs, waiters, food service suppliers, gourmet market personnel, event planners, chefs, cooks
Commercial Art	Graphic designers, advertising executives, industrial designers, product and package designers, curators, art professors, agents
Culinary Arts	Restaurant owners, managers, staff, sommeliers; food service suppliers; caterers; hotel, resort, club, and corporate dining service managers
Chemistry	Professors, other scientists, engineers, pharmaceutical personnel, lab technicians, physicians
Child Care	Teachers, social workers, child psychologists, nurses, pediatricians, dietitians, nannies, child care agencies

Civil Engineering	Architects, computer specialists, technicians and technologists, electricians, government officials, contractors, construction workers, electrical engineers, urban planners
Comedy	Agents, club managers and personnel, producers, publicists, writers, cartoonists, actors
Commercial Banking	Accountants, attorneys, auditors, loan officers
Commodities Brokerage	Financial analysts, stockbrokers, personal financial planners, investment bankers, agriculture specialists
Communications	Writers, graphic designers and artists, desktop publishers, printers, public relations, marketing, advertising personnel
Computer Programming	Computer engineers, systems analysts, compute operators, software developers, telecommunications specialists, computer salespeople, computer consultants
Contracting and Construction	Architects, carpenters, construction workers, suppliers, real estate developers, interior designers, electricians
Corporate Finance	Investment bankers, corporate attorneys, financial analysts, accountants, business school faculty, other corporate executives
Court Reporting	Attorneys, judges, transcribers, translators, court clerks, paralegals
Criminology	Lawyers, federal agents, law enforcement officials, pathologists, sociologists, professors
Curators	Art historians, archaeologists, anthropologists, historic preservationists, art galleries, art dealers, antique dealers, professors, librarians, historical societies
Dentistry	Dental lab technicians, oral surgeons, orthodontists, physicians, medical supply salespeople, hygienists, dental assistants

If you need contacts in...	Track them down through...
Directing (Film, TV, Theater)	Actors, agents, editors, producers, photographers, cinematographers, production assistants, script readers
Ecology	Biologists, environmentalists, scientists, waste management experts, botanists, horticulturists, urban and regional planners
Economics	Bankers, policy analysts, statisticians, professors, government officials
Editing (Books)	Literary agents, writers, reviewers, printers, publicists, proofreaders
Editing (Film)	Producers, actors, production assistants, technicians, cinematographers, photographers
Editing (Journals)	Literary agents, writers, reviewers, printers, publicists, proofreaders, professors, professional association personnel
Editing (Magazines)	Literary agents, writers, reviewers, printers, publicists, proofreaders
Educational Advising	Admissions reps, financial aid officers, independent educational consultants, guidance counselors, teachers, psychologists, career counselors (school and colleges)
Electrical Engineering	Computer programmers, technicians and technologists, electricians, architects, other engineers
Electricians	Construction workers, plumbers, carpenters, property managers, landlords, telecommunication specialists
Employee Assistance	EAP counselors and managers in hospitals and large corporations, substance abuse counselors, social workers, psychologists, physicians
Environmental Science	Biologists, ecologists, scientists, waste management experts, botanists, horticulturists, lobbyists, energy conservation specialists, soil scientists, oceanographers

Event Planning	Conference and meeting planners, party planners, restaurant and hotel banquet managers, caterers, travel agents, hotel employees, airline ticket agents, public relations and promotions executives, invitation and party favor designers and printers, calligraphers, tour guides
Fashion Design	Textile designers and manufacturers, buyers, advertising executives, production managers, models, photographers, retail managers and salespeople, milliners, tailors
Fine Arts	Art dealers, agents, gallery owners and employees, museum curators, photographers, professors, publishers, editors, art supply store managers and salespeople
Firefighting	Paramedics, police officers, safety inspectors, government officials, arson investigators
Floral Design	Florists, horticulturists, botanists, artists, photo stylists, photographers, interior decorators
Food and Wine	Sommeliers, restaurant owners and managers and staff, chefs and cooks, vintners, cookbook writers and editors, food service suppliers, wine importers, people who eat out a lot, food and wine magazine editors and writers, pastry chefs, bakers, bartenders, food stylists for photo shoots, cooking equipment reps, menu designers and consultants
Foreign Service	Policy analysts in government agencies and think tanks, government officials, politicians, tourism boards, translators, political scientists, economists, international affairs professors, people in international business
Forestry	Park rangers, tourism board members, fish and wildlife officials, fishing guides, botanists, horticulturists, environmental planners, paper industry executives, soil scientists

If you need contacts in...	Track them down through...
Fundraising and Development	Nonprofit organization personnel; school, college, and university administrators; foundation executives; event planners; corporate giving department executives; estate planners
Genetics	Medical research centers, people who work at clinics or hospitals, neuroscientists, oncologists, obstetricians, midwives, social workers
Geology	Geophysicists, land developers, petroleum engineers, surveyors, professors
Gerontology	Attorneys specializing in elder law, managers of residential retirement communities, physicians, nurses, social workers, estate planners
Graphic Design	Advertising executives, artists, market researchers, product managers
Guidance Counseling	Teachers, professors, university administrators, career counselors, students, independent educational consultants
Health Care Administration	Insurance agents, physicians, nurses, medical personnel
Holistic Health	Acupuncturists, yoga instructors, herbalists, nutritionists, movement specialists, fitness trainers, psychotherapists, midwives, natural food purveyors, macrobiotic chefs, massage therapists, naturopathic physicians, art therapists
Hotel Management	Event and meeting planners, party planners, food service workers, food service suppliers, travel agents, housekeepers
Human Resources	Anyone in a large corporation or nonprofit organization, employment agencies, executive search firms, management consultants, training consultants

Import-Export	Customs brokers, art dealers, antique dealers, lawyers, manufacturers, shippers, couriers
Industrial and Organizational Psychology	Human resources personnel, training consultants or in-house corporate trainers, management consultants, productivity experts, clinical psychologists, business school faculty
Information Systems	Computer engineers, computer programmers, systems analysts, financial analysts, production managers, librarians, researchers, telecommunications specialists, database managers, employee records administrators, security consultants
Insurance	Actuaries, attorneys, bankers, policyholders, employee benefits specialists, pension fund reps, underwriters
Interior Decoration and Design	Architects, carpenters, contractors, decorative arts suppliers, antique dealers, design magazine editors and writers, art historians, museum curators, historic preservationists, furniture manufacturer's reps, fabric and textile manufacturers and salespeople, homeowners
International Affairs	Translators, diplomats, ambassadors, people in international business, reporters, editors, government officials, linguists, political scientists, economists, nonprofit organization staff
Investment Banking	Commercial bankers, accountants, researchers, stockbrokers, attorneys, real estate developers
Jewelry Design	Jewelry store personnel, jewelry appraisers, gemologists, artists
Journalism	Editors, reporters, photographers, publishers, researchers, media specialists, broadcasters, publicists
Labor Relations	Attorneys, human resources personnel, mediators, conflict resolution specialists, social workers, union reps, arbitrators

If you need contacts in...	Track them down through...
Law	Paralegals, legal secretaries, accountants, other attorneys, bankers, judges, law professors. Depending on the specialty area within law, might also be tracked down by social workers, investment bankers, commercial bankers, realtors, corporate executives, medical professionals, etc.
Law Enforcement	Criminologists, lawyers, federal agents, paramedics, chemists, pathologists, private investigators
Lobbying	Politicians, political aides, political campaign workers, corporate government relations or public affairs reps, corporate human resources personnel, nonprofit organizations, union reps
Literary Agencies	Producers, directors, publishers, editors, writers, lawyers, market researchers
Management Consulting	Business people, including strategic planners, managers, financial analysts, scientists, economists, accountants, organizational development specialists, industrial and organizational psychologists, training and development consultants and specialists
Market Research	Marketing executives, advertising executives, statisticians, computer programmers, communications experts, public relations executives, demographers
Marketing	Advertising executives, market researchers, media specialists, public relations executives, anyone in a large corporation
Mathematicians	Actuaries, computer programmers, electrical engineers, statisticians, professors, financial analysts, economists
Medicine	Nurses, social workers, therapists and psychologists, nursing home administrators, child care centers, hospital administrators

Mortgage Brokers	Bankers, loan officers, real estate brokers, lawyers, accountants, personal financial planners
Multimedia	Computer programmers, software developers, educators, publishers, computer magazine writers, reporters, editors, graphic designers, musicians, artists
Musicians	Club managers, promoters, publicists, songwriters, talent agents, arts organization administrators
Nursing	Physicians, medical technicians, patients, pharmacists
Nutrition	Chefs and cooks, restaurateurs, teachers, school and college administrators, psychologists, physicians, eating disorder specialists, dietitians, natural food suppliers and stores, herbalists, fitness trainers, health club personnel
Package Design	Graphic artists, marketing executives, art design directors, advertising executives, production managers
Pharmaceuticals	Physicians, nurses, medical office managers, hospital and HMO administrators, pharmacists, chemists, biochemists
Pharmacoeconomics	Economists, management consultants, hospital administrators, government officials, insurance companies, HMOs, pharmaceutical companies
Photography	Advertising executives, art directors, party planners, graphic designers, reporters, magazine art directors, darkroom and lab technicians
Physical and Occupational Therapy	Physicians, nurses, sports medicine specialists, vocational therapy and rehabilitation counselors, social workers, speech pathologists, audiologists, nursing home administrators, hospital administrators, health care agencies, dance and movement therapists, chiropractors

If you need contacts in...	Track them down through...
Politics	Campaign workers, political aides, political researchers, policy analysts in think tanks and government, corporate government relations executives, lobbyists, speech writers, pollsters
Printing	Graphic designers, public relations specialists, publishers, editors, party and event planners
Private Investigation	Credit bureaus, police officers, government record clerks
Promotions and Publicity	Marketing executives, public relations specialists, advertising executives, market researchers, publicists, agents, corporate communications specialists, media, music, film, journalists, editors, event planners
Psychology	Physical and occupational therapists, psychiatrists, social workers, college and university administrators, school administrators, teachers, independent educational consultants
Public Health	Epidemiologists, physicians, nonprofit organizations, sociologists, anthropologists, demographers, biostatisticians, economists, government officials, health care administrators
Public Relations	Advertising and marketing executives, anyone in a business that uses a PR firm, media personnel, writers, journalists
Publishing	Bookstore reps and managers, writers, freelance editors, illustrators, intellectual property lawyers
Real Estate	Attorneys, bankers, construction workers, contractors, architects, electricians, plumbers, carpenters, tenants, interior designers and decorators, architects, loan officers, mortgage brokers

Social Work	Psychotherapists and psychologists, physicians, hospital and health care administrators, physical and occupational therapists, speech pathologists, nurses, medical technicians, nonprofit organization workers, lawyers, mediators
Speech Pathology and Speech Therapy	Psychotherapists, psychiatrists, teachers, voice therapy coaches, musicians, linguists, physical and occupational therapists
Sports Marketing	Athletes, coaches, team owners and managers, public relations, advertising, promotions, event planners, sports equipment manufacturers
Statistics	Mathematicians, professors, public health workers, government officials, computer programmers, economists, financial analysts, market researchers
Stockbrokers	Certified financial planners, traders, financial analysts, commodities brokers, lawyers, accountants, estate planners, any investors
Systems Analysis	Computer programmers, computer operators, office managers and secretaries, corporate purchasing managers, information systems specialists, computer salespeople, telecommunications specialists, electricians
Talent Agent	Actors, singers, producers, directors, publicists, publishers, editors, writers, lawyers
Telecommunications	Computer engineers, electrical engineers, electricians, telephone company employees, information systems managers
Theater	Actors, producers, directors, lighting designers, costume designers, trade unions, booking agents, casting directors, choreographers, entertainment lawyers, dancers, musicians
Travel	Travel agents, corporate travel planners, conference and event planners, hotel managers, airline employees, tour guides, travel magazine writers and editors, guidebook writers and publishers

If you need contacts in...	Track them down through...
Tutoring	Teachers, educational consultants, psychologists, social workers
Urban and Regional Planning	Civil engineers, government officials, politicians, sociologists, anthropologists, bankers, historic preservationists, archaeologists, landscape designers, architects, geographers, demographers, economists
Waste Management	EPA officials, chemists, garbage handlers, recyclers, biologists, environmental scientists
Writing	Editors, publishers, reporters, advertising executives, public relations executives, corporate communications executives, desktop publishers, librarians, copywriters, novelists, biographers
Zoology	Animal trainers, breeders, wildlife specialists, park rangers, biologists, ecologists, zookeepers, veterinarians, museum curators

Appendix B

A Sampling of Professional and Trade Associations

Professional and trade associations offer a wealth of networking opportunities. To encourage you to make use of these valuable resources, this appendix lists more than 300 associations representing more than 50 career fields and industries. Since there are literally tens of thousands of trade and professional associations in this country, this is by no means an exhaustive list—it contains just some of the more significant and useful associations within each field.

This list should serve simply as a starting point for you. To be thorough, I suggest you do a search of the association directories that can be found in your local library (see Appendix D). You can also consult the American Society of Association Executives on the Web at http://www.asaenet.org.

Accounting

Accountants for the Public Interest

(914) 345-2620
http://www.accountingnet.com
http://www.smartpros.com

American Accounting Association

(941) 921-7747
http://aaahq.org

American Society of Women Accountants

(800) 326-2163
(703) 506-3265
Fax: (703) 506-3266
http://www.aswa.org

Institute of Internal Auditors

(407) 937-1100
(407) 937-1101
http://www.theiia.org

National Association of Black Accountants

(301) 474-6222
http://www.nabainc.org

Actuaries

American Academy of Actuaries

(202) 223-8196
http://www.actuary.org

Advertising

The Advertising Council

(212) 922-1500
http://www.adcouncil.org

American Advertising Federation

(202) 898-0089
http://www.aaf.org

American Association of Advertising Agencies

(212) 682-2500
http://www.aaaa.org

International Advertising Association

(212) 557-1133
http://www.iaaglobal.org

Archaeology

Archaeological Institute of America

(617) 353-9361
http://www.archaeological.org

Center for American Archeology

(618) 653-4316
http://www.caa-archeology.org

Society of American Archaeology

(202) 789-8200
http://www.saa.org

Architecture

American Institute of Architects

(202) 626-7300
http://www.aia.org

American Society of Landscape Architects

(202) 898-2444
http://www.asla.org

Associated Landscape Contractors of America

(703) 736-9666
http://www.alca.org

Arts

American Association of Museums

(202) 289-1818
http://www.aam-us.org

American Crafts Council

(212) 274-0630
http://www.craftcouncil.org

Americans for the Arts

(212) 223-2787
http://www.artsusa.org

Art Dealers Association of America

(212) 940-8590
http://www.artdealers.org

Association of Hispanic Arts

(212) 727-7227
http://www.latinoarts.org

National Antique and Art Dealers Association of America

(212) 826-9707
http://www.dir-dd.com/naadaa.html

National Association of Artists' Organizations

http://www.naao.net

Professional Photographers of America

(800) 786-6277
(404) 522-8600
http://www.ppa-world.org

Society of Illustrators

(212) 838-2560
http://www.societyillustrators.org

Aviation/Airlines

Air Transport Association

(202) 626-4000
http://www.airlines.org

Association of Flight Attendants

(202) 712-9799
http://www.afanet.org

Banking

America's Community Bankers Association

(202) 857-3100
http://www.acbankers.org

American Bankers Association

(800) BANKERS
(202) 663-5000
http://www.aba.com

Mortgage Bankers Association of America

(202) 557-2700
http://www.mbaa.org

National Bankers Association

(202) 588-5432
http://www.nationalbankers.org

Woman's World Banking—USA

(212) 768-8513
http://www.swwb.org

Clerical/Administrative

American Society of Corporate Secretaries

(212) 681-2000
http://www.ascs.org

International Virtual Assistants Association

(877) 440-2750
http://www.ivaa.org

National Association of Executive Secretaries

(703) 237-8616
http://www.naesaa.com

Professional Secretaries International

(816) 891-6600
http://www.main.org/psi

Computers/Information Technology/Library Science

American Library Association

(800) 545-2433
(312) 944-6780
http://www.ala.org

American Society for Information Science and Technology

(301) 495-0900
http://www.asis.org

The Association for Communications Technology Professionals in Higher Education

(859) 278-3338
http://www.acuta.org

Association for Computing Machinery

(800) 342-6626
(212) 626-0500
(202) 478-6312
http://http://www.acm.org

Association for Women in Computing

(415) 905-4663
http://www.awc@acm.org

Association of Personal Computer User Groups

(301) 423-1618
http://www.apcug.org

Independent Computer Consultants Association

(314) 892-1675
http://www.icca.org

Information Technology Association of America

(703) 522-5055
http://www.itaa.org

Society for Information Management

(312) 527-6734
http://www.simnet.org

Software & Information Industry Association

(202) 289-7442
http://www.siia.net

Special Libraries Association

(202) 234-4700
http://www.sla.org

Consulting

American Consultants League

(866) 344-7201
http://www.americanconsultantsleague.com

Association of Management Consulting Firms

(212) 551-7887
http://www.amcf.org

Professional and Technical Consultants Association

(800) 74-PATCA
(408) 971-5902
http://www.patca.com

Culinary/Food & Wine

American Bakers Association

(202) 789-0300
http://http://www.americanbakers.org

American Culinary Federation

(800) 624-9458
http://www.acfchefs.org

International Association of Culinary Professionals

(502) 581-9786
http://www.iacp.com

National Restaurant Association

(202) 331-5900
http://www.restaurant.org

Sommelier Society of America

(212) 679-4190
http://sommeliersocietyofamerica.org

Dentistry

American Dental Assistants Association

(312) 541-1550
http://www.dentalassistant.org

American Dental Association

(312) 440-2500
http://www.ada.org

American Dental Hygienists' Association

(312) 440-8900
http://www.adha.org

National Association of Dental Laboratories

(800) 950-1150
(850) 205-5626
http://www.nadl.org

Design

American Design and Drafting Association

(731) 627-9321
http://www.adda.org

American Society of Furniture Designers

> (910) 576-1273
> http://www.asfd.com

American Society of Interior Designers

> (202) 546-3480
> http://www.asid.org

American Textile Manufacturers Institute

> (202) 862-0500
> http://www.atmi.org

Association of Professional Landscape Designers

> (717) 238-9780
> http://www.apld.com

Council of Fashion Designers of America

> (212) 302-1821
> http://www.cfda.com

Industrial Designers Society of America

> (703) 707-6000
> http://www.idsa.org

International Association of Lighting Designers

> (312) 527-3677
> http://www.iald.org

Society of American Florists

> (703) 836-8700
> http://www.safnow.org

Surface Design Association

> (707) 829-3110
> http://www.surfacedesign.org

Economics

American Economic Association

> (615) 322-2595
> http://www.vanderbilt.edu/AEA

National Association of Business Economists

> (202) 463-6223
> http://www.nabe.com

Education

American Association for Adult and Continuing Education

> (410) 767-0492
> http://www.aaace.org

American Association for Higher Education

> (202) 293-6440
> http://www.aahe.org

American Association of School Administrators

> (703) 528-0700
> http://www.aasa.org

American Association of University Professors

> (202) 737-5900
> http://www.aaup.org

American Association of University Women

> (800) 326-AAUW
> (202) 785-7700
> http://www.aauw.org

American Federation of Teachers

> (202) 879-4400
> http://www.aft.org

Independent Educational Consultants Association

> (703) 591-4850
> http://www.educationalconsulting.org

Institute of International Education

> (212) 883-8200
> http://www.iie.org

Modern Language Association

> (646) 576-5000
> http://www.mla.org

National Association of Student Personnel Administrators

> (202) 265-7500
> http://www.naspa.org

National Education Association

> (202) 833-4000
> http://www.nea.org

Women in Higher Education

> (608) 251-3232
> http://www.wihe.com

Energy

The Alliance to Save Energy

> (202) 857-0666
> http://www.ase.org

American Gas Association

> (202) 824-7000
> http://www.aga.org

American Petroleum Institute

> (202) 682-8000
> http://www.api.org

The National Coal Council

> (202) 223-1191
> http://www.nationalcoalcouncil.org

National Mining Association

> (202) 463-2600
> http://www.nma.org

National Petroleum Council

> (202) 393-6100
> http://www.npc.org

U.S. Dept. of Energy

> (800) DIAL-DOE
> http://www.doe.gov

Engineering

American Association of Engineering Societies

> (202) 296-2237
> http://www.aaes.org

American Institute of Chemical Engineers

> (212) 591-7338
> http://www.aiche.org

American Society of Civil Engineers

> (800) 548-2723
> (703) 295-6300
> http://www.asce.org

American Society of Mechanical Engineers

> (800) 843-2763
> (212) 705-7722
> http://www.asme.org

Institute of Electrical and Electronics Engineers

> (212) 419-7900
> http://www.ieee.org

Institute of Industrial Engineers

> (800) 494-0460
> (770) 449-0460
> http://www.iienet.org

Junior Engineering Technical Society

> (703) 548-JETS
> http://www.jets.org

Environment

Ecological Society of America

> (202) 833-8773
> http://www.esa.org

Environmental Protection Agency

> (202) 272-0167
> http://www.epa.gov

Student Conservation Association

> (603) 543-1700
> http://www.thesca.org

Water Environment Federation

> (800) 666-0206
> (703) 684-2452
> http://www.wef.org

Film/TV/Music/Radio

American Federation of Television and Radio Artists

> (212) 532-0800
> http://www.aftra.org

American Film Institute

> (800) 774-4AFI
> http://www.afi.com

American Women in Radio and Television

> (703) 506-3290
> http://www.awrt.org

Independent Feature Project

> (212) 465-8200
> http://www.ifp.org

Motion Picture Association of America

> (818) 995-6600
> http://www.mpaa.org

National Association of Black Owned Broadcasters

> (202) 463-8970
> http://www.nabob.org

National Association of Broadcasters

> (202) 429-5300
> http://www.nab.org

National Cable and Television Association

> (202) 775-3550
> http://www.ncta.com

National Television Academy

> (212) 586-8424
> http://www.emmyonline.org

Producers Guild of America

> (310) 358-9020
> http://www.producersguild.com

Radio-Television News Directors Association & Foundation

> (202) 659-6510
> http://www.rtnda.org

Recording Industry Association of America

> (202) 775-0101
> http://www.riaa.com

The Songwriters Guild of America

> (201) 867-7603
> http://www.songwriters.org

Finance

American Finance Association

> (212) 998-0370
> http://www.afajof.org

American Financial Services Association

> (202) 296-5544
> http://www.afsaonline.org

Association for Investment Management and Research

> (800) 247-8132
> http://www.aimr.com

The Financial Executives' Networking Group

> (203) 227-8965
> http://www.thefeng.com

Financial Women International

> (651) 487-7632
> http://www.fwi.org

Financial Women's Association of New York

> (212) 533-2141
> http://www.fwa.org

Investment Counsel Association of America

> (202) 293-4222
> http://www.icaa.org

National Association of Corporate Treasurers

> (703) 437-4377
> http://www.nact.org

National Association of Credit Management

> (410) 740-5560
> http://www.nacm.org

Security Traders Association

> (212) 867-7002
> http://www.securitytraders.org

Graphic Design/Arts

American Institute of Graphic Arts

> (212) 807-1990
> http://www.aiga.org

Graphic Artists Guild

(212) 791-3400

http://www.gag.org

Health Administration/ Public Health

American Association of Healthcare Consultants

(888) 350-2242

http://www.aahc.net

American College of Healthcare Executives

(312) 424-2800

http://www.ache.org

American Health Care Association

(202) 842-4444

http://www.ahca.org

American Health Information Management Association

(312) 233-1100

http://www.ahima.org

American Health Lawyers Association

(202) 833-1100

http://www.healthlawyers.org

American Hospital Association

(312) 422-3000

http://www.hospitalconnect.com

American Public Health Association

(202) 777-2742

http://www.apha.org

Association for Healthcare Philanthropy

(703) 532-6243

http://www.ahp.org

National Health Council

(202) 785-3910

http://www.nationalhealthcouncil.org

Health Care/Medicine

American Academy of Physician Assistants

(703) 836-2272

http://www.aapa.org

American Association for Respiratory Care

(972) 243-2272

http://www.aarc.org

American Association of Medical Assistants

(312) 899-1500

http://www.aama-ntl.org

American College of Nurse-Midwives

(202) 728-9860

http://www.acnm.org

American Medical Association

(800) 621-8335

http://www.ama-assn.org

American Nurses Association

(800) 274-4ANA

http://www.nursingworld.org

American Occupational Therapy Association

(301) 652-2682

http://www.aota.org

American Optometric Association

(314) 991-4100

http://www.aoa.org

American Physical Therapy Association

(800) 999-2782

http://www.apta.org

American Psychiatric Association

(703) 907-7300

http://www.psych.org

American Society of Radiologic Technologists

(505) 298-4500

http://www.asrt.org

American Speech-Language-Hearing Association

>　(800) 498-2071
>　http://www.asha.org

Gerontological Society of America

>　(202) 842-1275
>　http://www.geron.org

International Chiropractors Association

>　(800) 423-4690
>　http://www.chiropractic.org

National Association for Home Care and Hospice

>　(202) 547-7424
>　http://www.nahc.org

National Association of Emergency Medical Technicians

>　(800) 346-2368
>　(601) 924-7744
>　http://www.naemt.org

National League for Nursing

>　(800) 669-1656
>　(212) 363-5555
>　http://nln.org

National Society of Genetic Counselors

>　(610) 872-7608
>　http://www.nsgc.org

Society of Diagnostic Medical Sonographers

>　(800) 229-9506
>　(214) 473-8057
>　http://www.sdms.org

The Society of Nuclear Medicine

>　(703) 708-9000
>　http://www.snm.org

History

American Association for State and Local History

>　(615) 320-3203
>　http://www.aaslh.org

American Folklore Society

>　(614) 292-3375
>　http://www.afsnet.org

National Trust for Historic Preservation

>　(202) 588-6000
>　http://www.nthp.org

Society of American Archivists

>　(312) 922-0140
>　http://www.archivists.org

Hospitality

American Hotel and Motel Association

>　(202) 289-3100
>　http://www.ahma.com

Club Managers Association of America

>　(703) 739-9500
>　http://www.cmaa.org

Independent Innkeepers Association

>　(269) 789-0393
>　http://www.innbook.com

The International Council on Hotel, Restaurant and Institutional Education

>　(804) 346-4800
>　http://www.chrie.org

National Restaurant Association

>　(202) 331-5900
>　http://www.restaurant.org

Human Resources/Training/Labor Relations

American Arbitration Association

>　(212) 716-5800
>　http://www.adr.org

American Society for Training and Development

>　(703) 683-8100
>　http://www.astd.org

International Public Management Association
for Human Resources

> (703) 549-7100
> http://www.ipma-hr.org

Society for Human Resource Management

> (800) 283-SHRM
> (703) 548-3440
> http://www.shrm.org

Insurance

Insurance Information Institute

> (212) 346-5500
> http://www.iii.org

Reinsurance Association of America

> (202) 638-3690
> http://www.raanet.org

International

American Association of Exporters and Importers

> (202) 661-2181
> http://www.aaei.org

American Translators Association

> (703) 683-6100
> http://www.atanet.org

International Trade Administration

> (800) USA-TRAD
> http://www.ita.doc.gov

Law

American Bar Association

> (312) 988-5000
> http://www.abanet.org

National Association of Legal Assistants

> (918) 587-6828
> http://www.nala.org

National Court Reporters Association

> (800) 272-6272
> (703) 556-6272
> http://www.ncraonline.org

National Federation of Paralegal Associations

> (206) 652-4120
> http://www.paralegals.org

National Legal Center for the Public Interest

> (202) 466-9360
> http://www.nlcpi.org

Law Enforcement/Corrections/ Investigation

American Correctional Association

> (800) 222-5646
> (301) 918-1800
> http://www.aca.org

American Federation of Police and Concerned Citizens

> (321) 264-0911
> http://www.aphf.org/afp_cc.html

American Jail Association

> (301) 790-3930
> http://www.corrections.com/aja

American Probation and Parole Association

> (859) 244-8203
> http://www.appa-net.org

American Society of Criminology

> (612) 292-9207
> http://www.asc41.com

National Association of Investigative Specialists

> (512) 719-3595
> http://www.pimall.com/nais/dir.menu.html

World Association of Detectives

> +44 1482-665577 (England)
> http://www.world-detectives.com

Management

American Management Association

(212) 586-8100

http://www.amanet.org

American Society for Public Administration

(202) 393-7878

http://www.aspanet.org

American Society of Association Executives

(800) 950-2723

(202) 626-2723

http://www.asaenet.org

Institute of Management Consultants

(800) 221-2557

(202) 367-1134

http://www.imcusa.org

National Association for Female Executives

(800) 927-NAFE

http://www.nafe.com

Project Management Institute

http://www.pmi.org

Women in Management

(213) 740-4721

http://www.usc.edu/org/wim

Manufacturing

National Association of Manufacturers

(202) 637-3000

http://www.nam.org

Marketing

American Marketing Association

(800) AMA-1150

(312) 542-9000

http://www.ama.org

Direct Marketing Association

(212) 768-7277

http://www.the-dma.org

Marketing Research Association

(800) 488-4845

(262) 523-9090

http://www.mranet.org

Mathematics

Mathematical Association of America

(202) 387-5200

http://www.maa.org

Society for Industrial and Applied Mathematics

(215) 382-9800

http://www.siam.org

Meeting/Event/Party Planning

Association of Bridal Consultants

(860) 355-0464

http://www.bridalassn.com

International Special Events Society

(800) 688-4737

(312) 321-6853

http://www.ises.com

Meeting Professionals International

(972) 702-3000

http://www.mpiweb.org

Multimedia

The HTML Writers Guild

http://www.hwg.org

Not-for-Profit/Public Sector/ Social Service

American Society for Public Administration

(202) 393-7878

http://www.aspanet.org

Association of Fundraising Professionals

(703) 684-0410

http://www.nsfre.org

Center for Community Change

(202) 342-0519

http://www.communitychange.org

Council on Foundations

(202) 466-6512

http://www.cof.org

National Congress for Community Economic Development

(202) 289-9020

http://www.ncced.org

National Network of Grantmakers

(718) 643-8814

http://www.nng.org

Society for Nonprofit Organizations

(734) 451-3582

http://danenet.danenet.org/snpo/

Nutrition

American Dietetic Association

(800) 877-1600

http://www.eatright.org

American Society for Clinical Nutrition

(301) 530-7110

http://www.ascn.org

Operations/Logistics/ Production

American Production and Inventory Control Society

(703) 354-8851

http://www.apics.org

The American Society for Quality

(414) 272-8575

http://www.asq.org

American Supply Association

(312) 464-0090

http://www.asa.net

Council of Logistics Management

(708) 574-0985

http://www.clm1.org

Institute for Operations Research and the Management Sciences

(800) 4-INFORMS

http://www.informs.org

International Facility Management Association

(713) 623-IFMA

http://www.ifma.org

Performing Arts

Actors' Equity Association

(212) 869-8530

http://www.actorsequity.org

The American Dance Guild

(212) 932-2789

http://www.americandanceguild.org

American Federation of Musicians

(212) 869-1330

http://www.afm.org

American Guild of Musical Artists

(212) 265-3687

http://www.musicalartists.org

International Society for the Performing Arts Foundation

(914) 921-1550

http://www.ispa.org

League of Historic American Theaters

(410) 659-9533

http://www.lhat.org

Screen Actors Guild

(323) 954-1600

http://www.sag.org

Theater Communications Group

(212) 609-5900

http://www.tcg.org

Pharmaceuticals

American Pharmaceutical Association

> (202) 628-4410
> http://www.aphanet.org

Pharmaceutical Research and Manufacturers of America

> (202) 835-3400
> http://www.phrma.org

Psychology/Counseling

American Counseling Association

> (800) 347-6647
> (703) 823-0252
> http://www.counseling.org

American Psychological Association

> (800) 374-2721
> (202) 336-5510
> http://www.apa.org

American School Counseling Association

> (703) 683-2722
> http://www.schoolcounselor.org

Public Relations/Promotions

International Communication Association

> (202) 530-9855
> http://www.icahdq.org

Promotion Marketing Association

> (212) 420-1100
> http://www.pmalink.org

Public Relations Society of America

> (212) 995-2230
> http://www.prsa.org

Public Relations Student Society of America

> (212) 460-1474
> http://www.prssa.org

Publishing/Journalism/Writing/Communications

American Copy Editors Society

> http://www.copydesk.org

American Society of Journalists and Authors

> (212) 997-0947
> http://www.asja.org

American Society of Magazine Editors

> (212) 872-3700
> http://www.magazine.org/Editorial/ASME/

The Association for Women in Communications

> (410) 544-7442
> http://www.womcom.org

Association of American Publishers

> (212) 255-0200
> http://www.publishers.org

National Newspaper Association

> (573) 882-5800
> http://www.nna.org

National Writers Union

> (212) 254-0279
> http://www.nwu.org

The Newspaper Guild

> (202) 434-7177
> http://www.newsguild.org

Society for Technical Communication

> (703) 522-4114
> http://www.stc.org

Writers Guild of America-East

> (212) 767-7800
> http://www.wgaeast.org

Purchasing

Institute for Supply Management

> (602) 752-6276
> http://www.ism.ws

National Association of State Purchasing Officials

> (859) 514-9159
> http://www.naspo.org

Real Estate

Institute of Real Estate Management

> (312) 329-6000
> http://www.irem.org

National Association of Real Estate Brokers

> (301) 552-9340
> http://www.nareb.com

National Association of Realtors

> (805) 557-2300
> http://www.realtor.com

Retailing

National Retail Federation

> (800) NRF-HOW2
> http://www.nrf.com

Sales

American Telemarketing Association

> http://www.ataconnect.org

American Teleservices Association

> (317) 816-9336
> http://www.ataconnect.org

National Association of Sales Professionals

> (480) 951-4311
> http://www.nasp.com

National Association of Wholesaler-Distributors

> (202) 872-0885
> http://www.naw.org

Science (Including Social Sciences)

Academy of Political Science

> (212) 870-2500
> http://www.jstor.org/journals/aps.html

American Academy of Political and Social Science

> (215) 746-6500
> http://www.aapss.org

American Anthropological Association

> (703) 528-1902
> http://www.aaanet.org

American Astronomical Society

> (202) 328-2010
> http://www.aas.org

American Chemical Society

> (800) 227-5558
> (202) 872-4600
> http://www.chemistry.org

American Geological Institute

> (703) 379-2480
> http://www.agiweb.org

American Institute of Biological Sciences

> (202) 628-1500
> http://www.aibs.org

American Meteorological Society

> (617) 227-2425
> http://www.ametsoc.org

American Physical Society

> (301) 209-3200
> http://www.aps.org

American Physiological Society

> (301) 634-7164
> http://www.the-aps.org

American Political Science Association

> (202) 483-2512
> http://www.apsanet.org

American Society for Microbiology

> (202) 737-3600
> http://www.asm.org

American Sociological Association

> (202) 383-9005
> http://www.asanet.org

Botanical Society of America

> (314) 577-9566
> http://www.botany.org

Genetics Society of America

> (301) 634-7300
> http://www.genetics-gsa.org

Marine Technology Society

> (410) 884-5330
> (202) 775-5966
> http://www.mtsociety.org

National Science Foundation

> (703) 292-5111
> http://www.nsf.gov

Skilled Trades/Technicians

American Welding Society

> (305) 443-9353
> http://www.amweld.org

The Associated General Contractors of America

> (703) 548-3118
> http://www.agc.org

Association of Manufacturing Technicians

> (703) 893-2900
> http://www.mfgtech.org

Automotive Service Association

> (817) 283-6205
> http://www.asashop.org

Electronics Technicians Association, International

> (765) 653-8262
> http://www.eta-sda.com

Independent Electrical Contractors

> (703) 549-7448
> http://www.ieci.org

National Association of Women in Construction

> (800) 552-3506
> http://www.nawic.org

National Electrical Contractors Association

> (301) 657-3110
> http://www.necanet.org

Small Business/Entrepreneurs/Franchising

African American Women Entrepreneurs@Home

> http://www.vsscyberoffice.com/aaweh.htm

American Home Business Association

> (800) 664-2422
> http://www.homebusiness.com

American Woman's Economic Development Corp.

> (917) 368-6100
> http://www.awed.org

Chamber of Commerce of the United States

> (202) 659-6000
> http://www.uschamber.org

International Franchise Association

> (202) 628-8000
> http://www.franchise.org

National Association for the Self-Employed

> (800) 232-6273
> http://www.nase.org

U.S. Small Business Administration

> (800) 827-5722
> http://www.sba.gov

World Entrepreneurs' Organization and Young Entrepreneur's Organization

> (703) 519-6700
> http://www.yeo.org

Social Work

National Association of Social Workers

> (202) 408-8600
> http://www.naswdc.org

Telecommunications

Cellular Telecommunications and Internet Association

> (202) 785-0081
> http://www.wow-com.com

National Association of Telecommunications Officers and Advisors

> (703) 519-8035
> http://www.natoa.org

National Cable & Telecommunications Association

> (202) 775-3550
> http://www.ncta.com

Society of Telecommunications Consultants

> (530) 336-7070
> http://www.stcconsultants.org

Travel

American Society of Travel Agents

> (703) 739-2782
> http://www.astanet.com

Cruise Lines International Association

> (212) 921-0066
> http://www.cruising.org

Society of American Travel Writers

> (919) 861-5586
> http://www.satw.org

The Travel Institute

> (781) 237-0280
> http://www.icta.com

Urban/Regional Planning

American Planning Association

> (312) 431-9100
> http://www.planning.org

International Downtown Association

> (202) 393-6801
> http://www.ida-downtown.org

Veterinary Medicine/Animals

American Association of Zookeepers

> (913) 273-1980
> http://www.aazk.org

American Veterinary Medical Association

> (847) 925-8070
> http://www.avma.org

The American Zoo and Aquarium Association

> (301) 562-0777
> http://www.aza.org

The Humane Society of the United States

> (202) 452-1100
> http://www.hsus.org

The Society for Integrative and Comparative Biology

> (800) 955-1246
> (703) 790-1745
> http://www.sicb.org

Waste Management

Air and Waste Management Association

> (412) 232-3444
> http://www.awma.org

National Solid Wastes Management Association

> (800) 424-2869
> http://www.nswma.org

Where to Find Experts to Help with Your Networking

Chapter 4 introduced you to the STARS concept of seeing your network as consisting of Strategists, Targets, Allied Forces, and Role Models. Each of the STARS in your network has a role in helping you look your best, sound professional, write well, plan effective strategies, make the right choices, find employment, develop a business, and stay healthy and relaxed while doing all that.

This appendix is designed to help you track down many of the professionals who can support your networking efforts. It is arranged according to categories of professional expertise, and within each category, you will find contact information for associations, organizations, individuals, service businesses, and Web sites that can provide the help you need or may refer you to someone who can.

Business Strategy Consulting

American Women's Economic Development Corporation (AWED)

(212) 692-9100

http://www.awed.org

AWED is a national organization headquartered in New York that offers individual counseling, mentoring, workshops, seminars, conferences, publications, and other resources to established and new businesses owned by women.

Business Owners' Idea Cafe

http://www.businessownersideacafe.com

A fun approach to serious business where you can find small business ideas, grants, and plans to start and run a business. Also provides opportunities to e-network and talk with experts in small business ownership.

Center for Entrepreneurial Management

(212) 925-7911

http://www.ceoclubs.org

http://www.ceoclubs.com

A national, not-for-profit organization that offers a variety of services including networking opportunities for entrepreneurs.

Entrepreneur.com and Entrepreneur Magazine

http://www.entrepreneur.com

Whether for a home-based business or franchise opportunity or a major company, this informative site is a valuable resource. Click on the Magazine link to read articles from *Entrepreneur Magazine*.

Entreworld

http://www.entreworld.org

Recognized by *USA Today, Forbes, Inc.,* and *Fast Company* as a premier online resource for small business owners, the EntreWorld search engine delivers useful information, guidance, and contacts for entrepreneurs.

Fast Company *Magazine online*

http://www.fastcompany.com

Fast Company's guides are collections of articles hand-picked by the editors from the Web-exclusive features and archived stories from the magazine.

Inc. *Magazine online*

http://www.inc.com

The Web site for *Inc.* magazine delivers advice, tools, and services to help business owners and CEOs start, run, and grow their businesses more successfully. You'll find information and advice covering virtually every business and management task, including marketing, sales, capital, managing people, and more.

SCORE: The Service Corps of Retired Executives

Contact the Small Business Administration for referral to a SCORE office near you. The retired executives who volunteer for SCORE use their many years of business experience to advise you about your small business or one you're thinking of starting.

Small Business Administration (SBA)

SBA Answer Desk: (800) 827-5722

http://www.sba.gov

The SBA offers a wide range of services for small businesses and has offices across the country.

Small Business Development Councils (SBDC)

http://www.sba.gov/sbdc

The U.S Small Business Administration (SBA) administers the Small Business Development Center Program to provide management assistance to current and prospective small business owners. SBDCs offer one-stop assistance to individuals and small businesses by providing a wide variety of information and guidance in central and easily accessible branch locations. The program is a cooperative effort of the private sector; the educational community; and federal, state, and local governments. It enhances economic development by providing small businesses with management and technical assistance.

Working Solo

http://www.workingsolo.com

Working Solo, Inc. (WSI) was founded by Terry Lonier in 1991 as an outgrowth of her experience as an independent professional since 1978. Its focus is threefold: (1) To help individuals create professional success through the mastery of self-employment and related business practices; (2) To advise corporations in understanding how their organizations can best communicate with and serve SOHO (small office/home office) business owners; 3) To serve as an advocate for micro-businesses and to foster the creative entrepreneurial spirit in both individuals and larger organizations. This is a wonderful, informative site from a guru of the SOHO world.

Career Advice and Jobs Online

There are many sites that post useful advice on career choice, career management, and job search topics as well as hosting career seminars in online auditoriums and information exchanges on bulletin boards and in chat rooms. Some sites also offer actual counseling online in "real-time" sessions or link you to a counselor who can work with you by phone. Other career-related Web sites focus on job listings or resume posting rather than advice. Both types are listed next.

America's Job Bank

http://www.ajb.dni.us

The Black Collegian *Online*

http://www.black-collegian.com

The online version of *The Black Collegian* magazine, this site is a great place for African Americans to network. It includes career advice, lots of resources, and job listings.

Career America

http://www.careeramerica.com

Career Center for Workforce Diversity

http://www.eop.com

Career City

http://www.careercity.com

Career Crafting

http://www.careercrafting.com

This site focuses solely on career advice rather than on jobs. Career information is posted at the site, and free career counseling is available if you call a posted 800 number.

Career Resource Center

http://www.careerresource.com

The Career Resource Center provides an extensive index of career resources on the Web with links to more than 7,500 sites.

CareerXroads

http://www.careerxroads.com

EOP

http://www.eop.com

This is an excellent networking resource for women, Hispanics, African Americans, and disabled people. It provides information about conferences, job fairs, employment opportunities, and career advice, all with an eye toward diversity issues.

Help Wanted-USA

http://www.iccweb.com

JIST Publishing

http://www.jist.com

This site provides information on JIST's many career planning, job search, educational, and life skills products and training tools/programs.

JobWeb

http://www.jobweb.org

Latino Web

http://www.public.iastate.edu/~savega/us_latin.htm

This site is full of resources, information, and links to other sites of interest to Latinos.

Monster

http://www.monster.com

A good general-purpose site for job searching, career search, and other items. Be sure to check out Monster Networking, where you can join a community of other professionals to share leads, information, and support. It's a great way to expand your network exponentially.

MonsterTRAK

http://www.monstertrak.com

Backed by the knowledge and experience of Monster, MonsterTRAK is the #1 Web site for students and alumni looking for full-time and part-time positions, internships, and on-campus employment.

Net Temps

http://www.americasemployers.com

"Net-Temps is the leading online recruiting service for the Staffing Industry serving their direct placement and temporary (contract) requirements.

The company has been ranked in the top 10 of all job posting Web sites for the past 8 years by comScore Media-Metrix and Nielsen//Net Ratings."

NetworkMoves

http://www.networkmoves.com

NetworkMoves is a free monthly source for professional networking interviews, news, opportunities, and success stories.

The Riley Guide

http://www.rileyguide.com

Margaret Riley is known in the career counseling and job coaching world as a pioneering figure and reliable authority on Internet job searching. Her site is an excellent starting point for networking and job searching online. It includes an annotated index of job sites and links to most of the sites where you can apply for jobs.

Career and Job Search Counseling and Coaching

Academic and Community-Based Career Centers

If you're in college or graduate school, be sure to take advantage of your campus career counseling services. And, as an alum, you may still have access to career counseling, job listings, and other resources at your alma mater. Contact your schools to see what they have to offer locally and long distance. Many career counseling services (individual advising and workshops) are also available to the general public in such settings as nonprofit agencies; churches and other religious institutions; adult education centers, such as The Learning Annex; and the continuing education or adult learning division of universities.

Career Masters Institute

(800) 881-9972

http://www.cminstitute.com

This organization's diverse membership includes career coaches, counselors, outplacement consultants, resume writers, recruiters, college and university career development professionals, government and military career transition specialists, HR professionals, and more. Contact the organization by phone or browse their Web site for a referral to the best career or job search coach for you.

Career Planning and Adult Development Network

(650) 359-6911

http://www.careernetwork.org

This international network based in California consists of over 1,000 career development professionals, many of whom are in private practice or work in organizations that serve the general public. The main office in San Jose can tell you how to get in touch with the Network contact person in your area (there's at least one in most U.S. states and in several other countries). Your local contact can then refer you to a career counselor.

The Five O'Clock Club

(800) 538-6645

(212) 286-4500

http://www.fiveoclockclub.com

Headquartered in Manhattan with affiliates across the U.S. and abroad, The Five O'Clock Club offers coaching and networking opportunities in small groups for job hunters and those who want to change careers. The organization's director, Kate Wendleton, is the author of several excellent job search books (see Appendix D). You may contact the New York office or browse their site to find out if there is a Five O'Clock Club near you.

Forty Plus Clubs

(212) 947-4230

http://www.fortyplus-nyc.org

For job seekers forty years old or older, these nationwide clubs offer great networking opportunities and job search guidance. You can contact the New York club for information on a location near you.

Communication Consulting

Association of Professional Communication Consultants (APCC)

http://www.consultingsuccess.org

APCC is an international network of professionals providing communication expertise and solutions. Members include consultants, trainers, facilitators, executive coaches, writers, editors, corporate communication specialists, educators, and technical communicators.

Executive Coaching

Association of Career Professionals International (ACPI)

http://www.acpinternational.org

ACPI's members work in outplacement firms, corporate career development and human resources departments, consulting firms, and other settings in which they assist individuals and groups in developing and managing their careers. Many members maintain full-time or part-time private practices that often include executive coaching services along with career-management and job-search coaching. Others may provide executive coaching through the outplacement or career management firms for which they work. For the current ACPI regional rep in your area, consult the ACPI Web site.

National Association for Female Executives (NAFE)

(800) 927-NAFE

http://www.nafe.com

NAFE offers conferences, training programs, and other resources to promote success among female executives.

Executive Recruiters/ Employment Agencies

The best way to find a good career search firm or employment agency is through word of mouth— by asking friends and colleagues for referrals to anyone who has placed them in a job in the past. In addition, many recruiters can be found through the jobs they list in the help wanted section of newspapers or on online job boards. You can also consult the following sources to learn more about recruiters:

- American Staffing Association: http://www.staffingtoday.net
- Association of Executive Search Consultants: http://www.aesc.com
- SearchFirm.com: http://www.searchfirm.com

Image Consulting

Association of Image Consultants International (AICI)

(972) 755-1503,

Fax: (972) 755-2561

http://www.aici.org

info@aici.org

This organization can refer you to a consultant in your area who has professional member status with AICI. To find additional names (or ones who might charge less than those endorsed by AICI, but are nonetheless well qualified), consult your local Yellow Pages.

Color Me Beautiful

(800) COLOR-ME

http://www.colormebeautiful.com

Call this 800 number or go online for a referral to an independent consultant who is certified to do a color analysis according to the Color Me Beautiful system.

Professional Organizers

National Association of Professional Organizers

(847) 375-4746

http://www.napo.net

NAPO is a nonprofit association that can refer you to a professional organizer in your area. These people can help you get organized and manage your time more effectively.

Psychotherapy/Mental Health/ Wellness

The following professional associations can refer you to members who are qualified psychologists or psychotherapists.

American Psychological Association

(800) 374-2721

(202) 336-5510

http://www.apa.org

ETherapyWeb, National Directory of Online Counselors

http://etherapyweb.com

Locate licensed mental health professionals with Web offices set up to provide therapy via the phone and/or online.

National Association of Social Workers

(202) 408-8600

http://www.naswdc.org

National Institute of Mental Health

(866) 615-NIMH

http://www.nimh.nih.gov

Psychotherapy/Mental Health/ Wellness: Other Perspectives

The remaining organizations in this section offer referrals to professionals who can address your mental (and physical) health from other perspectives.

American Holistic Health Association

(714) 779-6152;

http://www.ahha.org

This association can refer you to wellness and holistic health professionals to keep you healthy, centered, and relaxed as you network.

IDEA: The Association for Fitness Professionals

http://www.ideafit.com

IDEA has a membership of more than 25,000 professionals in the areas of dance, exercise, and fitness training. They can refer you to a personal trainer or movement specialist to help with your personal presentation.

Public Speaking

The following organizations offer seminars and workshops in public speaking and other business communication skills. Some offer individual sessions as well.

Dale Carnegie Courses

http://www.dalecarnegie.com

The Executive Technique

(800) 992-1414

(312) 266-0001

http://www.executivetechnique.com

Fred Pryor Seminars

(800) 780-8476

http://www.pryor.com

Publicity/Public Relations

One of the best ways to find a freelance publicist to help with your self-promotion or marketing is simply to ask someone who seems to be getting lots of good publicity! In addition to a word-of-mouth referral, though, you can also find someone through many of the professional groups listed in the Business Strategy Consulting section of this appendix and through the following organizations.

Public Relations Society of America (PRSA)

(212) 995-2230

http://www.prsa.org

PRSA has a placement service for public relations professionals seeking temporary project work. If you need to hire a freelance publicist, you can list your project as a job with this service.

Resume Writing

Career Masters Institute

(800) 881-9972

http://www.cminstitute.com

This organization's diverse membership includes career coaches, counselors, outplacement consultants, resume writers, recruiters, college and university career development professionals, government and military career transition specialists, HR professionals, and more. Contact the organization by phone or browse their Web site for referral to the right resume expert for you.

National Résumé Writers' Association (NRWA)

(888) NRWA-444

http://www.nrwa.com

NRWA's members are professional resume writers who can assist you with developing a resume from scratch or revising an existing one. Their site has a user-friendly directory where you can search for a resume expert by geographic location, keywords, and other criteria.

Professional Résumé Writing and Research Association (PRWRA)

(800) 225-8688

http://www.prwra.com

As with NRWA, PRWRA's members are professional resume writers and career services professionals. You may search their member directory online to find an expert to help with your resume and related job search materials.

Resume Deli

(866) 2-RES-DELI

http://www.resumedeli.com

Unlike many resume writing businesses, where the qualifications of the resume writers are questionable, Resume Deli has assembled a top-notch team of highly experienced career counselors, published authors, and industry specialists to ensure that they offer the finest career services available. The Resume and Cover Letter Revamp service is professional, comprehensive, and targeted to your particular career needs. An especially nice feature of this business is that you see their prices right up front on the site's home page, and the prices are on a sliding scale based on your level of career experience. They also offer career counseling by the hour. I highly recommend this site.

Voice Coaching/Speech Therapy

American Speech-Language-Hearing Association

(800) 498-2071

http://www.asha.org

This is the principal professional association for speech pathologists and speech therapists who treat serious speech disorders as well as help those who simply need to improve their speaking style or voice. Their site has a helpful online directory to find an appropriate specialist in your area.

Also see listings in the "Public Speaking" section for organizations that provide voice coaching.

Books to Guide You in Networking

During the process of networking, you are likely to be dealing with a lot of complicated issues, such as making career decisions, conducting a job search, trying to advance in your career, or dealing with the ups and downs of running your own business. You might also find that as you practice the networking techniques recommended in this book, you need to work on related personal issues, such as your speaking voice or professional wardrobe. This bibliography includes books and other resources to guide you through these various aspects of networking. You'll also find resources for readers with special interests, such as networking in other countries or with special populations.

The information in this appendix is just a brief survey of what's available. The books, directories, and technology listed here are the ones I consider to be the best of the bunch. My assessment is largely based on what clients have told me about how well these resources have worked for them, as well as my own review of many of these resources.

Most of the guidebooks listed in this appendix can be found in the career, business, or self-help sections of any bookstore. Many of the directories included here (such as those that list companies, professional associations, and other organizations) are either not readily available in bookstores or are very expensive. They can be found in the reference or business section of most public and academic libraries, as well as in the libraries of college and graduate school career offices. Note that some branches of the public library have extensive career resource collections containing books on career planning, job search, and occupational information, among other resources. Check with your local public library system to find out if there is a career resource library near you.

Books to Help with Your Job Search

Complete Job Search Handbook, Howard Figler, New York: Owl Books/Henry Holt & Co., 1999.

Cyberspace Job Search Kit, Mary B. Nemnich and Fred E. Jandt, Indianapolis: JIST, 2001.

Dare to Change Your Job and Your Life, Carole Kanchier, Indianapolis: JIST, 2000.

Getting the Job You Really Want, Michael Farr, Indianapolis: JIST, 2002.

The Quick Interview & Salary Negotiation Book, J. Michael Farr, Indianapolis: JIST, 1995.

The Quick Job Search, Michael Farr, Indianapolis: JIST, 2002.

Targeting the Job You Want, Kate Wendleton, Franklin Lakes, NJ: Career Press, 2000.

What Color Is Your Parachute? Richard Bolles, Berkeley, CA: Ten Speed Press (annual).

Books to Help You Target a Career Direction

Do What You Are, Paul Tieger and Barbara Barron-Tieger, New York: Little, Brown, 2001.

I Could Do Anything If Only I Knew What It Was, Barbara Sher, New York: Bantam Doubleday Dell, 1995.

Zen and the Art of Making a Living: A Practical Guide to Creative Career Design, Laurence Boldt, New York: Penguin USA, 1999.

Books on Changing Careers

Career Change, David Helfand, New York: McGraw-Hill, 1999.

The Lawyer's Career Change Handbook: More Than 300 Things You Can Do with a Law Degree, Hindi Greenberg, Quill, 2002.

Books to Help Manage Your Career

Job Savvy: How to Be a Success at Work, LaVerne Ludden, Indianapolis: JIST, 2003.

Love It, Don't Leave It: 26 Ways to Get What You Want at Work, Beverly Kaye and Sharon Jordan-Evans, San Francisco, Berrett-Koehler, 2003.

Work Smart: 250 Smart Moves Your Boss Already Knows, Marci Taub and Michelle Tullier, The Princeton Review, 1998.

Books for Researching Career Fields and Industries

America's Top 101 Computer and Technical Jobs, Michael Farr, Indianapolis: JIST, 2005.

America's Top 101 Jobs for College Graduates, Michael Farr, Indianapolis: JIST, 2005.

America's Top 101 Jobs for People Without a Four-Year Degree, Michael Farr, Indianapolis: JIST, 2005.

America's Top 300 Jobs, U.S. Department of Labor, Indianapolis: JIST, 2004.

Occupational Outlook Handbook (OOH), U.S. Department of Labor. Also published by JIST.

Books for Students and Recent Grads

Best Resumes for College Students and New Grads, Louise Kursmark, Indianapolis: JIST, 2003.

Exploring Careers: A Young Person's Guide to 1,000 Jobs, Editors at JIST, Indianapolis: JIST, 2003. (Grades 6-12)

Kick Off Your Career, Kate Wendleton, Franklin Lakes, NJ: Career Press, 2002.

Quick Guide to College Majors and Careers, Laurence Shatkin, Ph.D., Indianapolis: JIST, 2002.

Books on Resumes, Portfolios, Cover Letters, and other Correspondence

America's Top Resumes for America's Top Jobs, Michael Farr, Indianapolis: JIST, 2002.

Cover Letter Magic, Wendy Enelow and Louise Kursmark, Indianapolis: JIST, 2004.

Gallery of Best Resumes, David F. Noble, Indianapolis: JIST, 2004.

Gallery of Best Resumes for People Without a Four-Year Degree, David F. Noble, JIST, 2002.

Portfolio Power, Martin Kimeldorf, SearchInc, 2003. (eBook)

The Quick Resume & Cover Letter Book, Michael Farr, Indianapolis: JIST, 2005.

Resume Magic, Susan Britton Whitcomb, Indianapolis: JIST, 2003.

Sales and Marketing Resumes for $100,000 Careers, Louise Kursmark, Indianapolis: JIST, 2004.

Your Career and Life Plan Portfolio, Editors at JIST, Indianapolis: JIST, 2003.

Other Good Books for Networking

Endless Referrals: Network Your Everyday Contacts into Sales, Bob Burg, New York: McGraw-Hill, 1998.

Make Your Contacts Count: Networking Know-How for Cash, Clients, and Career Success, Anne Baber and Lynne Waymon, New York: AMACOM, 2002.

Networking at Writer's Conferences: From Contacts to Contracts, Steven Spratt and Lee Spratt, New York: Wiley & Sons, 1995.

Networking in the Music Business, Dan Kimpel, Vallejo, CA: MixBooks/Hal Leonard Corp, 2000.

Nonstop Networking, Andrea Nierenberg, Sterling, VA: Capital Books, 2002.

Success Runs in Our Race: The Complete Guide to Effective Networking in the African-American Community, George Fraser, William Morrow, 1994.

Books Related to Networking Online

CareerXroads, Gerry Crispin and Mark Mehler, Kendall Park, New Jersey: MMC Group, annual.

The Complete Idiot's Guide to the Internet, Peter Kent, New York: Alpha Books, 2001.

The Invisible Web: Uncovering Information Sources Search Engines Can't See, Chris Sherman and Gary Price, Medford, NJ: CyberAge Books, 2001.

Books for Cross-Cultural Networking

Gestures: The Do's and Taboos of Body Language Around the World, Roger Axtell, New York: Wiley & Sons, 1997.

Kiss, Bow, or Shake Hands: How to Do Business in Sixty Countries, Terri Morrison, Avon, MA: Adams Media, 1995.

Multicultural Manners: New Rules of Etiquette for a Changing Society, Norine Dresser, New York: Wiley & Sons, 1996.

Passport to the World Series, World Trade Press. This series includes books on business etiquette, customs, and culture for many countries, including Thailand, the Philippines, India, Germany, and Italy. Sample title: *Passport Argentina: Your Pocket Guide to Indian Business, Customs & Etiquette,* 1999.

World Chamber of Commerce Directory, Published by World Chamber of Commerce Directory, annual.

Resources for Developing or Expanding Your Network

Professional and Trade Association Directories

Encyclopedia of Associations, Gale Research Company, Gale Research, annual. This is the most comprehensive of all association directories, listing over 22,000 professional and trade associations and other nonprofit organizations in the United States. This encyclopedia is organized in three volumes, with one entire volume as a keyword/subject index. It is an essential networking resource.

Minority Organizations: A National Directory, Chicago: Ferguson Publ., 1997.

NTPA: National Trade and Professional Associations of the United States, Columbia Books, annual. This is not as comprehensive as the *Encyclopedia of Associations,* but it is less cumbersome to use, as everything is in one volume. It includes most major associations for any field. Also useful is Columbia Books' *SRA: State and Regional Associations.*

Organized Obsessions: 1,001 Offbeat Associations, Fan Clubs, and Microsocieties You Can Join, Deborah Burek, Martin Connors, and Christa Brelin, Detroit, Michigan: Visible Ink Press, 1992.

Books and Directories Listing Companies

There are so many resources for identifying corporations that might become part of your networking efforts that a full listing is beyond the scope of this book. Your best bet is to consult a business librarian or search the Internet. Also, to find a directory of just about anything, consult *Directories in Print,* published by Gale Research. It has 3,500 subject headings and lists over 15,000 directories.

In this section, I have listed the resources that are typically considered the most popular and helpful. Many of these are also available on CD-ROM or online. (Note that most of these directories are published annually, so publication dates have not been listed for most.)

Directory of Management Consultants, Kennedy Publications.

Dun & Bradstreet Million Dollar Directory, Dun & Bradstreet Information Services.

Government Job Finder, Daniel Lauber, River Forest, Illinois: Planning/Communications, 2003.

Hidden Job Market: A Guide to America's 2000 Little-Known Fastest Growing High-Tech Companies, Peterson's.

Hoover's Directory of Human Resources Executives, Reference Press, Inc.

Hoover's Handbook of American Businesses, Reference Press, Inc.

Hoover's Handbook of Emerging Companies, Reference Press, Inc.

Hoover's Masterlist of Major U.S. Companies, Reference Press, Inc.

The Job Bank Series, Bob Adams, Inc.

The Job Seeker's Guide to Socially Responsible Companies, Katherine Jankowski, Gale Research, Inc.

National Business Telephone Directory, Gale Research, Inc.

National Directory of Minority-Owned Business Firms, Gale Research, Inc.

National Directory of Women-Owned Business Firms, Gale Research, Inc.

Owners and Officers of Private Companies, Taft Group.

Peterson's Business and Management Jobs, Peterson's.

Polk's Directories, R. L. Polk & Co.

Standard & Poor's Register of Corporations, Directors and Executives, Standard & Poor's Corporation.

Standard Directory of Advertising Agencies, Reed Elsevier Publ.

Ward's Business Directory of U.S. Private and Public Companies, Gale Research, Inc.

Books to Help You Get or Stay Organized

Complete Idiot's Guide to Overcoming Procrastination, Michelle Tullier, New York: Alpha Books, 1999.

If You Haven't Got the Time to Do It Right, When Will You Find the Time to Do It Over? Jeffrey Mayer, New York: Fireside, 1991.

Organizing for the Creative Person, Dorothy Lehmkuhl and Dolores Cotter Lamping, New York: Crown, 1994.

Organizing from the Inside Out, Julie Morgenstern, New York: Owl Books/ Henry Holt, 1998.

Ready, Set, Organize! Pipi Campbell Peterson, Indianapolis, IN: JIST, 2002.

The Seven Habits of Highly Effective People, Steven Covey, New York: Simon & Schuster, 1990.

Resources for Understanding Your Networking Personality

Beyond Shyness: How to Conquer Social Anxieties, Jonathan Berent and Amy Lemley, New York: Fireside/Simon & Schuster, 1994.

The Hidden Face of Shyness: Understanding and Overcoming Social Anxiety, Franklin Schneier and Lawrence Welkowitz, New York: Avon Books, 1996.

The Introvert Advantage: How to Succeed in an Extrovert World, Marti Olsen, New York: Workman Publishing, 2002.

Myers-Briggs Type Indicator (MBTI), Consulting Psychologists Press. The MBTI is one of the world's most widely used measures ("tests") of personality style. Based on Carl Jung's theories of personality and grounded in solid test construction methods and decades of research, the MBTI is a useful tool for understanding why you do the things you do in the way that you do them. The MBTI can be administered only by qualified specialists (typically career counselors, human resources specialists, management consultants, training specialists, and psychotherapists, among others) and should be accompanied by a thorough explanation of your results and adequate counseling to apply the results to your career and personal goals. Taking the MBTI can help you understand how your personality type affects your networking style.

There are several good books that discuss personality type or the MBTI specifically. They include the following:

Do What You Are, Paul Tieger and Barbara Barron-Tieger, New York: Little, Brown, 2001.

Gifts Differing, Isabel Briggs Myers and Peter Myers, Palo Alto, California: Consulting Psychologists Press, 1995.

Type Talk at Work, Otto Kroeger and Janet Thuesen, New York: Dell Publishing, 2002.

Shyness: What It Is, What to Do About It, Philip Zimbardo, Reading, Massachusetts: Addison-Wesley, 1999.

Books on Business Etiquette and Protocol

At Ease Professionally: An Etiquette Guide for the Business Arena, Hilka Klinkenberg, Chicago: Bonus Books, 1992.

Class Acts: How Good Manners Create Good Relationships and Good Relationships Create Good Business, Mary Mitchell, New York: M. Evans & Co., 2003.

Letitia Baldrige's New Complete Guide to Executive Manners, Letitia Baldrige, New York: Scribner, 1993.

Books on Image, Attire, and Self-Presentation

Chic Simple Dress Smart for Men, Kim Johnson Gross and Jeff Stone, New York: Warner, 2002.

Chic Simple Dress Smart for Women, Kim Johnson Gross and Jeff Stone, New York: Warner, 2002.

Color Me Beautiful's Looking Your Best: Color, Makeup, and Style, Mary Spillane and Christine Sherlock, Lanham, MD: Madison Books, 1995.

Dress Casually for Success...for Men, Mark Weber, New York: McGraw-Hill, 1996.

You Are the Message: Getting What You Want by Being Who You Are, Roger Ailes, New York: Doubleday, 1995.

Books on Voice, Speech, and Making Conversation

The Articulate Executive: Learn to Look, Act, and Sound Like a Leader, Granville N. Toogood, New York: McGraw-Hill, 1997.

Crucial Conversation: Tools for Talking When Stakes Are High, Kerry Patterson et al., New York: McGraw-Hill, 2002.

High-Impact Public Speaking for Business and the Professions, J. Regis O'Connor, New York: McGraw-Hill, 1997.

Managing Your Mouth, Robert Genua, New York: AMACOM, 1993.

Winning Telephone Tips: 30 Fast and Profitable Tips for Making the Best Use of Your Phone, Paul R. Timm, Hawthorne, New Jersey: Career Press, 1997.

Books on Written Communication

The 100 Most Difficult Business Letters You'll Ever Have to Write, Fax, or E-Mail, Bernard Heller, New York: HarperCollins, 1994.

The Elements of Business Writing, Gary Blake and Robert Bly, New York: Macmillan, 1992.

Books for Entrepreneurs and Freelancers

Getting Business to Come to You, Paul Edwards, Sarah Edwards, New York: J.P. Tarcher/ Putnam, 1998.

The Harvard Entrepreneurs' Club Guide to Starting Your Own Business, Poonam Sharma, New York: Wiley & Sons, 1999.

Mind Your Own Business, LaVerne Ludden, Indianapolis, IN: JIST, 1999.

Self-Employment: From Dream to Reality! Linda Gilkerson and Theresia M. Paauwe, Indianapolis, IN: JIST, 2003.

The Six-Figure Consultant: How to Start (or Jump-Start) Your Consulting Career and Earn $100,000+ a Year, Robert Bly, Chicago, IL: Upstart Publishing, 1999.

Working from Home, Paul & Sarah Edwards, New York: J. P. Tarcher/Putnam, 1999.

Working Solo, Terri Lonier, New York: Wiley & Sons, 1998.

Interesting Books for Networkers with a Scholarly Bent

Composing a Life, Mary Catherine Bateson, New York: Grove Press, 2001.

Conflict & The Web of Group Affiliations, Georg Simmel, New York: Macmillan, 1964.

The Great Good Place: Cafes, Coffee Shops, Bookstores, Bars, Hair Salons, and Other Hangouts at the Heart of a Community, Ray Oldenburg, New York: Marlowe & Co., 1999.

A New Outline of Social Psychology, Martin Gold, Washington, DC: American Psychological Association, 1997.

The Social Animal, Elliot Aronson, Salt Lake City, Utah: W. H. Freeman & Co., 1999.

Index